IS GOD HAPPY?

Also by Leszek Kołakowski:

IS GOD HAPPY?

Selected Essays

———•———

LESZEK KOŁAKOWSKI

BASIC BOOKS

A Member of the Perseus Books Group
New York

Published by Basic Books,
A Member of the Perseus Books Group

Books published by Basic Books are available at special discounts for bulk purchases in the United States by corporations, institutions, and other organizations. For more information, please contact the Special Markets Department at the Perseus Books Group, 2300 Chestnut Street, Suite 200, Philadelphia, PA 19103, or call (800) 810-4145, ext. 5000, or e-mail special.markets@perseusbooks.com.

A CIP catalog record for this book is available from the Library of Congress.

LCCN: 2012949200
ISBN: 978-0-465-08099-1 (hardcover)
ISBN: 978-0-465-07574-4 (e-book)

10 9 8 7 6 5 4 3 2 1

Contents

Contents

Introduction

The essays in this volume span over fifty years: a lifetime of work and thought. They have been selected to reflect both the author's main philosophical interests and the remarkable constancy of those interests over this long period. They also, of course, in some measure reflect his changing approaches to and assessments of questions and ideas to which he returned again and again throughout his life.

They are arranged thematically rather than chronologically, in three sections which correspond roughly to three categories of connected topics. A number of essays are published here in English for the first time. They are: 'The Death of Gods', 'Erasmus and his God', 'An Invitation from God to a Feast', 'Why a Calf? Idolatry and the Death of God', 'Is God Happy?', 'In Praise of Unpunctuality', 'In Praise of Snobbery', 'Is there a Future for Truth?', 'On Reason (and Other Things)' and 'Our Merry Apocalypse'.

The work for which Leszek Kołakowski is perhaps best known in the West is his three-volume *Main Currents of Marxism*,[1] an analysis of the origins and philosophical roots, golden age and breakdown of that ideology. In his epilogue to that work, he describes Marxism as 'the greatest fantasy of the twentieth century', a dream of a perfect society which in practice became the foundation for 'a monstrous edifice of lies, exploitation and oppression'. He argues that the Leninist-Stalinist version of communist ideology and practice is not a distortion or degenerate form of Marxism but one of its possible interpretations. The dangers, delusions and falsehoods of this ideology and the nature of totalitarianism were prominent themes in his writing from 1955 onwards. The first section of this volume contains essays which deal with Marxism, communism, socialism, totalitarianism and ideology.

The best and simplest way of introducing this section is to use Leszek Kołakowski's own words, from his preface to another collection in which some of these essays appeared:[2]

'. . . part of this collection deals with questions and burdens imposed on us by communism and its historical vicissitudes. After all that has happened since 1989, the topic might seem obsolete, or of interest only as a historical study. I wish it were obsolete, but I am not sure it is. Communism was not a crazy fantasy of a few fanatics, nor the result of human stupidity and baseness; it was a real, a very real part of the history of the twentieth century, and we cannot understand this history of ours without understanding communism. We cannot get rid of the spectre by saying it was just "human stupidity" or "human corruptibility". The spectre is stronger than the spells we cast on it. It might come back to life.'

The opening essay in this section – 'The Death of Gods' – appears here in English for the first time. Written in 1956, it is one of the earliest essays in this volume. It is also one of the most important from both a political and a biographical point of view. By 1956 Kołakowski was known as a 'revisionist' and had become a very prominent thorn in the side of the authorities. The essay is an extremely strong attack on the ideology and practice of communism, demolishing the false justifications of the regime and the myths which it propagated. It is astonishingly forthright for that time, and breathtaking in its lucidity and forcefulness. It was seized by the censor and remained unpublished in Poland until after the fall of communism, although it was circulated in underground manuscript copies.

'What is Socialism?' was another important early essay and a typically 'revisionist' text which satirised the reality of the regime as a travesty of the ideals of socialism. Also written in 1956, also censored (indeed the journal for which it had been intended was shut down) and also unpublished in Poland until the fall of communism, it lived a brief public life pinned up on a bulletin board at

Warsaw University until the authorities had it taken down. It, too, was later circulated in manuscript.

Both these essays were of great significance at the time; they are two 'landmark' texts which caused a stir and remain important today. Another essay which stands out in this way is 'Jesus Christ, Prophet and Reformer', in the second section of the present volume. It, too, is an early essay, again written in 1956.

In 1966, on the tenth anniversary of the 'Polish October', Leszek Kołakowski delivered a speech at Warsaw University which was to become famous: a devastating condemnation of the Party and the communist authorities, of opportunities missed and hopes unfulfilled since October 1956. For this he was expelled from the Party. In March 1968 he was expelled from his Chair at the university and banned from teaching and publishing.

The second section of this volume brings together essays on subjects connected with religion. Many of the topics touched upon here – divine omnipotence and the existence of evil, the meaning of the sacred, idolatry and sacrilege, faith and reason, individual responsibility and divine Grace, reformist movements in the Catholic Church and those regularly re-emerging currents within it which were nourished by the hope of renewing Christianity and returning to the religion of the Gospels (discussed here in the essay on Erasmus) – were explored by the author at greater length in a number of books, among them: *Metaphysical Horror*, *Religion*, and his works on the seventeenth century. The essay 'Leibniz and Job: The Metaphysics of Evil and the Experience of Evil' is one of many texts on the problem of evil in this best of all possible worlds. The idea of the sacred is also a prominent subject in many of Kołakowski's writings. The sacred as an essential and ineradicable element in human spiritual life is one of the topics explored in an important early book, *The Presence of Myth*, and later in *Religion* and in *Metaphysical Horror*. It is touched upon here in the essay about idolatry, 'Why a Calf?' and in 'Anxiety About God in an Ostensibly Godless Age'.

Religious faith as the experience of the sacred, particularly in the form of mysticism, was a prominent subject in Kołakowski's writings on seventeenth-century thought, most notably in a major 1965 work about non-confessional Christian movements in seventeenth-century Holland and France. It is a work about religious thinkers, reformers and mystics who denied the need for a 'visible' Church and rejected all institutionally controlled forms of religious life. It is also about religious freedom, the problems of orthodoxy and heresy, and the conflicts between individual religious consciousness and an organized Church. It appeared in French as *Chrétiens sans église* but never in English, except for parts of a chapter in a collection entitled *The Two Eyes of Spinoza*.[3] In that volume, too, are some essays written in the 1960s: on Uriel da Costa, Gassendi, Bayle and Luther. The essay on Erasmus in the present volume, which touches on some of these themes, was also written in 1965 and was hitherto unpublished in English.

It was in large measure Kołakowski's early immersion in the ideas and disputes of the seventeenth century that inspired much of his writing on the diverse but closely interconnected subjects which became such important themes in his later work: orthodoxy and heresy (in ideology as well as religion), faith and reason, freedom (theological, Augustinian, Spinozan, religious, political), the sacred and the experience of the sacred, individual responsibility, divine Grace – and even Marxist ideology and communism, where, as he often pointed out, dogma and the notion of heresy and orthodoxy, and indeed the idea of the sacred, functioned in ways analogous to their functioning in the Church, just as the structure and functioning of the Party hierarchy in many ways resembled that of the Church.

His PhD in 1953 had been on Spinoza. His book on Spinoza, *Freedom and Antinomies of Freedom in the Philosophy of Spinoza*,[4] was an analysis of all the aspects – moral, metaphysical, anthropological, political and cognitive – of Spinozan freedom, its limits and the insuperable contradictions in which Spinoza's idea of freedom was entangled. Some of the topics which had been central there are also an important theme in his later writings: Spinoza's conception of philosophy as the study of man and the nature and limits of freedom and toleration. He wrote of Spinoza's philosophy as an attempt '. . . to interpret classical problems of philosophy as problems of a moral nature, to reveal their hidden human content; in other words, to present the problem of God as a problem of man, the problem of heaven and earth as a problem of human freedom', and saw his metaphysics as 'a search for man's place in the world, a place he must find in order to be able to live without despair, bitterness or false hopes'. In particular the vast annals of the conflict between faith and reason in religious thought – of the 'emancipation of faith from reason and of reason from faith' and of the various attempts to reconcile the two – were a subject to which he returned in a variety of different contexts, historical, religious and political. It is, of course, in the context of the Augustinian theory of Grace and predestination, a prominent theme in his book on Pascal and the Jansenists, *God Owes us Nothing*. The present volume includes a short essay on Pascal, in dialogue form, entitled 'An Invitation from God to a Feast'.

The question of happiness, while perhaps not directly related to any of the themes mentioned here as central, nevertheless occupies an important place in religious thought and was a traditional subject of philosophical reflection both ancient and modern. But the question of God's happiness is less commonly raised. That is the subject of the title essay 'Is God Happy?', which appears at the end of this section. If not unique, it is certainly a subject seldom found in the historiography of philosophy.

Many of the concerns which emerge as prominent both in Leszek Kołakowski's writings on religion and the history of religious thought and in those on communism and ideology, particularly on communism as a secular religion – freedom and toleration, faith and scepticism, the role of heresy and orthodoxy and of dogma and doctrine, myth and the idea of the sacred – were also central themes in his many essays about the problems of modernity and the legacy of the Enlightenment, both in political and in religious contexts. Some of these are represented in the third section of this volume, which deals with modern and post-Enlightenment man, truth and relativism, and the various ideologies, illusions and delusions of modern civilization.

Several of the essays in this third section – certainly 'Lot's Wife' and 'On Reason', but perhaps also 'Is There a Future for Truth?' – could have found an equally comfortable home in another section of this volume. Such is the fundamental nature of the problems raised in these essays and their centrality to so many areas of philosophical, political and religious thought that no single text slots neatly into one category. 'Lot's Wife', for instance – another essay seized by the censor and never published in communist Poland – would have been no less at home in the section on socialism (as the censors clearly realized). One of the Biblical tales in a 1966 collection entitled *The Key to Heaven*,[5] it appears here in a new translation. Equally the essay 'On Reason', which deals with reason and faith, could have been housed in the section on religion. 'Is There a Future for Truth?', while it discusses the various philosophical theories of truth, is also about religious truth and the importance of the idea of Truth with a capital T. 'Our Merry Apocalypse', too – an essay about science and faith, myth and the sacred, modernity and the Enlightenment – could have been filed under 'religion'. The essays about collective identity, natural law, crime and punishment and the demise of historical man were somewhat easier to categorize; they clearly belong in this third section.

I have also included two early essays written in a playful vein – to give an idea of Kołakowski's wit and range of styles. They are the two brief exercises in self-parody, 'In Praise of Snobbery' and 'In Praise of Unpunctuality', both written in the early 1960s. They, too, appear in English for the first time.

Perhaps the most salient feature of Leszek Kołakowski's work, and the one which characterizes him best, is his attitude towards truth and certainty. On the one hand, a critical scepticism and suspicion of claims to certainty pervades his work. Its philosophical underpinnings are laid out in the essay 'The Priest and the Jester', perhaps his most famous essay in Poland, not included in this volume but published in English in *The Two Eyes of Spinoza*.[6] He writes in his preface to *My Correct Views on Everything*:

'None of these dilemmas is properly solved; everything is left ambiguous. I want to believe that this is not just a result of my ineptitude, but perhaps also of the incurable ambiguity of reality itself.'

At the same time there is also in these essays, and throughout Kołakowski's work, a strong rejection of relativism and defence of the idea of truth; a defence, too, of the validity of metaphysical questions, and an insistence on the importance of the metaphysical dimension in human life.

Agnieszka Kołakowska, 2012

Notes

1. Recently reissued in one volume by Norton.

2. *My Correct Views On Everything*, St Augustine's Press, 2005.

3. Published by St Augustine's Press.

4. Warsaw, 1959, recently reissued in Poland but never translated into English.

5. University of Chicago Press, 1989.

6. St Augustine's Press, 2005.

IS GOD HAPPY?

I. *Socialism, Ideology and the Left*

The Death of Gods

When, at the ripe age of eighteen, we become communists, equipped with an unshakeable confidence in our own wisdom and a handful of experiences, undigested and less significant than we like to imagine, acquired in the Great Hell of war, we devote very little thought to the fact that we need communism in order to harmonize relations of production with the forces of production. It rarely occurs to us that the extremely advanced technological standards here and now, in Poland in 1945, require the immediate socialisation of the means of production if crises of overproduction are not to loom over us like storm clouds. In short, we are not good Marxists. For us, socialism, however we go about arguing for it in theoretical debates, is everything but the result of the operation of the law of value. Defended with clumsy arguments cobbled together from a cursory reading of Marx, Kautsky or Lenin, it is really just a myth of a Better World, a vague nostalgia for human life, a rejection of the crimes and humiliations of which we have witnessed too many, a kingdom of equality and freedom, a message of great renewal, a reason for existence. We are brothers of the Paris communards, the workers during the Russian Revolution, the soldiers in the Spanish Civil War.

We thus have before us a goal that justifies everything. We abhor the nationalist slogans which bedevil the political life of our party and treat them as an awkward and inconvenient tool for masking temporary tactics – tactics which will shortly bring a common world without barriers or frontiers. And we abhor all the more those who, in pure, thin, melodious voices like the voices of castrati, call for prudence and moderation and in times awash with fresh blood know only one rallying cry: Wash your hands! Wash your hands!

When at this time of grave crisis in the communist conscious-ness – a crisis of whose depth, extent and consequences we are not all fully aware – we look back anxiously at the road travelled, at the work accomplished with so much effort and labour, so much faith and devotion, we see the following picture:

We believed in a utopia. We believed that socialism would auto-matically eradicate all social inequalities; we believed that in a socialist system work and individual talents would be the only factors deter-mining people's social position and role. Instead we found that the process called 'building socialism' generated its own social classes, its own system of privileges, drastically at odds with the principles of traditional egalitarianism, its own mechanism for creating elites, and its own set of rules, serving to perpetuate an ossified hierarchy and caste system as inflexible, immutable and conservative as it was happy to conceal itself behind a phraseological veil of egalitarianism.

We believed that socialist rule would naturally lead to the swift and total disappearance of national hostility, nationalist prejudice and tribal conflict. Instead we found that political activity which goes by the name of socialist can encourage and exploit the most absurd forms of chauvinism and blind nationalist megalomania. In culture these manifest themselves in the form of naive deceptions and infantile sophistry, but in politics, concealed behind a thin façade of traditional internationalist slogans, they assume the much more dangerous and sinister form of colonialism.

We believed that socialism would ruthlessly extirpate that most despicable curse of our times – racism. Instead, wherever we looked in this allegedly socialist politics and ideology, we found the sinister shadow of *Der Stürmer* looming behind every patriotic slogan.

We were well acquainted with Engels's famous phrase about socialism as the leap to the kingdom of freedom. But we found that socialist industrialization can develop with the aid of mass slave labour, and that the superstructure of a state of socialized produc-tion can degenerate into a system of total police terror, a military dictatorship of lawlessness and fear.

We were convinced that one of the chief gains of the revolution would be a system of universal participation in government, a genuine rule of the people based on the consciousness of the proletariat. Instead we found the so-called socialist system transforming itself before our eyes into a travesty of its own watchwords: into a radical autocratic or oligarchic centrism, more crippling to social initiative than any form of bourgeois democracy.

We had learnt from Marx that socialism, in giving society control over the processes of its own material reproduction, would do away with ideological smoke screens, render social relations transparent and liberate man from alienation, which gives rise to fetishes and myths. Instead we found that it is here, in the so-called socialist system, that the obfuscation of real social relations attains its zenith and new forms of religious mystification oppress the social consciousness as never before; never before has the reflection of collective life in the human mind been so distorted and so false.

We thought it an obvious truth that socialism would mean the end of wars and conquests. Instead we found that the policies of this allegedly socialist state could be described variously as hovering on the brink of war or aggressive and interventionist.

For the naive imagination socialism was to be a time of tremendous cultural richness and expansion of the human spirit, which would flourish free and unconstrained, liberated at last from all dependence. Instead we found that the blossoming of socialist culture meant the wholesale destruction of the greatest traditions of that culture, the transformation of literature and art into instruments for the basest kind of toadying to authority, the reduction of philosophy and sociology to vague expositions of official doctrine reflecting the political tactics of a given moment, the promotion of hacks and the crushing of genuine artists, and the construction of a system in which the great destroyer of culture Andrei Zhdanov regularly announces his hideous triumphs.*

---

* Andrei Zhdanov, a leading Soviet ideologue under Stalin, known principally for his condemnation of 'bourgeois literature', his imposition of socialist realism, later known as the 'Zhdanov doctrine', and his persecution of writers in the 1940s.

We knew that with socialism would come an end to humiliation, a consciousness of human dignity and a sense of participation in a common enterprise as free and equal citizens. It was hard to admit that the thing they called socialism perpetuated conditions where humiliation and the trampling of human dignity were everyone's daily bread.

One could go on expanding this long and sad list of lost illusions, each exposing a successive stretch of the fast lane to 1984. But it is not a list of complaints from the disenchanted and the deceived. We are perfectly clear about the situation in which we find ourselves. We do not claim that we were deceived: falling victim to deception is no excuse. Nor do we claim that the situation deprived us of the courage to speak when we saw the crimes that were being committed. Lack of courage is no excuse, even if it can be explained historically; we are responsible for everything we do. Nor, finally, do we claim that we did not know what was going on: even if we knew less than we know today, we knew enough, more than enough, to be fully aware of the abyss between our idea of socialism and the reality, Soviet and our own. We were not blind; thousands of facts evoked horror or laughter. But both the horror and the laughter were platonic: harmless and defanged.

So let us not delude ourselves that it was only when faced with new knowledge and new facts that we found ourselves in a land of silence, abandoned by the gods.

It was not lack of knowledge that fostered our illusions. They were fostered by the way in which, morally and intellectually, we dealt with the knowledge we had: by a system in which every inconvenient fact was given a simple explanation within a set of ideological myths, with which we deliberately blinded ourselves to the reality. The crisis of the communist consciousness did not come about through lack of new knowledge about the world; it came about through the collapse of the mythology which gave shape to that knowledge. If the idea of socialism is to recover its original, pristine radiance, untainted by lies and deceit, a mercilessly clear awareness of that mythology, its existence and its mechanisms, must lead to its collapse.

Here, then, are some of the myths in which the grain of truth grew warped and became a fetish.

The myth of the fortress under siege

Communists are in a permanent state of war with the old world; they are defending a fortress besieged on all sides by the forces of the old order. In this besieged fortress there is only one goal: to withstand the siege. And whatever furthers this goal is a good thing. In the besieged fortress every conflict, every dispute, is catastrophic, every sign of weakness a triumph for the enemy, every relaxation of the penal system a calamity. The army abhors democracy; in the army, better to obey a stupid leader than sow anarchy, however astute and penetrating the mind behind it. So if we know that Joseph Stalin is a poor and primitive philosopher, better that we should turn our brains to demonstrating the opposite than that we should, even in this one domain, weaken the authority whose existence is the condition of victory. If we know that Gide is a great writer, still it will be better if the rifleman in the fortress never hears of him than that, absorbed in his reading, he should miss even once when he fires. And if the commander of the fortress is a criminal, better to pass this over in silence than run the risk that his subordinates, absorbed in giving him his comeuppance, should leave the gates unguarded.

The myth of the besieged fortress is not entirely unjustified. Nevertheless, its main effect is to contribute to communism's undoing. In a besieged fortress communists are isolated; in a besieged fortress it is out of the question to seek allies in the enemy camp. The sense of being under siege has two tactical consequences, both catastrophic. It requires the besieged to perceive the whole visible world outside the fortress as the enemy, preventing them from swelling their ranks and so strengthening their forces, and cutting them off from all values and possibilities that lie outside. And within the fortress itself it creates a military hierarchy based on blind obedience and intolerant to criticism.

The myth of the fortress is a dangerous one. A besieged fortress cannot hold out for decades. And when the rifleman, still reeling from the smoke, at last opens the gates, he walks out into city streets thronged with people; among them are many enemies but also many friends, at whom, he now realizes, he has been shooting indiscriminately. But worse is to come: he goes on to discover that the brutal corporal whose orders he had obeyed without question, convinced that in war this was just what you did and how it had to be, enjoys giving orders so much that he would rather deceive his soldiers by inventing a siege than do anything to promote peace, for with peace his power would vanish. Power is dangerous; it wants to last forever, and the less it is controlled, the more easily it can maintain itself. This is why power – not just on a subjective whim, but by virtue of the workings of a historical mechanism – invents its own myths.

The Myth of Power:
Remarks on the Life of Myths

We sometimes forget an obvious point: that Marx and Lenin, because of the different circumstances of their political activity, saw things from different points of view. For Marx socialism was above all the result of a country's economic maturity; he saw the proletarian revolution and the socialization of the means of production as a kind of inevitable social explosion resulting from what one might call the chemistry of economic life. For Lenin socialism was a problem of political power, which can and should be seized if the opportunity presents itself: wherever political conditions for seizing power arise, they should be fully exploited. This is the point of view of a revolutionary, and one which every revolutionary must accept. But with one caveat: by 'conditions for seizing power' we mean conditions in a particular country, never conditions which would allow seizing power somewhere else. Exporting the revolution is out of the question; of that there is no doubt. Only a counter-revolution can be exported, whatever it calls itself and whatever the slogans it hides behind. Now it is not hard to see that the conditions for seizing power are much more easily created in underdeveloped countries, where not only socialist but anti-feudal and national liberation movements can still find fertile soil, so that a revolution which is in fact socialist can at the same time present itself as democratic and thus attract those parts of the population which have not attained socialist consciousness, namely the peasantry and subjugated nations. But the very conditions which facilitate the seizing of power make it particularly difficult to hold on to it in the long run. Power which is threatened and concentrates all its political effort on itself becomes an end in itself; it becomes power for its own sake. Communists, when they assume power, know in theory that it is only a means to an end, that of liberating society, and that in time it will self-destruct. But power has its own rules of evolution, and they are unyielding and merciless. The harder power is to maintain, the more it must surround itself with an aura of adoration and promote a cult for its own worship. It is all too easy to forget that power is the instrument of a class and the spokesman for the interests of that class. To put it more specifically: 'The time will come,' we say, 'for all the purposes to which this power is supposed to be put; for the moment the important thing is to maintain it.' But this 'moment' goes on for years, until it turns out that it is too late: power has become an end in itself. It has stopped being the instrument of the class which seized it and become the instrument of those who possess it. The apparatus of power has spread like a malignant growth and no longer seeks justification for its existence in the common interest. As an apparatus of power it has its own interests: the interests of a caste or an autonomous organization which continues to hide behind the façade of the Great Rallying Cry. And the ideology of those who rule becomes the ruling ideology. This simple observation we owe to Marx.

The myth of power as the highest justification seeps into the consciousness of those who are not themselves participants in it (although efforts are made to delude them into thinking that they are). In this way the pernicious belief that possessing power is the highest end becomes entrenched. No price is too high for power. That price can be aggression, intervention, the extermination of an entire nation, mass catastrophe, the repudiation of one's own original principles, moral corruption and contempt. It has indeed been all those things. But once it becomes apparent that power feeds on blood and depends on it for its continued existence, that it will stop at nothing, and that it has a natural tendency to unlimited growth, then the myth of power is unmasked and shows its shameful face – the face for so long hidden by the leader in the daily paper. And once exposed, the myth of power is extinguished; it can no longer survive in the minds of those who have seen it.

Of course, mystification and manipulation of the social consciousness produces results that can endure; they can take on a life of their own. Sometimes a pious believer will not waver in his faith even when he sees that the wooden figure which spoke to him is hollow and conceals a priest; he, too, is capable of preferring to believe a myth rather than the evidence of his own eyes. So the extinction of myths requires certain conditions. But it will be a mass extinction: once one myth is exposed, the rest will follow, hurtling down like an avalanche. It will be enough, too, if just one priest is exposed – or, better still, if another priest exposes him, for whatever reason; for the faithful believe no one, not even the exposer. The first step is the hardest; the rest comes easily. Even if the believer has only stopped believing in the efficacy of the rosary, it is safe to predict that he will shortly be an atheist. This is why – priests, take note – a mythology, if it is to be effective, must be all-encompassing. The death of gods is a chain reaction; each drags another down into the abyss. *Abyssus abyssum invocat.* Hence the necessity – of which experienced priests are well aware – of maintaining the mythology as a system in which every detail is equally important and equally holy. The logic of mythology is familiar to every priest; it is there in his mind when he says: today you will miss Mass, tomorrow you will curse God, and the day after that you will become a Bolshevik. This is why only

Stalinism, because it was all-encompassing, was a viable mythology. Stalin's priests said: today you will admire a painting by Paul Klee, tomorrow you will cease admiring socialist-realist architecture, the day after that you will start to doubt the leap from quantity to quality, and the day after that you will renounce your loyalty to Caesar. And since Caesar's rule is the rule of the people, you will be an enemy of the people. So by admiring a painting by Paul Klee you become an enemy of the people *in potentia*; you are 'objectively' an enemy of the people, a spy and a saboteur. The power of this strategy, confirmed by centuries of historical experience, is undeniable. And its collapse had to be as total as its rule had been: a chain of divinities, collapsing like a pack of cards. What folly to imagine it was possible to extract just one!

Of course, even when the myths functioned efficiently, occasionally something horrifying would happen that could not be justified by the myth of the besieged fortress or the myth of power. A system of additional myths was then needed to explain such things, and on the whole these explanations, even if not always entirely rational nor entirely soothing to the conscience, were nevertheless adequate for the purpose, producing a sort of self-imposed vegetative intellectual state which made it possible to pass over them and go on as before. There were three such chief myths: the myth of two sides to every question, the myth of the words 'relics of the past' and 'distortions', and finally that king of myths, the myth of unity.

The Myth of Two Sides to Every Question

This myth is based on a primitive dialectic connected with a word that features prominently in the poor man's version of Stalinist philosophy: 'concretely'. A fact must be considered 'concretely'; this means that it must be considered within the context in which it takes place, not 'in general' or 'beyond space and time'. And different contexts can reveal entirely different sides to the same question – indeed, entirely contradictory sides. This applies in particular to moral and political judgements. The proletariat has a supreme goal: the communist society. The bourgeoisie also has a supreme goal: to maintain its power, which is based on exploitation. To consider a question 'concretely' is to consider whether it furthers one or other of these two supreme goals. In a socialist country a lie is not a lie from the point of view of the supreme goal, because it serves the cause of truth. In a socialist country murder is not murder, aggression is not aggression, and slavery is not slavery if it serves the cause of freedom; concentration camps are not concentration camps, torture is not torture, chauvinism is not chauvinism. The supreme goal sanctifies everything done in its name. The bourgeoisie deceives the people in order to rule, but the socialist state, by its very nature, cannot deceive the people; its ostensible lies and deceptions are precisely that: ostensible only, because they serve the cause of truth and its future triumphs. Its deceit is not deceit. In a capitalist state, poverty is part of the 'essence' of social life; where there are pockets of plenty, they are merely a deceitful ploy by the rulers to pacify the masses. In a socialist state, ostensible poverty is only a means to future plenty; thus every instance of poverty is in fact potential plenty, just as lies are potential truth and tyranny potential freedom. A decline in the standard of living is in fact an increase if we keep in mind, as we must, the supreme goal, just as any rise in the standard of living in a capitalist country is in fact – 'in essence' – a decline, in that it serves to maintain bourgeois rule. Concretely, comrade; you must judge things concretely. You say that the introduction of school fees in a socialist country limits access to schools for the children of workers? On the contrary, it serves to improve socialist education and thus in fact – 'essentially' and in view of the supreme goal – broadens access to education. You say that displacing an entire nation by force and expelling it from its land violates the principle of self-determination? But this is metaphysical reasoning. The displacement safeguards socialist power, which upholds the principle of national self-determination; 'essentially', therefore, it does not violate this principle, but, on the contrary, defends and strengthens it.

This, then, is the myth of two sides to every question. Need one add that the principle of national self-determination realized through its violation can only be the purest humbug, and that it transforms the Supreme Goal into the Supreme Deception?

The Myth of 'Relics' and 'Distortions'

The myth of the phrase 'relics of the past' and the word 'distortions' works somewhat differently. While the myth of two sides to every question justifies crimes, this one serves to identify the real criminal – the one who acts in the shadows. Things are sometimes rotten in the state of Denmark, or rather not exactly rotten, of course, but perhaps not quite perfect; there are temporary setbacks to be overcome before true perfection can be achieved. Sometimes, too, an abrupt political about-turn is required: yesterday's watchwords must be condemned; decisions made an hour ago must be vehemently denounced. But at the same time it has to be explained that nothing has really changed: that the political 'essence' remains the same. This is where 'distortions' and 'relics of the past' come in useful. In prehistoric times, about a year ago, there was a debate about whether evil is 'immanent' in socialism: in other words, whether the evil that we see here and now is only a relic of the capitalist past or also a product of these new conditions and in part at least specific to socialism. Today this debate seems anachronistic, because it presupposes that our historical present is the genuine realization of socialism. And yet the myth of these words continues to function. No past evil, already condemned as such, can be accepted as the product of really existing socialism; it must be called a 'distortion' or a 'relic'. Who would defend bureaucracy? Everyone has reasons enough to condemn it. But bureaucracy has no connection with the current system of government; it is a 'distortion'. The 'essence' of the system of government is perfectly hale and hearty, and remains unchanged. If this is not evident to the observer, it is because his vision is shallow; he 'skates on the surface of appearances' and misses the 'essence'. The 'essence' cannot be discerned through mere observation; it must be revealed through the insight provided by abstraction, which will show that in reality, the appearance of terror conceals perfect freedom, just as the rule of law lies behind the appearance of bureaucracy and perfect equality reigns behind the appearance of hierarchy. Everything can be explained by philosophical reasoning if this latter is armed with the categories of 'essence' and 'appearance'. Shallow critics might latch on to 'distortions' and 'relics' – the mere journalist, in his thoughtlessness and frivolity, is incapable of seeing beyond them – but the deeper insight of the philosopher and politician can skim off the external froth of appearances and grasp the reality beneath: the pristine, untouched, unpolluted root of socialism. Therefore politicians need philosophers, who by judicious use of the myth of 'distortions' and 'relics' can indefinitely prolong the belief in the untainted and ever vital, albeit invisible, essence of socialism. 'Distortions' and 'relics' provide an unsurpassed moral and intellectual refuge: they allow us to dispense with any analysis of social phenomena, explain everything that needs to be explained and build up an eminently convenient picture of the criminal – the criminal known in advance to be responsible for all the evils which have, will and may come to pass, always triumphantly, in socialism. Glory to the philosophers.

The Myth of Unity

Finally we come to that king of myths: the myth of unity. The principle of the unity of the workers' movement as a condition of its effectiveness has a long history, but one that has not always survived in that movement's social memory; we sometimes even forget that Bolshevism began as a break-off faction. Stalinism made the watchword of unity into an instrument of permanent blackmail, used by the ruling bureaucracy against the movement; this latter, unable to maintain itself as an organic whole, was transformed into an atomized mass with no political life or will of its own and subordinated to the uncontrolled decisions of the ruling oligarchy. Thus was bureaucratic unity born: the unity of a heap of stones flung into a sack and bound together with the string of military discipline. This kind of unity has its advantages, especially for those who hold the string: a sack of stones can be used to smash skulls. If, in addition, the stones can be made to believe that they are acting of their own free will and towards a worthy and noble end, the myth has achieved its goal. Unity achieved through the total annihilation of political life does indeed make significant differences of opinion within the Party impossible, for the simple reason that there are no opinions to have differences about. All political life is concentrated within the (ever narrowing) circle of the ruling leadership, which enjoys absolute freedom of action.

Another type of unity is created when, as the result of a crisis or shock of some kind, genuine political life suddenly blossoms in a bureaucratized and atomized party: when the stones in the sack begin to speak with human voices and the Party is faced with divisions and dissent. Not long ago a split in the international communist movement seemed likely before the week was out. It was averted – and the blood runs cold at the thought of the means whereby this was achieved. But where powerful forces are at work to maintain the movement in a state of rotting stagnation, the watchword of unity is fatal. Unity in such a situation is the unity of a gangrenous organism with its gangrene; appeals for it are in practice tantamount to appeals for the toleration of the movement's most reactionary currents – currents which always seek ways of maintaining their toxic enclaves within it, endangering the life of the whole. An artificially maintained façade of unity cannot survive in conditions where a consciousness of moral and political crisis has seeped through and taken root, irreversibly. No one could now re-impose unity on the sack-of-stones principle. The present appearance of unity bears more resemblance to a haystack which spontaneously starts smouldering from inside and at some unexpected moment will burst into flame. The slogan of unity has ceased to exert its hypnotic and paralysing influence. It has become the weapon of those who are terrified by the prospect of a battle of ideas, in which they would inevitably be exposed; of those who would come plummeting down from their paper Olympian heights in any system of power that was subject to social control; of those whose utter vapidity harmonizes nicely with their unthinking reliance upon doctrine, just as their love of power fits with their sergeant-major style and their anti-Semitism with their fondness for military dictatorship. They like appealing for unity – unity imposed with the aid of cudgels and gags.

And so for a number of years we worked hard to discredit the idea of socialism as thoroughly as possible. Happily, we were successful only in part, though there are plenty of forces which continue to pursue this aim with admirable consistency. For a long time identification of the idea of socialism with the most unfortunate forms of its implementation has led to a state of affairs in which one of the chief tasks is explaining to everyone that socialism as a system of organizing society has never been implemented anywhere in the world, and that the idea of building socialism in one underdeveloped country is the costliest utopia in the history of mankind. Belief in this utopia, and attempts to realize it, became the main source of the mythology whose logic is laid out above.

We are now gathered at the funeral of this mythology. At the same time it is the moral funeral of those forms of the revolutionary movement which have proved incapable of spearheading social progress. But it is not an ordinary funeral. It is horrifying and grotesque, for the corpse, unaware of its own death and convinced that it is at the head of a joyful demonstration, continues enthusiastically shouting slogans and hitting out at those in the funeral procession, provoking macabre laughter. But the death of gods has some singular features, not met with in ordinary life. When we make our farewells to a dying person, it is with an unshakeable certainty that we shall not meet again. Farewells to gods are riskier; one can never be entirely certain that they will not return in a new incarnation. And their reincarnation skills are astonishing. Revolutions topple emperors, but history teaches that often a true child of the revolution will place the imperial crown on his head and then issue a decree forbidding the masses to sing '*ça ira!*' The death of gods has its disturbing and dangerous side.

But it also has an optimistic side. The death of gods is the liberation of man – always partial and imperfect, and, like childbirth, often painful, violent and brutal, and yet always to be welcomed.

We are back where we started. Back at the point where the political and theoretical work of resuscitating a workers' movement that is viable and capable of evolving must begin anew; once again faced with the need to analyse contemporary society so that a new revolutionary humanism can be created, based on the forces of the working class and an adequate knowledge of the modern world. Back at the point described by a well-known French nursery rhyme:

Si cette histoire vous amuse

Nous allons la recommencer;
Si au contraire elle vous ennuie
Nous allons la répéter.

1956

This essay was seized by the censor and remained unpublished in Poland until after the fall of communism.

What is Socialism?

We intend to tell you what socialism is. But first we must tell you what it is not – and our views on this matter were once very different from what they are at present.

Here, then, is what socialism is not:

- a society in which someone who has committed no crime sits at home waiting for the police;
- a society in which it is a crime to be the brother, sister, son, or wife of a criminal;
- a society in which some people are unhappy because they say what they think and others are unhappy because they do not;
- a society in which some people are better off because they do not think at all;
- a society in which some people are unhappy because they are Jews and others are happier because they are not;
- a state whose soldiers are the first to set foot in the territory of another country;
- a state where people are better off because they praise their leaders;
- a state where one can be condemned without trial;
- a society whose leaders appoint themselves;
- a society in which ten people live in one room;
- a society that has illiterates and plague epidemics;
- a state that does not permit travel abroad;
- a state that has more spies than nurses and more room in prisons than in hospitals;

– a state where the number of bureaucrats increases more quickly than that of workers;

– a state where people are compelled to lie;

– a state where people are compelled to steal;

– a state where people are compelled to commit crimes;

– a state that possesses colonies;

– a state whose neighbours curse geography;

– a state that produces superb jet planes and lousy shoes;

– a state where cowards are better off than the courageous;

– a state where defence lawyers are usually in agreement with the prosecution;

– a tyranny, an oligarchy, a bureaucracy;

– a society where vast numbers of people turn to God to comfort them in their misery;

– a state that gives literary prizes to talentless hacks and knows better than painters what kind of painting is the best;

– a nation that oppresses other nations;

– a nation that is oppressed by another nation;

– a state that wants all its citizens to have the same views on philosophy, foreign policy, the economy, literature, and morality;

– a state whose government determines the rights of its citizens but whose citizens do not determine the rights of their government;

– a state in which one is responsible for one's ancestors;

– a state in which some people earn forty times as much as others;

– a system of government that is opposed by the majority of the governed;

– one isolated country;

– a group of underdeveloped countries;

– a state that employs nationalist slogans;

– a state whose government believes that nothing matters more than its being in power;

– a state that makes pacts with criminals and adapts its worldview to these pacts;

– a state that wants its foreign ministry to shape the worldview of all mankind at any given moment;

– a state that is not very good at distinguishing between slavery and liberation;

– a state that gives free rein to proponents of racism;

– a state that currently exists;

– a state with private ownership of the means of production;

– a state that considers itself socialist solely because it has abolished private ownership of the means of production;

– a state that is not very good at distinguishing between social revolution and armed invasion;

– a state that does not believe that people under socialism should be happier than people elsewhere;

– a society that is very sad;

– a caste system;

– a state whose government always knows the will of the people before it asks them;

– a state where people can be pushed around, humiliated, and ill-treated with impunity;

– a state where a certain view of world history is obligatory;

– a state whose philosophers and writers always say the same things as the generals and ministers, but always after the latter have said them;

– a state where city maps are state secrets;

– a state where the results of parliamentary elections can always be unerringly predicted;

– a state where slave labour exists;

– a state where feudal bonds exist;

– a state that has a monopoly on telling its citizens all they need to know about the world;

– a state that thinks freedom amounts to obedience to the state;

– a state that sees no difference between what is true and what it is in its interest for people to believe;

– a state where a nation can be transplanted in its entirety from one place to another, willy-nilly;

– a state in which the workers have no influence on the government;

– a state that believes it alone can save mankind;

– a state that thinks it has always been right;

– a state where history is in the service of politics;

– a state whose citizens are not permitted to read the greatest works of contemporary literature, or to see the greatest contemporary works of art, or to hear the best contemporary music;

– a state that is always exceedingly pleased with itself;

– a state that claims the world is very complicated, but in fact believes that it is very simple;

– a state where you have to go through an awful lot of suffering before you can see a doctor;

– a state that has beggars;

– a state that is convinced that no one could ever invent anything better;

– a state that believes that everyone simply adores it, although the opposite is true;

– a state that governs according to the principle *oderint dum metuant*;

– a state that decides who may criticize it and how;

– a state where one is required each day to say the opposite of what one said the day before and to believe that one is always saying the same thing;

– a state that does not like it at all when its citizens read old newspapers;

– a state where many ignorant people are considered scholars;

– a state where the content of all the newspapers is the same;

– a state whose government wants to control all forms of social organization;

– a state where there are many decent and courageous people, but a study of the politics of its government will not allow you to discover this;

– a state that does not like it at all when its regime is analysed by scholars, but is very happy when this is done by sycophants;

– a state that always knows better than its citizens where the happiness of every one of its citizens lies;

– a state that, while not sacrificing anything for any higher principles, nevertheless believes that it is the leading light of progress.

That was the first part. And now, pay attention, because we are going to tell you what socialism is. Here is what socialism is:

Socialism is a system that . . . But what's the point of going into all these details? It's very simple: socialism is just a really wonderful thing.

1956

This essay was seized by the censor and the student journal for which it had been written was closed down. The essay was then pinned up on a bulletin board at Warsaw University until – very shortly afterwards – the authorities took it down. From then on underground copies of it were circulated. It remained unpublished in Poland until after the fall of communism.

Communism as a Cultural Force

There is a Polish joke about a little girl who is told at school to write an essay entitled, 'Why I love the Soviet Union.' Uncertain of the answer, she asks her mother: 'Mummy, why do I love the Soviet Union?' 'What are you talking about,' cries her mother, 'the Soviets are criminals, nobody loves them, everybody hates them!' She asks her father. 'What sort of rubbish are you talking now,' he says, growing angry, 'they are the oppressors whose troops are occupying our country, the whole world loathes them!' Distressed, the girl asks several other adults the same question, but receives the same reply from all of them. In the end she writes: 'I love the Soviet Union because nobody else does.'

I would like to proceed in more or less the same manner as the girl. I would like, namely, to consider a question that is seldom seriously considered (except in communist propaganda, but even there its authors don't take it seriously): communism as a source of cultural inspiration in this century. Anthropologists generally use the word 'culture' in a neutral, non-value-laden sense, to denote the various systems of communication particular to a given society: law, tradition, educational institutions, the mechanisms of power, religious belief, art, family relationships, sexual norms, etc.; and all these are things that can of course be described without any value judgements and without presupposing that some cultures are higher or lower than others. In this sense of the word, Mayakovsky's poems are as much a part of communist culture as the lifeless jargon of a hack from any provincial propaganda department; so are the pictures produced by Maoist artists (which still have a long way to go before they attain the standards of American comic strips), just as much as the classics of Chinese painting. But I have in mind 'culture' in a much more limited sense, and one that does presuppose certain value judgements. I have in mind, namely: (1) works that are original works of literature, art, or scholarship in the humanities, not attempts to copy already existing models; and (2) works of which it is safe to say that they have been absorbed into, and become integral elements of, that culture which is co-extensive with what we traditionally call the 'Christian world', and which grew out of Greek, Roman, Jewish and Christian roots (Russia, even if in its politics it is perhaps closer to its Tatar traditions, does to a great extent belong to this sphere).

My question, then, is the following: how do we explain the fact that international communism, both where it was a ruling ideology and where it only aspired to power, has proved, at certain historical periods, culturally so fertile – able both to inspire works of genuine worth, still considered part of European civilization, and to attract such a significant following among the cultural elite, including some truly outstanding individuals? The question is worth considering because the destructive and anti-cultural function of communism is very well known to us all; indeed, and more importantly, there is good reason to believe – and this is what makes the question particularly interesting – that it was built into the system from the start. This aspect of communist rule has been widely described, so there is no need to go into it here. It is worth noting, however, that communism, in contrast to other tyrannies, past and present, performed its culture-destroying function not only, and not even mainly, by negative means, such as censorship, repression and prohibitions. Traditional tyrannies are less destructive insofar as their aim is limited to suppressing political opposition and eradicating from cultural life such elements as could pose a threat to their authority. As a rule such tyrannies limit their goals: they want to remain undivided and indestructible, but not necessarily to extend their control over all spheres of life. They can thus tolerate cultural expression if it is politically indifferent.

Communism, on the other hand, from the beginning conceived of itself as an all-embracing system of power; it seeks not only to eliminate threats to its existence but also to regulate all spheres of collective life, including ideology, literature, art, science, the family, even styles of dress. Such an ideal state of total control is of course extremely difficult to achieve; nevertheless, we can recall a time when the drive to achieve it was very strong, and ideological norms were established for everything: from the only correct view of the theory of relativity through the only correct kinds of music to the width of trousers that uniquely satisfied the requirements of socialist life. The most impressive results in this drive towards omni-regulation were achieved by the People's Republic of China; the Soviet Union during the last years of the Stalin era also did very well, though its results were not quite so outstanding. A partial retreat from this ideal was imposed by the pressures of reality; the abandonment of ideological criteria in the natural sciences was one such example. Other laws proved too troublesome to enforce, for instance those that concerned modes of dress. In most of the Soviet Union's European protectorates, and particularly in Poland, regulation never achieved such levels; not, however, because the principle itself was abandoned, but rather because the extent to which it can be implemented depends on the strength of the apparatus of power when confronted with the natural tendencies of social life. In this regard Poland was for many years, and indeed still is today, closer to the model of a traditional tyranny than to that of a totalitarian regime, for its ruling apparatus concentrates mainly on negative means of control, such as censorship and repressive measures against the opposition and people it considers politically suspect; it does not attempt, or does so very feebly and ineffectually, to impose ideological norms on cultural life. This is not, needless to say, because of any benevolent intentions on its part, merely because of its weakness.

This, however, is not what I want to discuss here; on the contrary, the object of my interest is communism as a culturally active force. That it was such a force seems unquestionable. Talented writers like Mayakovsky, Yesenin, Babel, Pilnyak, Fadeyev and Ehrenburg; outstanding film directors such as Eisenstein and Pudovkin; avant-garde painters such as Malevich, Dejneka, Rodchenko and for a short while even Chagall – all these, and a significant part of the intelligentsia, identified themselves ideologically with the Bolshevik revolution of 1917. The later fates of this quite considerable body of artists and writers were varied, as we know: some killed themselves, others were killed by executioners; a few prostituted their talents to the new tyrant or ended their days idle and embittered. In the 1920s communism also attracted a number of Western intellectuals, including members of the literary and artistic avant-garde: Aragon, Éluard, and Picasso were Communist Party members all their lives, as were many other people of unquestionable distinction in France, Italy and Germany. Even in countries where communism never established itself as a political force of any significance, such as the US or Great Britain, the number of intellectuals, writers, and artists who at some stage, for varying lengths of time, had been, if not CP members, then Trotskyite or Stalinist sympathizers, is impressive. The same can be said of the intelligentsia in Mexico and Brazil. In inter-war Poland, where the political influence of communism was marginal (although more noticeable in the trade-union movement) and naturally checked by its associations with a country that was an age-old enemy, it still managed to attract a certain number of genuine artists: Broniewski, Jasieński, Wandurski, Wat, Zegadłowicz, and Kruczkowski, or intellectuals like Stefan Czarnowski (in the later years of his life), Nowakowski and Natalia Gasiorowska. In the first decade after the Second World War the communist government enjoyed the support of a considerable number of writers and artists, many of them outstanding. The same was true in Czechoslovakia and Hungary.

There is no need to multiply examples and names; the list is long. It is indisputable that in certain historical conditions communism not only exerted a powerful attraction for a great number of artists, but also inspired many works of art which had a major impact on the artistic and intellectual life of this century. Thus it was not only a distinct form of civilization, one that devastated and continues in its attempts to devastate Europe's historical continuity, destroying spiritual expression wherever its influence reaches, but also a source of energy which inspired that expression.

The least plausible and most naive way of explaining this is by generalizations of the type, 'People are easily deceived, easily corrupted and intimidated, and this is the secret of communism's success.' Dismissing the history of communism with such formulas is as easy as it is futile, even counter-productive, because it makes important historical phenomena impossible to understand. Furthermore, such formulas have the advantage that they can be applied to anything we don't like or are outraged by; their all-explanatory power betrays their uselessness. The history of communist culture is not so easily accounted for; it consisted of social processes which should be analysed as such, not as the suspect motivations of individuals. If the question could be disposed of so simply, it would be impossible to explain why communist governments today, with all the instruments of deception, corruption, and intimidation still at their disposal, have entirely lost not only the ability to stimulate artistic and intellectual creativity, but also the power to attract cultural elites; and that they lost this ability not only within their sphere of power but also outside it, in Europe and America. How is it that Stalin could build up such support among intellectuals while present regimes, less cruel and bloodthirsty, cannot? Why do various other revolutionary and despotic regimes lack this ability? Fascism and Hitlerism were pure destroyers of culture and left nothing but desolation in their wake; and although they aroused the sympathy of a few members of Western cultural elites (Heidegger, Ezra Pound, Céline and Knut Hamsun to name the best known), they proved extremely weak in this respect when compared with Stalinism.

In only one important discipline did communism prove completely barren, and that is philosophy. Official Soviet philosophy has left nothing of note; its history could be studied only as an example of the inevitable debasing of the intellect when it is reduced to being a servile instrument of the Party. Lukács and Bloch, two genuinely interesting thinkers who are still studied, are only partial counterexamples. Lukács is worth reading as a rare example of an outstanding thinker who throughout his life, despite conflicts and disagreements, put his intellect at the service of a tyrant; his books inspire no interesting thought and are considered 'things of the past' even in Hungary, his native country. The only components of Bloch's thought that might conceivably be of some interest are those that have little connection with communism, or even with Marxism. In Poland and Czechoslovakia, too, the philosophy produced by the spirit of communism is a rubbish heap – though to archeologists even rubbish heaps can be of interest.

Communism has a centuries-old history. Even in its earliest guise – the utopian literature of the Renaissance and the Enlightenment (often religiously inspired, invoking the Apostolic community of goods which condemned private property as a sin) – it betrayed its incurable contradictions. These utopias were at the same time egalitarian and despotic; they promoted the ideal of perfect equality, but also rule by an enlightened elite to safeguard this equality. Communism, which came on the scene not just as a literary genre but as a political movement, had its roots in the Jacobin Left. Here the contradiction between equality, considered the supreme and absolute value, and freedom, was even more prominent: the ideal society was to be at the same time strictly egalitarian and despotically governed – a squaring of the circle. In the nineteenth century, the century of Marx, which witnessed the birth and growth of the modern socialist movement, communism did not find fertile soil in which to flourish. It had developed some theoretical offshoots, but it scarcely existed as a political movement; the First International was far from being its organ; Marx himself, despite his theoretical authority, was insignificant as a political activist; and the socialist parties of the Second International, although sometimes in conflict and split into factions, in their overwhelming majority (and this included Marxists) believed in the legitimacy of democratic institutions and in cultural freedom. Social criticism in the nineteenth-century novel was strongly developed and sometimes very sharp, but it had no connection with communism.

Modern communism in the proper sense was born at the beginning of the twentieth century, in the form of Lenin's faction. Until the First World War its influence within the socialist movement was nugatory outside Russia; the fact that it was a completely new ideological and political phenomenon, not merely a tactical or doctrinal faction within a movement, went unheeded for a long time, and gradually began to become apparent only after 1910. The movement made no secret of its embryonic despotism; its totalitarian potential was present at birth. If it managed, in time, to harness the revolutionary wave in Russia and establish itself on its crest, this was, admittedly, owing to an exceptional series of historical accidents, but not only to these. It was also thanks to an ability that later, in more developed form, became the keystone of Soviet success: the ability to absorb and assimilate all major social grievances and turn them to its advantage.

From the very beginning, ideologically as well as tactically, communism was a parasite. It efficiently exploited all social ills, attaching itself to causes that were not only important but also worthy, and supported by much of an intelligentsia nurtured on the ideals of enlightenment and humanism. Communism before the First World War not only defended workers' interests, but also exposed national oppression, took on board the aspirations of poor peasants and protested against censorship. In short, it allied itself, in a non-doctrinaire fashion, with all potential sources of opposition to czarist autocracy and tried to channel them all in one direction. There was almost no communist involvement in the February Revolution or the overthrow of the czar, and absolutely nothing communist in the slogans of the October Revolution: 'peace' and 'land for the peasants.' The dominant ideology of the masses in the revolutionary process was not communism but anarchy, expressed in the slogan: all power to the soviets (councils). The Bolsheviks took over this slogan, then dropped it (when most of the soviets were Menshevik), and then adopted it again in order to exploit the anarchist utopia to smash still-existing government structures and impose their own rule on a demoralized and disorganized society. Lenin openly admitted that the Bolsheviks won because they adopted the Socialist Revolutionaries' agrarian programme. The third slogan which, together with 'peace' and 'land for the peasants,' played an important role in the disintegration of the former state was the 'right to self-determination.' We all know how this programme turned out: 'land for the peasants' meant mass expropriation of the peasantry and chaining peasants to the land on principles similar to those of feudal servitude; 'peace' meant building the most militarized empire on earth, unequalled in aggression and insatiable in its greed for conquest; and 'self-determination' meant the systematic stifling of all national aspirations and traditions.

Many intellectuals, however, saw Bolshevism not so much as a collection of policies to alleviate immediate social grievances, however severe, but as a global sort of utopian technology, the beginning of a new world, a new era, in which all human problems would be resolved and all misery eradicated once and for all. The most urgent problem was of course that of peace and war, and the connected issue of internationalism. World communism as we know it today is the product of the First World War. We Poles have a natural tendency to see that war in the light of one of the greatest events in our history, the re-emergence of an independent Polish state after years of subjugation. This outcome, however, had not been among the aims of any of the powers that launched the war. The war itself was an appalling slaughter of millions, and the longer it lasted the clearer it became that it was indeed, as left-wing socialists claimed, an imperialist war – a conflict between ruling elites carried out by the people. It would be hard to overestimate the role played by antiwar feeling in the sympathetic attitude of European intellectuals toward Bolshevism during the early 1920s. The Bolsheviks reaped the harvest from the disaster suffered by the Second International in 1914, when it became clear that international workers' solidarity, the ideological backbone of the socialist movement, was an empty slogan that disappeared without trace as soon as it was put to the test. The USDP, the German social-democratic anti-war faction set up in 1917, was thus a natural incubator of communism; and for the European writers who joined communist parties or sympathized with them at that time – like Arnold Zweig, Bertolt Brecht, Henri Barbusse, Romain Rolland, Anatole France, Jaroslav Hašek, to name the best known – the horror of war was the main motivation. Communism was the promise of a world without wars. It exploited the human desire for peace, which has become one of the most powerful social emotions of this century. Before the war, the communists were little more than a minor sect, even in Russia; in the period between the first and second Russian revolutions, the influence of Marxism and communism declined sharply among the Russian intelligentsia, and many distinguished intellectuals launched violent attacks on the historical and philosophical dogmas they had recently supported. It was not without reason that, at the 1934 Writers' Congress, Maxim Gorky, by then a wholly devoted Stalinist, described the years 1907–17, a great era in the history of Russian poetry, as 'the most disgraceful and shameful decade in the history of the Russian intelligentsia.'

But other motives played their part. There was the fascination with barbarism that is sometimes found among intellectuals; what fascinated here was the absolute beginning of a new era, a break with the past, freedom from the shackles of a bygone age. In Russia as in the West, this ethos of a culture unbound and unembedded, the (illusory, needless to add) freedom from inherited tradition, the cult of youth unhampered by the burdens of history, the desire to shock, to *épater la bourgeoisie* – all this, too, made the Bolsheviks attractive. They represented the radically New; they were the hammer that would smash the dragging, restricting weight of the past, responding to the call of the *Internationale: 'du passé faisons la table rase.'* For Blok and for Mayakovsky, for the French Surrealists, for the Futurists, this was an important aspect of the attraction. Its presence at that time as one of the factors of communism's magnetic powers is perhaps explicable by the historical circumstances. The real end of the nineteenth century, the real beginning of a new era in all areas of human experience, was the First World War. The Bolsheviks appreciated this more clearly and sooner than anyone else, and were thus able, for a time, to carve out a place for themselves in European culture as the embodiment of this new era – which in turn contributed to lending a semblance of authenticity, however short-lived, to communist civilization.

The first half of the 1930s brought new social upheavals which the communists succeeded in exploiting: the Great Depression, the triumph of National Socialism in Germany, and later the Spanish Civil War and the turbulent events in China. These were all burning, tragic issues. The Great Depression, with its millions of unemployed, its misery and despair, was a perfect opportunity for communism, which now presented itself as the promise of a society without unemployment and insecurity, and also as the most energetic enemy of the fascist cancer which seemed to be devouring Europe (also by exploiting the miseries of the time). At a time when millions were dying from the Soviet government's artificially induced famine in the Ukraine, from cold, torture and exhaustion, from execution in Stalin's prisons and camps, or during the various stages of transportation, a significant number of Western intellectuals saw the Soviet state as a bastion of peace and revolutionary humanism, as the harbinger of a new world in which people would be equal, free from insecurity and confident of the future. Among those who sympathized or identified themselves with communism were people like André Malraux, Walter Benjamin, Theodore Plivier, Jean-Richard Bloch, Theodore Dreiser, John Dos Passos and Upton Sinclair. Leon Feuchtwanger and Romain Rolland greeted the macabre farce of the Moscow Trials as a triumph of justice.

Here, too, it is futile to bemoan human naiveté and blindness; here, too, social and cultural processes are at work which must be analysed as such and explained. The Popular Front in the 1930s was of course a form of Soviet manipulation, but it was not merely manipulation: to the extent that it was effective, this was because its slogans reflected the real hopes, fears and experiences of Europe. Fascism was not a communist-invented bogeyman, but a very real, and deadly, threat to civilizations and nations; although it fed off the same social diseases as communism, it attracted people of an entirely different sort, and it had almost no cultural vitality. The shaky and sometimes timid policies of the Western powers in the face of this threat were skillfully exploited by the communists; anti-fascism could be, and indeed was, a culturally inspiring force. The social upheavals resulting from inflation and the Depression were very real. The two-year Molotov–Ribbentrop pact must have come as a shock to many people, certainly, but the later course of the war soon blotted this embarrassing stain, and from 1941 to 1945 the Soviet colossus once again adopted, with some success, its role as the world's main protector from Hitler's barbarity; and it used its military successes as a strong base on which to build a new ideological invasion of Europe. After the war it adopted, also with some success, the role of ideological herald of decolonization.

Similar processes can be observed in the case of the Polish cultural elite: those of its members who came out in unequivocal support of the communist regime after the war tended mostly to come from socialist or left-liberal rather than communist backgrounds, and their allegiance was determined largely by their negative attitudes toward pre-war Poland, especially in the most recent years, after the death of Marshal Piłsudski. We tend, understandably, to idealize this pre-war period, because it was a time when Poland, for all its failings, was independent. Moreover, its failings seem insignificant when compared to those of the new 'progressive' regime: press restrictions and censorship were minimal in comparison with the systematically destructive effects of the progressive muzzle imposed on Polish culture by the communist regime, and pre-war acts of police illegality pale beside the lawlessness which prevails in the People's Republic of Poland. But that part of the intelligentsia which in 1945 or 1946, after the horror of war and occupation, identified itself, with greater or lesser enthusiasm, with the new regime, saw things differently. Those who remembered the Brest trial, the Bereza concentration camp, the repellent wave of virulent anti-Semitism and the oppressive clericalism, saw communism as a continuation of the Enlightenment: as a force that would combat the chauvinist and clerical current in the Polish tradition which it regarded as poisonous and pernicious. (Here, too, they were continuing a certain tradition, for this was a current that had been combated since at least the seventeenth century – long before the formation of the intelligentsia in the modern sense of the word – by the more critical and cosmopolitan segments of the educated Polish nobility.) Similarly, the social reforms announced by the communists reflected many of the traditional demands of the non-communist Left in Poland.

To say this is not to excuse anything, least of all the role of the intelligentsia in the massive communist lie. But communism is – to repeat a banal observation – a historical phenomenon of immense importance which needs to be explained; it is not enough simply to condemn the gullibility and corruptibility of its followers. If communism successfully exploited genuine social grievances, many of them the preoccupation of both liberals and socialists in Europe, this does not mean that it resolved these problems in any way, or even that it tried to resolve them. On the contrary, it brought disaster in all the social, cultural, national and international issues it championed. The only ostensible exception was an issue which the Soviets endlessly trumpet as their great achievement: the issue of unemployment. I say ostensible because unemployment in the Soviet Union was eliminated by a system of forced labour; and indeed, there has never been unemployment among slaves. Hitler, too, triumphed over the plague of unemployment. However, in democratic societies unemployment remains a very real and thorny problem. In conditions of great unemployment, the promises of communism begin to seem attractive, and the hope flourishes that many people will be prepared to exchange their freedom for the security of slaves.

Communism was a gigantic façade, and the reality concealed behind it was the sheer drive for power, for total power as an end in itself. The rest was merely instrumental – a matter of tactics and some necessary self-restrictions to achieve the desired end. But the façade was more than mere decoration: it was communism's only means of survival; its respiratory system. It was also the ineradicable residue of the tradition of the Enlightenment and nineteenth-century socialism, of which communism was indeed a deformed descendant. As with all descendants, however deformed, some inherited traits are always visible, and in communism, too, these were evident. The rationalism, contempt for tradition, and hatred for the mythological layer of culture to which the Enlightenment gave birth developed, under communism, into the brutal persecution of religion, but also into the principle (practised rather than directly expressed) that human beings are expendable: that individual lives count only as instruments of the 'greater whole' or the 'higher cause,' i.e., the state, for no rational grounds exist for attributing to them any special, non-instrumental status. Thus rationalism was transformed under communism into the idea of slavery. And romantic and early socialist strains – the search for a lost community and human solidarity, the protest against social disintegration caused by the industrial revolution and urbanization – developed, under communism, into caricature: solidarity imposed by force, in an attempt to create a fake, merely ostensible unity – the unity of despotism.

Nevertheless, both the rationalist and the Promethean phraseology, as well as the phraseology of solidarity, were highly visible in the language of communism from the outset, testifying to its links, however deformed, with the tradition of the Enlightenment and Romanticism. They also lent the communist ideology a certain pathos, and this in turn, since it was certainly authentic in the minds of adherents, inevitably lent communism a semblance of truth. In the period of communism's ideological nascency this was, of course, an advantage, but it also had its dangers. For the façade, to the extent that it was taken seriously within the movement, tended inevitably to take on an independent life of its own and to question its own purely instrumental role; and taking the façade seriously also meant confronting it with the reality of the political movement, or the state. This is how communism was able, indeed forced, constantly to produce its own internal critics, heretics, and apostates, who appealed to the original sources – ever-present in the ideological jargon – in order to expose the poverty of the reality. This phenomenon is almost entirely absent from other totalitarian movements, where the gap between the façade and reality was small – as a rule the ideology made its true intentions brutally plain – and the ideological tradition frail. Hitler could have been Stalin's equivalent, but there was no Nazi Marx or Engels, not even a Lenin, to back him up. He replaced them with an artificial, invented genealogy.

Thus communism was forced, to use its own phrase about the bourgeoisie, constantly to produce its own grave diggers. In the intellectual and moral criticism which eventually brought about the bankruptcy of the communist ideology, a particularly important and effective role was played, as we know, by former communists and left-wing socialists – people who not only were well acquainted with its political mechanisms and psychology, but had also 'internalized' them, finding no adequate substitute for their experiences. Arthur

Koestler, Ignazio Silone, Boris Souvarine and Bertram Wolfe were all communists; George Orwell was a left-wing socialist. Starting with Milovan Djilas, the role of former communists in the ideological dis-integration of the European Peoples' Democracies in the 1950s and 1960s was tremendous. In Poland, the names in this category are legion. Similarly in France.

But there is an important distinction to be made here. When we speak of the attractive power of the communist idea and of its cultural fecundity, we can have in mind one of two things: the work, in general and as a whole, of artists, writers, and intellectu-als who identified or sympathized with communism; or specifi-cally those of their works which bear the distinct stamp of communist ideological inspiration. The problem is that many out-standing artists and writers with communist sympathies either did not leave behind any work which unambiguously testified to their political leanings, or made only indirect reference to communism in their work. Sometimes their work dealt with causes which, while championed by communism and in line with communist ideology, were not identifiable as communist by their content alone; one could defend them without being either a communist or a fellow-traveler. Aragon was undoubtedly an outstanding poet, whose place in French literature is assured; but we can distinguish between his poetry and his mendacious Stalinist apologetics, or propaganda novels. Some of Pablo Neruda's poetry is distinctly and recognizably communist, while nothing in the work of the Mexican muralist Siqueiros, a first-rate artist, betrays the fact that he, too, was a thoroughly committed Stalinist. Theodore Dreiser was a communist sympathizer who toward the end of his life joined the Communist Party, but his novels belong to the rich tra-dition of American social criticism rather than to communist propaganda. In the pre-war poetry of Władysław Broniewski, the lyrical is easily distinguished from the political, but even the latter contains some things worthy of note: political poems which – unlike his post-war eulogy to Stalin – do somehow testify to the fact that communism was able, at a certain period, to absorb the energies arising from genuine social conflicts, not just from the history of Soviet imperialism. Similar distinctions can be made in the case of most of the artists mentioned above.

There have been – and I stress the past tense – some specifically communist works of art, literature and thought, unambiguous in their political content, that have nevertheless endured as part of our cultural heritage. But one can safely say that the longer the communists have been in power, the fewer such works there have been. Genuinely original work inspired by communist ideas, work of any real worth, virtually disappeared in the Soviet Union in the 1930s. This was owing not only, perhaps not even chiefly, to purges and killings, but above all to the growing stranglehold of a totalitarian system that left no room for individual expression, which was replaced with the obligatory agit-prop pap. This effectively eliminated those vestiges of authenticity that still remained in communist ideology. A certain amount of good writing did emerge from the Second World War, but the best of it was inspired by patriotism rather than communism: it depicted the horror of the war from the point of view of people who, in desperate circumstances, fought for their own life and for the life of their country, not for the triumph of the revolution. In Poland and other Soviet protectorates, post-war art inspired by the communist ideal produced very little of lasting value; socialist realism in art and literature was a stillbirth. Similarly, post-war writers who had seriously adopted the communist faith did not fully enter the national literature until they had forsaken it.

This is, I admit, a rough-hewn and summary account. It ignores transitional stages, possible exceptions, and works of art in which various ideological strains were mixed. But there is no space here to discuss individual lives and works in detail. If there were any communist-inspired works whose artistic merits are worth serious consideration, it remains indisputable that very soon after the communists came to power, everything of any cultural worth that was being produced in the countries of the Soviet bloc arose either in spite of the communist ideology or parallel to it, by-passing it, as it were.

It should be said, however, that when an ideology aims to be all-embracing and all-powerful, to work alongside it or parallel to it is to work against it. Work that simply ignores ideology, doctrine, and the authorities is tolerated, to be sure – even, to some extent, in the Soviet Union. But this is a symptom of the ideology's senility and decrepitude, not an intentional tribute paid to liberal values. Internal criticism of communism has practically ceased to exist; it has become socially superfluous. Communism no longer produces its own critics who appeal to its own doctrinal assumptions; every critical remark is aimed at principles, not at their supposed deformations. Neither in Western Europe, nor in the United States, nor in communist countries, are there any culturally significant artists who are inspired by communism. The collapse has been total and is certainly irreversible. Only in Latin America, with its enormous social problems, poverty, backwardness, and glaring inequalities, has communism retained something of its former appeal. In the Soviet Union, however, the only ideology with any signs of vitality is not communism but imperialism. In short, communism as a cultural force in the sense I have outlined here – as a force capable of producing works of enduring cultural value – has ceased to exist in the civilized world. Clearly it is still a political and military power capable of terror and conquest, and of mobilizing those forces in the Third World which hope to achieve power as cousins of the great empire. But it can no longer spread its influence through the intermediary of intellectual elites.

To say this is not to explain how communism came into being and was able to establish itself as such a powerful focus of ideological identification for so many people, including a considerable number of intellectuals. That would require a separate analysis, which I do not intend to undertake here. I will only repeat that the process cannot be explained by talking about stupidity or terror; that is a crude simplification of the problem. We might equally well explain the rise and success of Islam by saying that the Arabs were stupid, and this was why, instead of believing in Christ, they chose to believe in the false prophet Mohammed. In any case, I do not think the rise and spread of communism is causally explicable in the same way as drought or floods are explicable. Viewed in retrospect, all great historical events seem to have been determined by circumstances, and this holds true also for the sudden eruption of great religious movements. With hindsight we can always find causes. But the fragility of such explanations becomes evident when we consider that if they really laid bare all the mechanisms and sufficient conditions of historical change, we would be able to predict them. But we cannot. Communism was born as a quasi-religious movement, i.e., as the ideological expression of the need for ultimate salvation. This need is probably a permanent and ineradicable element of all civilizations, but its presence alone does not explain why, at certain times and in certain places, it comes to the fore in the form of intense historical convulsions, engulfing enormous numbers of people and leading to unexpected and violent upheavals which overturn the existing order. Communism, which grew out of a desperate need for ultimate salvation, for a new era, is an instance of such a convulsion. The product of the tradition of the Enlightenment, emerging at a time when educated elites had largely forsaken their traditional faiths, it took the (inconsistent) form of a secular religion; and the psychological mechanisms thanks to which it was able to advance were similiar to those that underlay the vitality of those traditional faiths in their most dynamic periods. The missionary force of its militant atheism was driven by a similar mechanism. However, its doctrinal form was a caricature of religion, for communism demanded both blind obedience and the recognition that it was a rational interpretation of the world. But it could not have both; and, floundering between these two inconsistent demands, it brought about, within the sphere of its influence, the collapse of both rationalism and religion. Its ideological bankruptcy was at the same time a defeat for the Enlightenment, of which it was the ultimate and most consistent – and therefore also the most self-destructive – expression.

Again, none of this explains the genesis of communism. At best, it explains the authenticity that initially characterized its message, and thus the reasons for its brief success as a catalyst in cultural life. But why history should have chosen those particular times and places to realize the self-destructive potential of the Enlightenment – this we do not know. Every powerful and significant social movement is the result of a combination of circumstances, among them the mentality of a particular age, the political and economic conditions, and the psychology, energy and initiative of the individuals involved. No one can claim to possess a method of quantifying all these historical circumstances and measuring them on a single scale which would provide a causal explanation of historical events. There is little doubt, however, that this particular convulsion is drawing to a close, and the loss of its ability to mobilize culturally active forces is the outstanding symptom of this decline. Communism is becoming more and more visibly a question of brute force, and it would be untrue to say that this is all it ever was. As to the form this decline will take, and the timescale in which it will happen, we can only consult the fortune-tellers.

1985

The Heritage of the Left

Long shelves can be filled with books written by ex-communists, be they writers, intellectuals or philosophers, like Ignazio Silone, Arthur Koestler, Boris Souvarine, Henri Lefebvre, Edgar Morin, Annie Kriegel, Pierre Daix, Dominique Desanti, or by former appa-ratchiks and leaders like Ruth Fischer, André Marty, Charles Tillon, Milovan Djilas, Wolfgang Leonhard, to name only a few. (We can leave aside a number of spies.) Some of their books are auto-biographical, some analytical or historical. However, in all of them the authors have tried to come to grips with, to explain and to understand the phenomenon of communism, and their own past commitment to it. These books constitute an important part of the political life of our century. The often quoted prediction of Ignazio Silone that the struggle between communists and ex-communists would be decisive in the future may have been an exaggeration, but it contains a kernel of truth: ex-communists did indeed play a sig-nificant role in bringing communism to ruin.

It would be difficult to think of books of this kind written by Leftists – whether European or American. I mean books that explain and analyse, in historical or psychological terms, the Leftists' own misguided commitments, wrong beliefs, and false hopes. It seems that these people jumped from one fellow-travellership to another without explanation and without thinking about the past. The Soviet Union doesn't look quite so good any more? We have the glory of a new socialism being built in China and the immortal thoughts of Chairman Mao. Something wrong with China, too? There is Cuba, the great hope of a people fighting the imperialist dragon. Fidel also not quite perfect any more? Then let's look for something else. There was not much else to be found, though, at least in the positive sense. There were some admirers of Pol-Pot and Khomeini among Leftist intellectuals (there is no limit to human stupidity), but admittedly only a few.

So there was a never-ending search for a good, noble cause, and once a good cause was abandoned for any reason it was immediately forgotten, and a new cause was found. For a long time there were, of course, genuinely good negative causes but fewer and fewer, it seemed: Franco's Spain (cross off), Salazar's Portugal (cross off), Pinochet's Chile (cross off), apartheid in South Africa (cross off). The worst tyrannies in Africa were mentioned only to the extent that one could, however implausibly, blame Western democracies for their existence.

Why is it that, while communists tried so obstinately to analyse communism and their own involvement with it, such analyses are so unusual among Leftists? Communism was a serious business, and committed communists meant business. They knew what they were after; theirs was real power politics on a world-scale. Very often they lied, of course, but they were usually lucid in going about it. Communists felt personally responsible for an impersonal Great Cause. Leftists, on the other hand, enjoyed a purely mental commitment without responsibility. Communist leaders appeared to have no great respect for their progressive helpmates; the latter were flattered and used, but they were not treated seriously, and for good reason. Communists were hawks; Leftists were irritated butterflies. This might be a reason why communists, once they had abandoned their creed and their parties to become social-democrats or liberals (or left politics for good), only rarely or temporarily joined the ranks of the Left.

Almost any cause, even a good cause, can testify to this comfortable irresponsibility of Leftists. There were, no doubt, serious political, moral and military reasons for the US to withdraw its troops from Vietnam, and the horrible 'mistakes' committed in the course of that war are hardly disputed today. But the Great Reason that was most loudly and most systematically invoked – the belief that once North Vietnam was taken over, South Vietnam would be 'liberated' – never existed. However nasty and corrupt the South Vietnamese regime may have been, one did not need to be clairvoyant to know that its communist successors would bring upon the Vietnamese people incomparably worse horrors and calamities. Didn't the Leftists of the 1970s know what Asiatic Stalinism meant? Most of them probably didn't, but theirs was not an excusable ignorance; they preferred not to know. Are there any books written by Leftists or former Leftists analysing this experience without lying? I cannot say with certainty that there are *none*, but I have never come across such an analysis. The Chinese 'great leap forward' produced many millions of corpses and the 'great cultural revolution' many millions more. Have the former adulators of the Great Chairman come up with their own examination of the monstrosities the Leftists pretended not to have noticed? Have the enthusiasts of the great oppressor of Cuba done so? (Again, I have not heard of such an analysis, but I am prepared to admit my mistake if I am wrong.) Progressive people, when confronted with evidence showing that they were supporting regimes based on slavery, torture and mass slaughter, normally would reply: 'A fabrication of the CIA!' And later, when the evidence became too overwhelming even for them, they just forgot about the whole business.

We can remember the time, admittedly not very recent but not very remote either, when, if you said that there were concentration camps in the Soviet Union, you were automatically labelled a 'cold warrior.' And since a cold warrior was wrong by definition, it followed logically that there were no concentration camps in the Soviet Union. When the glory of the Soviet Union faded, new lights appeared and at every stage we saw the same pattern: adore the despots and then escape and forget.

There was, however, one Great Cause that has persisted more or less intact throughout the past decades in the Leftist mentality: the loathing of democratic countries. Allegiances changed, but if there was something enduring in Leftist politics, it was this: in any conflict between a tyrannical and democratic country, the tyrants were right and democracy wrong: the US *versus* the Soviet Union, the US *versus* Cuba, Israel *versus* Syria. Even in the case of Argentina under military dictatorship *versus* Britain the tyrants were right. To show this there was no need to argue that one or another tyrannical regime was the most glorious achievement of mankind; it simply so happened that in any conflict with democracy, the tyrants were right.

Tony Judt makes this remark in his book *Past Imperfect: French Intellectuals 1944–1956* (University of California Press, 1992). His book deals with an earlier period than that referred to above, but the basic patterns are the same. Indeed, France during those years was the main source of the *gauchisme* that was later to spread throughout the Western, democratically governed world. My wife read this book before I did and said: 'Look, we must have read a lot of this stuff in the 1950s and then it did not strike us as something extraordinary; read today it looks almost unbelievable.'

The focus of the book is neither communists nor liberals, nor conservatives, but precisely the *gauchistes*, the *engagés* spokesmen of Progress. Judt's purpose is not simply to depict the mass of long-forgotten absurdities but to understand and explain them against the background of French history before and during World War II. French reactions to political show-trials in Eastern Europe are investigated with particular attention. Along with the most famous figures, like Jean-Paul Sartre and, on the Catholic side, Emmanuel Mounier, a large number of both famous and lesser-known writers and intellectuals appear on the pages of this interesting report.

While the Third Republic, its political establishment and its bourgeoisie, were, Judt says, attacked in the 1930s both by the Left and by the Maurrasists, there were some idols of the past, like Proudhon or Péguy, that were common to both movements. The horrors of World War I were still relatively fresh in people's minds and unconditional pacifism was strong, but the attractive force of communism was not, at least compared to the years after World War II. In any case, the Third Republic was considered irredeemable and neither Leftist nor Rightist critics regretted its demise. 'To take a stance against Pétain at this early stage would not only have required considerable foresight, not to speak of courage; it would also have meant a willingness to defend, albeit in some modified form, the very values with which the deceased Republic had been associated'

(p. 25). For some time a hope (which later on was to seem incomprehensible) of a national renewal built upon the ruins of the discredited democracy was widespread among the Left. These illusions were not long-lasting, however, and were soon replaced by another, and even shorter-lived, illusion of French society working in unity, after the war, for progress and social justice. The glory of the Soviet Union's huge war effort contributed enormously, of course, to the strength of French communism. To non-communist Leftists like Sartre, 'Revolution' became a 'categorical imperative,' an *'a priori existential requirement,'* Judt says, but it was an empty slogan, void of content and not supported by any analysis. The Liberation soon brought bitter disappointment, and the Resistance was inevitably transformed into a legend. Enormously inflated stories about the recent heroic past were naturally welcome; no one wanted to talk about the mass collaboration with the Nazis. It took many years before some people dared speak the truth – a truth known to everyone but conveniently forgotten. It was now anti-Americanism which offered itself as a natural continuation of the anti-Nazi resistance and which was warmly embraced by many intellectuals as a place for safe and comfortable heroism.

A digression is in order here. People who, like the present author, lived through the German occupation in Poland, later read French memoirs of the war years that seemed to describe a fairy-tale world. The French during the war continued to attend theatres, published without inhibition books and journals censored by the Germans, and gave each other literary prizes; high schools and universities functioned. Life was poorer, to be sure, but its continuity was not broken.

After the war, those who had been Pétainists for only a short time were busy condemning, with sanctimonious fury, those who left Marshal Pétain somewhat later. (There were, of course, cases of obviously horrible collaboration; but even Brasilliach, Judt says, was ultimately sentenced to death for his revolting opinions.)

Everything in French intellectual life, both during and after the war, was clouded in ambiguities. This is no doubt true of many political circumstances, but rarely has such ambiguity been used as a philosophical instrument to justify particular political choices. Merleau-Ponty, the great analyst of ambiguity, managed to avoid the worst, and those who, amid political ambiguities, preserved their lucidity and decency, like François Mauriac and Raymond Aron, were able to do so because they both clung to the simple distinction between good and evil (as opposed to the distinction between the politically 'correct' and 'incorrect'). Sartre did much to make this distinction meaningless. The case of Mounier's group and its self-inflicted blindness was perhaps more disturbing because of their Christian credentials. They declared that there was no point in condemning the 'excesses' of Stalinism because democracy is not innocent either, or they went so far as to actually approve judicial-political murders in Eastern Europe as necessary costs on the path to the kingdom of justice.

Unlike communists, who simply denied everything that was known about the monstrosities of 'really existing socialism' (the term was not yet in circulation), Leftist fellow-travellers admitted the facts to some extent, but justified them by appealing to the historical meaning of Stalinism, including its worst aspects. They assured their readers that socialism was growing despite 'certain excesses.' Some vilified the victims of show-trials, while others reflected sadly on the damage such trials inflicted on the reputation of socialist countries. But even those who were clearly uncomfortable with this display of cruelty still believed that there was no other option but to support communism in the East and its Western outposts. (Anti-Semitism, so prominent in the last period of Stalinism in the Soviet Union and Czechoslovakia, was not mentioned at all; but Israel was viciously attacked as a tool of imperialism.) Whatever the rulers of communist countries did, they were on the Left and thus they were friends. Moral indignation was reserved for Spain or colonized Algeria, that is to say, for crimes supposedly perpetrated by 'capitalism' as such. At best some (albeit few) Leftists condemned the atrocities of communism because in their view it was no longer communism but the same old capitalism restored. Thus defensive strategies varied among intellectuals, but there was always a way of defending and glorifying the 'land of the great lie' (the title of

Ciliga's book) if the will to believe was there. Communism proved extraordinarily successful in instilling in intellectuals the belief in the necessity of global and indivisible choices: either you opt for socialism and justice, in which case you must support the Soviet Union unconditionally, or you take the side of capitalist exploiters and oppressors. Today it seems incredible that this primitive and mendacious view of the world could have been so easily swallowed by so many people who took pride in their sophisticated philosophical education, and had indeed been educated at the École Normale or the Sorbonne.

It is pointless, however, to lament human blindness or wickedness (whichever word is more appropriate in any given case). The history of intellectuals who flattered despots is a long one, and it was well known before communism appeared; but the comparatively massive support intellectuals gave to the communist tyranny requires a more specific explanation. Naturally, aspects of human character and various cultural issues played a role: hatred of the bourgeois milieu, which was, for the great majority of French intellectuals, their own; latent national pride and envy, expressed in a rabid anti-Americanism; the belief (not entirely irrational) in the imminent victory of communism in Europe and the need to make sure one was on the winning side; all forms of ideological blindness; the cult of strength and violence, so common among intellectuals who were political leaders *manqués*; the genuine desire, however misguided in its practical expression, to support the cause of the exploited. But there always remains something still to be explained. The Leftism of the 1940s and 1950s was an appendix, wrapped in the specific language of French culture (and perhaps expressing the West's suicidal impulse), to the worldwide phenomenon of communism. And communism cannot be explained away by the base intentions of individuals. Despite all that we know about it, it still awaits an explanation in historical terms. The Bolshevik Revolution may have been – and I believe it was – an accident, but the fact that it established itself and began to spread like cancerous tissue is still intriguing. The anthology of all the absurdities ever uttered by Sartre or Mounier seems endless; one reads it today with mingled horror and amusement. Judt, in the last chapters of his book, depicts very well the peculiar French intellectual tradition against the background of the grotesque Leftist phraseology. He is less convincing in insisting that this tradition, whether or not accompanied by Marxism, is still very much alive; he seems to display a certain anti-French bias here. One cannot blame him for not attempting to explain the entire phenomenon of communism. Perhaps it is too early.

1994

Totalitarianism and the Virtue of the Lie

The validity of 'totalitarianism' as a concept is occasionally questioned on the grounds that a perfect model of a totalitarian society is nowhere to be found and that in no country among those which used to be cited as its best examples (the Soviet Union, especially under Stalin, Mao's China, Hitler's Germany) has the ideal of the absolute unity of leadership and of unlimited power ever been achieved.

This is not a serious obstacle. It is generally acknowledged that most of the concepts we employ in describing large-scale social phenomena have no perfect empirical equivalents. There has never been an absolutely pure capitalist society, which does not prevent us from making a distinction between capitalist and pre-capitalist economies, and the distinction is very useful. The fact that there is no such thing as total freedom does not make the distinction between free and despotic regimes any less cogent or intelligible. Indeed, the best examples of totalitarian societies were arguably closer to their conceptual ideal than any capitalist society was to its abstractly perfect description. (Among arguments purporting to do away with the concept of 'totalitarianism,' the most absurd says that the Soviet Union, for instance, is in fact a 'pluralist' system because there are always cliques or particular groups vying for power and influence in the establishment. If this is a symptom of pluralism, then the concept is useless and indeed quite meaningless, since all political regimes throughout history have been 'pluralist' in this sense.)

There is no single cause we could hold responsible for the emergence of a system that wants the state to have total power over all areas of human life, to destroy civil society entirely, and to extend state ownership over all things and all people. To be sure, power has always been sought by people as a value in itself, and not only as a means to gain wealth or other goods. This does not mean, however, that the phenomenon of totalitarianism may be explained by the thirst for domination inherent in human nature. Ambitions of power and struggles for it are quasi-universal, whereas the inner drive toward totalitarianism is not. Most of the despotic regimes we know in history were not totalitarian; they had no built-in tendency to regulate all realms of human activity, to expropriate people totally (physically and mentally) or to convert them into state property. Whether or not the term is properly used to describe some historical epochs in ancient China, or czarist Russia, or in certain theocratic societies and religious groups, or some primitive communities, modern totalitarianism is inseparably linked with the history of socialist ideas and movements. This does not mean that all the varieties of socialism are totalitarian by definition. European versions of totalitarianism – Russian Bolshevism, German Nazism, Italian Fascism – were bastard offshoots of the socialist tradition; yet in bastard children, too, a similarity to the parents is preserved, and can be clearly perceived.

The socialist idea emerged in the early nineteenth century as the moral response of a few intellectuals to social misfortunes brought about by industrialization – the misery and hopelessness of working-class lives, marked by crises, unemployment, glaring inequalities, the dissolving of traditional communities. In many respects the socialist critique of these characteristics of post-revolutionary societies clearly converged with the attacks coming from reactionary romanticism and from emerging nationalist ideologies. Socialism was essentially about 'social justice,' even though there has never been any agreement about the meaning of this vague term. All versions of socialism implied a belief in social control of production and distribution of material goods (not necessarily in the abolition of private property or in a controlled economy run by the state). All predicted that social control would secure the welfare of all, prevent waste, increase efficiency and eradicate 'unearned income' (another concept for which there has never been a satisfactory definition).

Most of them were not explicitly or intentionally totalitarian, and some strongly stressed the value of cultural freedom.

Yet in those versions of socialism that relied upon the power of the state to achieve a just and efficient economy, intimations of a totalitarian philosophy can be found at least with hindsight. Marxism was repeatedly attacked in the nineteenth century, especially by anarchist writers, as a programme for unabashed state tyranny. Historical developments perfectly bore out this assessment. Paradoxically, however, the despotic nature of Marxian socialism was to some extent limited by that component of the doctrine which was prominent in its late nineteenth-century version, and eventually entirely discredited (rightly so) as superstitious wishful thinking: the notion of historical determinism, some of whose elements Marx had taken up from Hegel and the Saint-Simonians. For the Marxists of the Second International, the determinist faith acted, on the one hand, as a source of their ideological confidence and, on the other, as a warning that the laws of history cannot be violated. This was a natural basis for an evolutionary concept of socialism, and it played this role in 'centrist' Social Democratic orthodoxy. The crisis of the socialist idea that revealed itself at the very beginning of the twentieth century was expressed in, among other signs, the (not quite unjustified) contention that if socialists relied upon 'historical laws' and expected the 'economic maturity' of capitalism to nurture the revolution, they could just as well bid farewell to all socialist hopes. There were those for whom revolutionary will and the political opportunity to seize power were all that counted, and they produced two totalitarian versions of socialism: fascism and Bolshevism (Domenico Settembrini emphasizes the essential similarity of Lenin's and Mussolini's ideological approaches very convincingly).

In both forms of totalitarian socialism – nationalist and internationalist – social control of production for the common good was stressed as essential. The model developed in the Soviet Union, China and other communist countries proved to be more consistent and more resilient than the fascist or Nazi varieties. It carried out the total nationalization of the means of production, distribution and information, pretending thereby to have created the foundation of the

Great Impossible – all-encompassing universal planning. It is clear, indeed, that a fully consistent totalitarian system implies complete state control of economic activity; therefore it is conceivable only within a socialist regime. Fascism and Nazism did not attempt wholesale nationalization (their tenure was relatively short; the Soviet Union waited twelve years before incorporating agricultural production and the peasants themselves into state property). To this extent they were less totalitarian, insofar as they left segments of society economically less dependent on state power. However, this does not at all imply that they were any 'better' in human terms; indeed, in various ways Nazism was more barbarous than Bolshevism.

In both cases the overriding ideology stressed the idea of social justice and proclaimed that some chosen parts of mankind (a superior race or nation, a progressive class or vanguard party) had the natural right to establish uncontrolled rule by virtue of historical destiny. And in both, the seizure of power was carried out under slogans that appealed to and incited envy as the driving revolutionary force. As in many (but not all) revolutionary movements, what was justice in doctrinal terms was, psychologically and in practice, the pragmatism of envy. The immediate aim was to destroy the existing elites – whether aristocratic or meritocratic, plutocratic or intellectual – and to replace them with a parvenu political class. Needless to say, egalitarian ideological ingredients, insofar as they played any role at all, could not long survive the seizure of power.

It is self-evident that no modern society can dispense with a principle of legitimacy, and that in a totalitarian society this legitimacy can only be ideological. Total power and total ideology embrace each other. The ideology is total in a much stronger sense, at least in its claims, than any that religious faith has ever achieved. Not only does it have all-embracing pretensions, not only is it supposed to be infallible and obligatory; its aim (unattainable, fortunately) goes beyond dominating and regulating the personal life of every subject to the point where it actually replaces personal life altogether, reducing human beings to replicas of ideological slogans. In other words, it annihilates personal life. This is much more than any religion has ever prescribed.

Such an ideology explains the specific function and specific meaning of the *lie* in a perfect totalitarian society, a function so peculiar and creative that even the word itself, 'lie,' sounds inadequate. The crucial importance of the lie in the communist totalitarian system was noticed long ago by Anton Ciliga, in his *Au pays du grand mensonge*, published in 1930; it took the genius of Orwell to reveal, as it were, the philosophical side of the issue.

What does the staff of the Ministry of Truth, where Orwell's hero works in 1984, do? They thoroughly destroy the records of the past; they print new, up-to-date editions of old newspapers and books; and they know that the corrected version will soon be replaced by another, re-corrected one. Their goal is to make people forget everything – facts, words, dead people, the names of places. How far they succeed in obliterating the past is not fully established in Orwell's description; clearly they try hard, and they achieve impressive results. The ideal of complete oblivion may not have been reached, but further progress is to be expected.

Let us consider what happens when the ideal has been effectively achieved. People remember only what they are taught to remember today and the content of their memory changes overnight, if needed. They really believe that something that happened the day before yesterday, and which they stored in their memories yesterday, did not happen at all and that something else happened instead. In effect, they are no longer human beings. Consciousness is memory, as Bergson would have put it. Creatures whose memory is effectively manipulated, programmed, and controlled from outside are no longer persons in any recognizable sense and therefore no longer human.

This is what totalitarian regimes unceasingly try to achieve. People whose memory – personal or collective – has been nationalized, become state-owned and perfectly malleable, totally controllable, are entirely at the mercy of their rulers; they have been deprived of their identity; they are helpless and incapable of questioning anything they are told to believe. They will never revolt, never think, never create. They have been transformed into dead objects. They may even, conceivably, be happy and love Big Brother, which is Winston Smith's supreme performance.

This use of the lie is interesting not only politically but epistemologically as well. The point is that if physical records of certain events and their recollection in human minds are utterly eradicated, and if consequently there is absolutely no way anybody can establish what is 'true' in the normal sense of the word, nothing remains but the generally imposed beliefs, which, of course, can be cancelled again the next day. There is no applicable criterion of truth except for what is proclaimed true at any given moment. And so the lie really becomes truth, or at least the distinction between true and false in their usual meaning has disappeared. This is the great cognitive triumph of totalitarianism: it can no longer be accused of lying, because it has succeeded in abrogating the very idea of truth.

We can thus see the difference between the common political lie and its totalitarian apotheosis. The lie has always been employed for political purposes. But the trivial lies and distortions used by politicians, governments, parties, kings or leaders are far removed from the lie that is the very core of a political system, the heart of a new civilization. The former are generally used for specific purposes, as an instrument to achieve specific goals. The normal political lie leaves the distinction between truth and falsity intact. The history of the Church provides a number of falsifications, distortions and legends fabricated for well-defined ends. Constantine's contribution was a forgery that legitimated the Church's claims to political supremacy. It was exposed by a great ecclesiastical scholar and eventually recognized for what it was; so were many other legends that Catholic and Protestant historians have examined and dismissed. The commemoration of the Three Kings was a contrivance to bolster the doctrine whereby the Church claimed supremacy over the secular powers. But the Church has not rewritten the Gospel of St Matthew in order to justify the legend; anyone can consult the text and see that it contains no hint that the three wise men who visited the infant Jesus were actually monarchs. The story remains alive as an innocent bit of folklore. Nobody knows who inserted the *Comma Johanneum* into the text of the Gospel; this was an unpleasant problem, to be sure, but eventually Catholic editors of the New Testament came to recognize the insertion.

During the last few centuries Catholic and Protestant cultures have produced a large number of outstanding historians who, far from employing various sorts of *pia fraus* to embellish the annals of the Church, have done pioneering work in subjecting Church documents to critical examination. They have produced many works of lasting value (and where are the communist historians who are worthy of such respect?). The Church purified itself of forgeries and gained by it. But its forgeries were aimed at specific targets – unlike the modern totalitarian lie, the ultimate goal of which is the total mental and moral expropriation of people.

The destructive work of totalitarian machinery, whether or not this word is used,* is usually supported by a special kind of primitive social philosophy. It proclaims not only that the common good of 'society' has priority over the interests of individuals, but that the very existence of individuals as persons is reducible to the existence of the social 'whole'; in other words, personal existence is, in a strange sense, unreal. This is a convenient foundation for any ideology of slavery.

So far I have been discussing an ideal totalitarian society, of which existing ones are (or were) only more or less successful approximations. Later Stalinism (and Maoism) was a reasonably fair approximation. Its triumph consisted not simply in that virtually everything was either falsified or suppressed – statistics, historical events, current events, names, maps, books (occasionally Lenin's texts) – but that the inhabitants of the country were trained to know what was politically 'correct.' In the functionaries' minds, the borderline between what is 'correct' and what is 'true,' as we normally understand this, seems really to have become blurred; by repeating the same absurdities time and again, they themselves began to believe or half-believe them. The vast and profound corruption of the language eventually produced people who were incapable of perceiving their own mendacity.

To a large extent this form of perception seems to survive, despite the fact that the omnipresence of ideology has been somewhat

* The adjective 'totalitarian' was used in a positive sense by Mussolini and Gramsci but never by Soviet ideologists or, to my knowledge, by the Nazis.

restricted recently. When the Soviet leaders maintain that they 'liberated Afghanistan,' or that there are no political prisoners in the Soviet Union, it is quite possible that they mean what they say: they have confounded their linguistic abilities to such an extent that they are incapable of using any other word than 'liberation' for a Soviet invasion and have no sense at all of the grotesque distance between language and reality. It takes a lot of courage, after all, to be entirely cynical; those who lie to themselves appear among us much more frequently than perfect cynics.

A very small and innocent anecdote. In 1950, in Leningrad, I visited the Hermitage in the company of a few Polish friends. We had a guide (a deputy director of the museum, as far as I remember) who was obviously a knowledgeable art historian. At a certain moment – no opportunity for ideological teaching must be lost – he told us: 'We have in our cellars, comrades, a lot of corrupt, degenerate bourgeois paintings. You know, all those Matisses, Cézannes, Braques and so on. We have never displayed them in the museum but perhaps one day we will show them so that Soviet people can see for themselves how deeply bourgeois art has sunk. Indeed, Comrade Stalin teaches us that we should not embellish history.' I was in the Hermitage again, with other friends, in 1957, a time of relative 'thaw,' and the same man was assigned to guide us. We were led to rooms full of modern French paintings. Our guide told us: 'Here you see the masterpieces of great French painters – Matisse, Cézanne, Braque and others. And,' he added (for no opportunity must be lost), 'do you know that the bourgeois press accused us of refusing to display these paintings in the Hermitage? This was because at a certain moment some rooms in the museum were being redecorated and were temporarily closed, and a bourgeois journalist happened to be here at that moment and then made this ridiculous accusation. Ha, ha!'

Was he lying? I am not sure. If I had reminded him of his earlier statement, which I failed to do, he would simply have denied everything with genuine indignation; he probably would have believed that what he told us was 'right' and therefore true. Truth, in this world, is what reinforces the 'right cause.' The psychological mechanism that operates in minds appropriately trained and put through a totalitarian mincer is a matter for Professor Festinger to analyse according to his principle of cognitive dissonance.

Lying as a matter of political expediency is itself not a particularly interesting phenomenon and scarcely worth investigation, so long as the lie is just a lie pure and simple, devised for a specific purpose: a minister says that he did not sleep with a girl, but in fact he did; a president claims he was not aware of what his subordinates had been doing, but in fact he was. Nothing mysterious and nothing exciting in such facts; they are ordinary by-products of politics. In totalitarian systems lying is interesting not because of its extent and frequency but because of its social, psychological and cognitive functions. For example, it would be very superficial to imagine that the lie as it appears in the Soviet press is just an amplification and intensification of the normal political lie. Certainly, if one wishes to collect political lies, any issue of *Pravda* ('Truth') or *Literaturnaya Gazeta* will do. Each issue is full of outright lies, suppressions and omissions; and in each case the purpose they serve is obvious. They become remarkable only when seen within the grand machinery of the education designed to build the New Civilization.

The cognitive aspect of this machinery consists in effacing the very distinction between truth and political 'correctness.' Its psychological function is important in that, by training people in this confusion and injecting them with the belief that nothing is true in itself and that anything can be made true by the decree of authority, it produces a new 'socialist man,' devoid of will and of moral resistance, stripped of social or historical identity. The art of forgetting history is crucial: people must learn that the past can be changed – from truth to truth – overnight. In this manner they are cut off from what would have been a source of strength: the possibility of identifying and asserting themselves by recalling their collective past. It is not that there is no teaching of history (though apparently there was hardly any in Mao's China; no books were available except for Mao's works and technical manuals); rather, people know that what they are taught today is both 'objectively' true and true for today only, and that their rulers are masters of the past. If they get accustomed to this, they become people without historical consciousness, thus without the ability to define themselves except in relation to the state; they are non-persons, *perduta gente*.

This mental and moral sterilization of society is, however, blistered with dangers. It works so long as the totalitarian regime, in dealing with its subjects, requires only ordinary passive obedience. If, in a moment of crisis, it requires personal motivation as well, the machinery fails. Stalinism was brought to such a crisis during the war with Germany, when the only way to mobilize the mass of Russians for defence was virtually to forget Marxism-Leninism and to use specifically Russian historical symbols and national feelings as an ideological weapon. An ideal totalitarian society consisting of malleable objects is strong in relatively stable conditions but very vulnerable in unstable ones. This is one of the reasons that a perfect totalitarian regime (or 'the higher stage of socialism') can never be built.

No matter how much has been done to realize the great ambition of totalitarianism – the total possession and control of human memory – the goal is unattainable. This is not only because human memory is highly intractable. Nor is it because the human being is an ontological reality: to be sure, human beings can be immobilized by coercion, but they will always strive to regain their rights at the first opportunity. Even in the best of conditions the massive process of forgery cannot be completed: it requires a large number of forgers who must understand the distinction between what is genuine and what is faked (the crudest example would be an officer in a military office of cartography, who must have unfalsified maps at his disposal in order to falsify the maps). The power of words over reality cannot be unlimited since, fortunately, reality imposes its own unalterable conditions. The rulers of totalitarian countries wish, of course, to be truthfully informed, but time and again they fall prey, inevitably, to their own lies and suffer unexpected defeats. Entangled in a trap of their own making, they attempt awkward compromises between their own need for truthful information and the quasiautomatic operations of a system that produces lies for everyone, including the producers.

In short, since totalitarianism implies the complete control by the state of all areas of life and the unlimited power of an artificial state ideology over minds, it can achieve its goals only if it succeeds in eliminating the resistance of both natural and mental reality, in other words, in cancelling reality altogether. Therefore, when we talk about totalitarian regimes, we do not have in mind systems that have reached perfection, but rather those that are driven by a never-ending effort to reach it, to swallow up all channels of human communication, and to eradicate all spontaneously emerging forms of social life. In this sense all Soviet-type regimes have been totalitarian, but they have differed from each other in their degree of achievement – in the distance that separates their real conditions from the inaccessible ideal.

It is fair to say, first, that in Central and East European communist countries, this distance has always been greater than in the Soviet metropolis: totalitarianism there has never achieved the Soviet degree of efficiency. And, second, in the Soviet Union itself we have observed a growth of this distance – a backward movement from totalitarian perfection. We cannot pretend, however, to know the exact meaning of this process or to foretell its future course.

This slow but real regressive movement of Soviet totalitarianism has nothing to do either with a lack of totalitarian will within the system and its ruling class or with any 'democratization' of the regime. It consists in some reluctantly given, or rather extorted, concessions to irresistible reality. (Back in the early fifties, Soviet ideologists even managed to hamper the development of military technology by their obscurantist attacks upon 'cybernetics.') For obvious reasons, totalitarian states – fortunately for the fate of mankind, but unfortunately for the generations who live in their darkness – are inescapably and irreparably inefficient in economic management. Hence all economic reforms in communist countries, to the extent that they yield any results, go in the same direction: partial liberation of market mechanisms – in other words, partial restoration of 'capitalism.' The omnipotence of ideology proved disastrous in many areas subjected to its rule, so its power had to be restricted. The crisis of legitimacy is patent, as is the desperate quest for reshaped ideological foundations. As a result, the state ideology becomes more and more incoherent and meaningless.

This does not mean that we can expect a gradual corrosion, which step by step will lead to a miraculous mutation and transform the totalitarian society into an 'open' one. At least, no historical analogies are helpful in making this sort of prediction. As long as the built-in totalitarian drive, supported by the powerful vested interests of privileged classes, operates in the Sovietized territories, there is little hope for the kind of progress that one day would imperceptibly cross the line separating despotism from democracy. The examples of Spain and Portugal are not very useful here, both because of the different international environment in which their transition took place and because they had never been very close to totalitarian perfection. Indeed, if the day came (let us give free rein to our fantasies and try to imagine it) when the Soviet political system were roughly similar to that of Spain in the last ten years of Franco's rule, this would be hailed by enlightened liberal opinion in the West as the greatest triumph of democracy since Pericles, and no doubt as ultimate proof of the infinite superiority of 'socialist democracy' over the bourgeois order.

Still, a relatively nonviolent collapse of totalitarianism is imaginable. The frail hope for such a development has so far been nourished most strongly by the example of Poland in 1980–81. Among the Soviet dependencies, Poland has notoriously been less consistent than others in its totalitarian progress, all the monstrosities of Stalinism notwithstanding. My strong impression is that in the early post-war years, committed communists (still in existence then, though no longer in the sixties and later) in Poland were intellectually less corrupt but more cynical than was the case in other countries. By 'cynical' I do not mean that they did not believe in the communist idea, but that they had little 'false consciousness': they knew that what the Party wanted to convey to the 'masses' was a pure lie, but they accepted and sanctioned it for the sake of the future blessings of the socialist community.

Nevertheless, despite all the efforts of the rulers, despite the overwhelming burden of organized mendacity, Poland's cultural continuity has not been broken. Throughout the post-war decades any relaxation of political conditions, whatever historical accidents might have brought it about, immediately pushed the suppressed historical identity of the Poles to the surface and revealed the glaring and incurable incompatibility between communism and Poland's deeply rooted traditional, national, religious, and political patterns. History books, whether printed in Poland or smuggled in from abroad, have always (if they were not tainted with official mendacity) enjoyed enormous popularity, not only among Poland's intelligentsia but – especially in recent years – among workers and young people.

The Polish 'Solidarity' movement, in its brief months of existence, seems to have opened a new, unexplored avenue: a way in which an inefficient and clumsy totalitarian system might conceivably be propelled toward a hybrid form that would include genuine elements of pluralism. The military dictatorship has temporarily crushed the organized form of this movement, but it has failed to destroy the hope. Indeed, the fact that the communist tyranny no longer even tries to assert its legitimacy, and that it has been compelled to appear without ideological disguise, revealing its true nature in acts of naked violence, is in itself a spectacular symptom of the decay of a totalitarian power system.

1983

What Is Left of Socialism?

Karl Marx – a powerful mind, a very learned man, and a good German writer – died 119 years ago. He lived in the age of steam; he never saw a car, a telephone or electric light, to say nothing of later technological devices. His admirers and followers used to say, and some still do, that this doesn't matter, and that his teaching is still perfectly relevant to our time because the system he analysed and attacked – capitalism – is still here. That Marx is worth reading is certain. The question is, however, whether his theory truly explains anything in our world, and whether it provides grounds for any predictions. The answer is no. Another question is whether or not his theories were ever useful. Here the answer is, obviously, yes: they operated successfully as a set of slogans that were supposed to justify and glorify communism and the slavery that inevitably goes with it.

When we ask what those theories explain or what Marx discovered, we may ask only about ideas that were specific to him, and not about commonsense platitudes. We should not make a laughing-stock out of Marx by attributing to him the discovery that in all non-primitive societies there are social groups or classes with conflicting interests that lead them to fight with one another; this was known to ancient historians. Marx himself did not pretend to have made this kind of discovery; as he wrote in a letter to Joseph Weydemeyer in 1852, he had not discovered the class struggle but rather had proved that it leads to the dictatorship of the proletariat, which in turn leads ultimately to the abolition of classes. It is impossible to say where and how he 'proved' this grandiose claim in his pre-1852 writings. To 'explain' something means to subsume events or processes under laws; but 'laws' in the Marxist sense are not the same as laws in the natural sciences, where they are understood as formulas stating that in well-defined conditions, well-defined phenomena always occur. What Marx called 'laws' are, rather, historical tendencies. There is thus no clear-cut distinction in his theories between explanation and prophecy. Besides, he believed that the meaning of both past and present may be understood only by reference to the future, of which he claimed to have knowledge. Hence, for Marx, only what does not (yet) exist can explain what does exist. But it should be added that for Marx the future *does* exist, in a peculiar, Hegelian, manner, even though it is unknowable.

All of Marx's important prophecies, however, have turned out to be false. First, he predicted growing class polarization and the disappearance of the middle class in societies based on a market economy. Karl Kautsky rightly stressed that if this prediction were wrong, the entire Marxist theory would be in ruins. It is clear that this prediction has proved to be wrong; rather, the opposite is the case. The middle classes are growing, whereas the working class in Marx's sense has been dwindling in capitalist societies as technological progress has increased.

Second, he predicted not only the relative but also the absolute impoverishment of the working class. This prediction was already wrong in his lifetime. It is worth noticing that in the second edition of *Capital* Marx updated various statistics and figures, but not those relating to workers' wages; those figures, if updated, would have contradicted his theory. Not even the most doctrinaire Marxists have tried to cling to this obviously false prediction in recent decades.

Third, and most importantly, Marx's theory predicted the inevitability of the proletarian revolution. Such a revolution has never occurred anywhere. The Bolshevik Revolution in Russia had nothing to do with Marxian prophesies. Its driving force was not a conflict between the industrial working class and capital, but rather was carried out under slogans that had no socialist, let alone Marxist, content: 'Peace' and 'Land for Peasants'. Needless to add that these slogans were to be subsequently turned into their opposite. What in the twentieth century perhaps comes closest to the working-class revolution were the events in Poland of 1980–81: the revolutionary movement of industrial workers (very strongly supported by the intelligentsia) against the exploiters, i.e., the state. And this solitary example of a working-class revolution (if indeed it may be counted as such) was directed against a socialist state, and carried out under the sign of the cross, with the blessing of the Pope.

Fourth, Marx predicted the inevitable fall of the profit rate, a process that was supposed to lead ultimately to the collapse of the capitalist economy. Like the others, this prediction proved to be simply wrong. Even according to Marx's theory, this could not be an inevitably operating regularity, because the same technical development that lowers the part of variable capital in production costs is supposed to lower the value of constant capital. Therefore the profit rate might remain stable or increase even if what Marx called 'living labour' declines for a given unit of output. And even if this 'law' were true, the mechanism whereby its operation would cause the decline and demise of capitalism is inconceivable, since the collapse of the profit rate can very well occur in conditions in which the absolute amount of profit is growing. This was noticed by Rosa Luxemburg, who invented a theory of her own about the inevitable collapse of capitalism, which proved no less wrong.

The fifth tenet of Marxism that has turned out to be wrong is the prediction that the market will hamper technical progress. The exact opposite has quite obviously proved to be the case. Market economies have proved extremely efficient in stimulating technological progress, whereas 'real socialism' turned out to lead to technological stagnation. Since it is undeniable that the market has created the greatest abundance ever known in human history, some neo-Marxists have felt compelled to change their approach. At one time, capitalism appeared horrifying because it produced misery; later, it turned out to be horrifying because it produces such abundance that it kills culture.

Neo-Marxists deplore what is called 'consumerism,' or the 'consumerist society.' In our civilization there are indeed many alarming and deplorable phenomena associated with the growth of consumption. The point is, however, that what we know as the alternative to this civilization is incomparably worse. In all communist societies, economic reforms (to the extent that they yielded any results at all) invariably led in the same direction: to a partial restoration of the market, that is to say, of 'capitalism.'

As for the so-called materialist interpretation of history, it has provided us with a number of interesting insights and suggestions, but it has no explanatory value. In its strong, rigid version, for which there is considerable support in many classic texts, it implies that social development depends entirely on the class struggle, which ultimately, through the intermediary of changing 'modes of production,' is determined by the technological level of the society in question. It implies, moreover, that law, religion, philosophy and other elements of culture have no history of their own, since their history is the history of the relations of production. This is an absurd claim, completely lacking in historical grounds.

If, on the other hand, the theory is taken in a weak, limited sense, it merely says that the history of culture must be investigated in such a way as to take account of social struggles and conflicting interests, and that political institutions depend in part, at least negatively, on technological development and on social conflicts. This, however, is an uncontroversial platitude which was known long before Marx. Thus the materialist interpretation of history is either nonsense or a platitude.

Another component of Marx's theory that lacks explanatory power is his labour theory. Marx made two important additions to the theories of Adam Smith and David Ricardo. First, he stated that in relationships between workers and capital, it is the labour force, rather than labour, that is sold; secondly, he made a distinction between abstract and concrete labour. Neither of these principles has any empirical basis, and neither is needed to explain crises, competition, and conflicts of interest. Crises and economic cycles are understandable by analysing the movement of prices, and the theory of value adds nothing to our understanding of them. It seems that contemporary economics – as distinct from economic ideologies – would not differ much from what it is today if Marx had never been born.

The tenets I have mentioned are not chosen at random: they constitute the skeleton of the Marxian doctrine. But there is hardly anything in Marxism that provides solutions to the many problems of our time, mainly because they were not urgent a century ago. As for ecological questions, we will find in Marx no more than a few romantic platitudes about man's unity with nature. Demographic problems are completely absent, apart from Marx's refusal to believe that anything like overpopulation in the absolute sense could ever occur. Neither will the dramatic problems of the Third World find help in his theory. Marx and Engels were strongly Eurocentric; they held other civilizations in contempt, and they praised the progressive effects of colonialism and imperialism (in India, Algeria and Mexico). What mattered to them was the victory of higher civilizations over backward ones; the idea of national determination was to Engels a matter for derision.

What Marxism is least capable of explaining is the totalitarian socialism that appointed Marx as its prophet. Many Western Marxists used to insist that socialism such as it existed in the Soviet Union, deplorable as it might be, had nothing to do with Marxist theory and was best explained by specific conditions in Russia. But if this is the case, how is it that so many people in the nineteenth century, especially the anarchists, predicted fairly exactly what socialism based on Marxist principles would turn out to be – namely, state slavery? Proudhon argued that Marx's ideal was to turn human beings into state property. According to Bakunin, Marxian socialism would consist in the rule of the renegades of the ruling class, and would be based on exploitation and oppression worse than anything previously known. According to the Polish anarcho-syndicalist Edward Abramowski, if communism were by some miracle to win in the moral conditions of contemporary society, it would result in class division and exploitation worse than what existed at the time (because institutional changes do not alter human motivations and moral behaviour). Benjamin Tucker said that Marxism knows only one cure for monopolies, and that is a *single* monopoly.

These predictions were made in the nineteenth century, decades before the Russian Revolution. Were these people clairvoyant? No.

Such predictions could be made rationally, and the system of social-ized serfdom inferred from the things Marx anticipated. It would be absurd, of course, to say that this was the prophet's intention or that Marxism was the efficient cause of twentieth-century communism. The victory of Russian communism resulted from a series of extraordinary accidents. But it might be said that Marx's theory con-tributed strongly to the emergence of totalitarianism, and that it provided its ideological form. It anticipated the universal nationali-zation of everything, and thus the nationalization of human beings. To be sure, Marx took from the Saint-Simonists the slogan that in the future there would be no government, only the administration of things; it did not occur to him, however, that one cannot admin-ister things without employing people for the purpose, so the total administration of things means the total administration of people.

None of this means that Marx's work is not worth reading; it is a part of European culture, and one should read it as one reads many classics – just as one should read Descartes's works on physics even though it would be silly to read them as a textbook about how to do physics today. Even in the former communist countries, the current repugnance for Marx and Marxist texts might pass; even there they will eventually be read as remnants of the past. One of the causes of the popularity of Marxism among educated people was the fact that in its simple form it was very easy; even Sartre noticed that Marxists are lazy. Indeed, they enjoyed having one key to open all doors, one universally applicable explanation for everything, an instrument that made it possible to master all of history and economics without actually having to study either.

Does the demise of Marxism automatically mean the end of the socialist tradition? Not necessarily. Everything, of course, depends on the meaning of the word 'socialism,' and those who still use it as their own profession of faith are usually reluctant to say what they mean, apart from empty generalities. And so some distinctions have to be made. The trouble is that the desire to detect 'historical laws' has led many people to conceive of 'capitalism' and 'socialism' as global 'systems,' diametrically opposed to each other. But there is no comparison. Capitalism developed spontaneously and organically from the spread of commerce. Nobody planned it, and it did not need an all-embracing ideology, whereas socialism was an ideological construction. Ultimately, capitalism is human nature at work – that is, man's greed allowed to follow its course – whereas socialism is an attempt to institutionalize and enforce fraternity. It seems obvious by now that a society in which greed is the main motivation of human action, for all of its repugnant and deplorable aspects, is incomparably better than a society based on compulsory brotherhood, whether in national or international socialism.

The idea of socialism as an 'alternative society' to capitalism amounts to the idea of totalitarian serfdom; the abolition of the market and overall nationalization can yield no other result. The belief that one can establish perfect equality by institutional means is no less malignant. The world has known pockets of voluntary equality, practised in some monasteries and in a handful of secular cooperatives. However, equality under compulsion inevitably requires totalitarian means, and totalitarianism implies extreme inequality, since it entails unequal access to information and power. Nor, practically speaking, is equality in the distribution of material goods possible once power is concentrated in the hands of an uncontrollable oligarchy; this is why nothing remotely close to equality has ever existed in socialist countries. The ideal is therefore self-defeating. We know very well why the idea of all-encompassing planning is economically catastrophic; Friedrich von Hayek's criticism on this point has been amply borne out by evidence from the experience of all communist countries without exception. Socialism in this sense means that people are prevented by repression from engaging in any socially useful activity except on orders from the state.

However, the socialist tradition is rich and varied; it includes many varieties apart from Marxism. Some socialist ideas did indeed have a built-in totalitarian tendency. This applies to most of the Renaissance and Enlightenment utopias, as well as to Saint-Simon. But some espoused liberal values. Once socialism, which started out as an innocent fantasy, became a real political movement, not all of its variants included the idea of an 'alternative society,' and of those that did, many did not take the idea seriously.

Everything was clearer before the First World War. Socialists and the Left in general wanted not only equal, universal and obligatory education, a social health service, progressive taxation and religious tolerance, but also secular education, the abolition of national and racial discrimination, the equality of women, freedom of the press and of assembly, the legal regulation of labour conditions, and a social security system. They fought against militarism and chauvinism. European socialist leaders of the period of the Second International, people like Jaurès, Babel, Turati, Vandervelle and Martov, embodied what was best in European political life.

But everything changed after World War I, when the word 'socialism' (and to a large extent 'the Left') began to be almost completely monopolized by Leninist-Stalinist socialism, which skewed most of these demands and slogans to mean their opposite. At the same time, most of these 'socialist' ideals were in fact realized in democratic countries with market economies. Alas, non-totalitarian socialist movements suffered for decades from ideological inhibitions and lacked the courage to denounce and fight consistently against the most despotic and murderous political system in the world (apart from Nazism). Soviet communism was supposed to be a kind of socialism, after all, and it embellished itself with internationalist and humanist phraseology inherited from the socialist tradition. Leninist tyranny thus succeeded in stealing the word 'socialism,' and the non-totalitarian socialists were complicit in the theft. There were some exceptions to this rule, but not many.

Be that as it may, socialist movements strongly contributed to changing the political landscape for the better. They inspired a number of social reforms without which the contemporary welfare state – which most of us take for granted – would be unthinkable. It would thus be a pity if the collapse of communist socialism resulted in the demise of the socialist tradition as a whole and the triumph of Social Darwinism as the dominant ideology.

While acknowledging that a perfect society can never be attained and that people will always find reasons to treat each other badly, we should not discard the concept of 'social justice,' much as it may have been ridiculed by Hayek and his followers. Certainly, it cannot be defined in economic terms. One cannot deduce from the expression 'social justice' the answer to questions about what particular taxation system is desirable and economically sound in given conditions, what social benefits are justified, or what is the best way for rich countries to aid the poorer parts of the world. 'Social justice' merely expresses an attitude toward social problems. It is true that more often than not the expression 'social justice' is employed by individuals or entire societies who refuse to take responsibility for their own lives. But, as the old saying goes, the abuse does not invalidate the use.

In its vagueness, 'social justice' resembles the concept of human dignity. It is difficult to define what human dignity is. It is not an organ to be discovered in our body, it is not an empirical notion, but without it we would be unable to answer the simple question: what is wrong with slavery? Likewise, the concept of social justice is vague, and it can be used as an ideological tool of totalitarian socialism. Yet the concept is a useful intermediary between an exhortation to charity, to almsgiving, and the concept of distributive justice; it is not the same as distributive justice because it does not necessarily imply reciprocal recognition. Nor is it simply an appeal to charity, because it implies, however imprecisely, that some claims may be deserved. The concept of social justice does not imply that there is such a thing as the common destiny of mankind in which everybody takes part, but it does suggest that the concept of humanity makes sense – not so much as a zoological category but as a moral one.

Without the market, the economy would collapse (in fact, in 'real socialism' there is no economy at all, only economic policy). But it is also generally recognized that the market does not automatically solve all pressing human problems. The concept of social justice is needed to justify the belief that there is a 'humanity' – and that we must look on other individuals as belonging to this collectivity, toward which we have certain moral duties.

Socialism as a social or moral philosophy was based on the ideal of human brotherhood, which can never be implemented by institutional means. There has never been, and there will never be, an institutional means of making people brothers. Fraternity under compulsion is the most malignant idea devised in modern times; it is a perfect path to totalitarian tyranny. Socialism in this sense is tantamount to a kingdom of lies. This is no reason, however, to scrap the idea of human fraternity. If it is not something that can be effectively achieved by means of social engineering, it is useful as a statement of goals. The socialist idea is dead as a project for an 'alternative society.' But as a statement of solidarity with the underdog and the oppressed, as a motivation to oppose Social Darwinism, as a light that keeps before our eyes something higher than competition and greed – for all of these reasons, socialism – the ideal, not the system – still has its uses.

1995

Genocide and Ideology

The Holocaust can be viewed from different perspectives: as the bloodiest chapter in the extraordinary history of the people of Israel or as an aspect of twentieth-century nationalism and totalitarianism. My remarks deal with the latter. I have nothing new to say about the history of the Holocaust, and I am not going to discuss the relevance of the massacre of Jews to the present state of the 'Jewish question,' in particular to the situation of the state of Israel. I do not deny the validity of such reflection, of course; on the contrary, this is probably almost the last moment when such questions can be discussed within the framework of living memory, and not as a matter of scholarly inquiry. In ten or fifteen years the world will be ruled by people for whom the Second World War will be a closed chapter of the past; the link between these events and the existence of the state of Israel will be forgotten, and political decisions will no longer be in the hands of people who were witnesses to or victims of the atrocities of those years. But that is not my subject on this occasion.

A short self-introduction is not out of place in discussing a topic which can hardly be treated in a strictly scholarly and dispassionate manner. I am not a Jew or of Jewish origin myself. I spent the war in Nazi-occupied Poland as a boy, from the age of twelve to seventeen. I lived in various places, including Warsaw. I remember the destruction of the Warsaw Ghetto, which I saw from outside; I lived among Poles who were active in helping Jews and who risked their lives every day trying to save those few who could be saved from the inferno. Most of the time I lived with Jews who were hiding from their hangmen. About 6 million Polish citizens perished in the genocide, about half of them Jews or Poles of Jewish descent. I, as well as everyone I knew in this period, had and still have a clear sense of a community of victims, and I admit that our memory does impose a bias on our analysis of these events.

We sometimes wonder what it was that was so horrifyingly new in the massacre of European Jews in the Second World War. Genocide is clearly not an invention of the twentieth century, let alone of the Nazis, aside from the more efficient technique they developed of killing people and of transporting them to slaughter. Neither is ideological genocide, by which I mean mass extermination that the exterminators justify not simply by their need to have more room for themselves or to enrich themselves, but by an elaborate 'philosophy,' implying that the victims *deserve* annihilation for metaphysical, historical, or moral reasons. As far as I know, the mass slaughter of Anatolian Armenians during the First World War was not supported by any ideological considerations; neither were the massacres of Indians in North America. In the history of European conquest in South America in the sixteenth and seventeenth centuries, we might occasionally find a kind of 'philosophical' argument for slaughter, to the effect that Indians were not properly human beings endowed with souls; yet this theory (soon denied by the Church) was seldom referred to, and even if adopted it did not provide a reason for mass killing. It could only yield the conclusion that in moral terms killing was indifferent. On the whole it seems that these massacres were not ideological and that the killers did not bother much about constructing theories to lend their actions legitimacy. They were after wealth and power; they knew what these were. At best, the total 'otherness' of their victims in terms of religion and culture helped the conquerors to overcome any inhibitions they may have had. The same may be said of most of the atrocities committed throughout the early stages of colonization, whether or not they deserved the label of 'genocide' (a word which is obviously impossible to define with perfect precision).*

But Nazis cannot claim to have been the inventors of ideological genocide either. Mass extermination in religious wars of the past

* On the definition of genocide, see V. N. Dadrian, 'A Typology of Genocide,' *International Review of Sociology* 2 (1975).

falls into this category, no matter what other reasons – more or less sophisticated than the victims' incorrect opinions about divine Grace and the Holy Trinity – were invoked. The massacre of the Cathars in Southern France at the beginning of the thirteenth century might deserve the name of ideological genocide. But heretics had a choice, at least theoretically: they could have converted to the orthodox doctrine, repented and renounced their errors. The Jews had no such option. Jewishness being hereditary, one could not (according to the doctrine) get rid of it; one was incurably corrupted and irrevocably condemned. Of the two components of the Nazi ideology which are relevant to this discussion – the innate superiority of the Germans and the intrinsic and incurable evil of Jewishness – neither was new.

We know of various attempts to trace the origin of this ideology back to German Romanticism, or even further back. Thomas Mann and George Lukács may be mentioned in this context or, in America, Peter Viereck. Even more effort has been devoted to explaining the historical background of the phenomenon of Nazism in terms of the economic, social, and emotional conditions in Germany after World War I. Some authors, mostly former Marxists, went further in philosophico-historical explanations and tended to the view that Nazism, far from being a monstrous accident, was a typical symptom of a general totalitarian trend, of which the Soviet system was another striking example, and that both announced a new political formation which, cruel and inhuman as it might be, was a natural product of tremendous changes in technological development. This gloomy outlook may be found in the writings of Bruno Rizzi, Friedrich Pollock and James Burnham. To them the specific Nazi ideology seemed of little importance; the general economic and political features of the new order being, as it were, fatefully preordained in the very nature of recent technical development, it *was* a matter of chance, or of contingent local tradition, which ideological shape the system would take in a given country – communist in Russia or Nazi in Germany. The particular ideology itself had no more than an instrumental function in mobilizing the resources for tasks which, however burdensome, were imposed by history.

We may set aside this last problem and state generally that, fortunately, there are no compelling reasons to accept this sinister prophecy: no grounds for believing that irresistible historical forces lead the world unavoidably to a totalitarian order. We may admit that some aspects of technological change seem to favour such a development (e.g., the increasing shift of important decisions to central powers), but others counteract it (e.g., the technological and economic inefficiency of totalitarianism), and it would be presumptous to maintain that we can predict the outcome of the clash between these opposite tendencies on the global scale.

However convincing the explanations of Nazism in terms of economic and cultural history might be, it is difficult to resist the impression that there was something demonically new in this ideology, and that its temporary success was to a large extent owing to the personal contribution of Hitler himself (and, of course, of Rosenberg). His creativity should not be underestimated or reduced to a simple expression of pre-existing trends that merely produced him as their necessary instrument. It might well have been the case that the militarization of the German economy was a solution to the country's problems, and that an official pseudo-religion involving worship of the state and dreams of power were likely to emerge as an auxiliary device. But the specificity of Nazi ideology is not properly accounted for by such considerations. This is owing perhaps to the natural reluctance of the human mind to admit that crucial historical events, events which changed the course of world affairs, were produced by mere chance and by a series of unpredictable coincidences, not by an intelligible sequence of necessities. And although it might be true that the result of the First World War made a second one very likely, possibly even inevitable, there was no preordained necessity in the rise and the victory of Nazism – nor, for that matter, in the fact that the Third Reich ultimately lost the war. Nazism was a creation of the human mind, not of impersonal historical forces, and its doctrine was not a fortuitous and passive instrument in the achievement of goals that were ready-made independently of this doctrine. However miserable intellectually and however abominable morally, the Nazi ideology was real not only in the sense that people actually believed in it, but also in the sense that it effectively influenced its leaders' behaviour as an independent variable.

This is particularly true in the case of anti-Semitism. It has been repeatedly pointed out by historians that the extermination of Jews in the last phase of the war was actually harmful to the Reich in terms of warfare, since the *Endlösung* required huge transportation resources that were badly needed for military purposes, and Jewish slave labor could usefully have been employed. Nonetheless, it continued, for ideological reasons. Nazi anti-Semitism was ideologically supported not only by specific accusations like those found in traditional Christian anti-Semitism. Essentially, the Jews were guilty of being Jews and therefore doomed to destruction. They were the embodiment of evil and simultaneously an abstract symbol of evil: whatever was touched by Jewishness was evil, and, conversely, whatever was evil seemed to be of Jewish origin. Plutocracy, communism, pacifism, liberalism, avant-garde art, and the theory of relativity – all these were Jewish. The Holocaust was not only a cunning way of achieving objectives that were set up independently of it; it was a goal in itself, an act of great historical justice, a definitive victory over evil.

In this context I would like to call attention to a book published in Poland under the title *Conversations with a Hangman*. The author, Kazimierz Moczarski, was an officer of the Polish Underground Army fighting against the Nazi occupation. He was also involved in organizing help for the Warsaw ghetto fighters before and during the 1943 uprising. Like many soldiers who had fought in the non-communist anti-German underground, he was imprisoned after the war by the Polish communist authorities, savagely tortured, and eventually sentenced to death. He was not executed, however, and was released in the late 1950s. During his ordeal in prison he spent nine months in one cell with SS Gruppenführer Jurgen Stroop, the hangman of the Warsaw ghetto. (Stroop himself was subsequently sentenced to death by a Polish court and executed in 1952.) After his release Moczarski wrote this fascinating book relating his long conversations with the Nazi criminal in a Warsaw prison. It is perhaps a unique document, the best portrait we have of a genuine Nazi who persisted to the end in his macabre creed: he believed that the reason the Nazis had lost the war was that they had been *too good*, not resolute enough in uprooting all the poisonous tendencies in Germany.

It is in this sense that the Nazi genocide may have been an ideological genocide of a new kind. But it leads us nowhere to say that this ideology was a product of madness or of paranoia. There are no paranoid states or mass movements, and the Nazi doctrine, though perhaps exceptional in its open barbarity, was not at all exceptional in the degree to which it outraged reason.

We now come to the main question I am purporting to discuss: what is the legacy of Nazi ideology in today's world? What changes in the contemporary clash of ideas may be reasonably attributed to the record and outcome of National Socialism?

In discussing this I would dismiss the marginal phenomena of contemporary Nazism in the literal sense. The small groups of fanatics here and there who still use the Nazi symbols and the phraseology of Hitler's Germany seem to me unimportant; hideous as they are, they have no future and no more role to play, and the amount of attention they attract in the press is disproportionate. The very fact that they use Nazi symbols reveals their hopeless position. Indeed, I believe that what remains of the Nazi heritage is not any direct or even indirect continuation of this ideology, but rather certain transformations which, as a result of the collapse of Nazism, have occurred in the post-war ideological struggle as a whole.

A remarkable aspect of Nazism was its overtness. It had very few elements of a mendacious façade. It displayed its goals openly and uttered them aloud: to erect a German superstate, to destroy the Jews, and to transform Poles and other Slavs into slaves after exterminating their educated classes and thus annihilating their culture. This programme was put into effect, and its executors in the army, the SS, police, and the Party scarcely needed what is called 'false consciousness': they did what the ideology explicitly expected them to do, however ridiculous the justifications of this ideology as a race theory may have been.

Though the physical extermination of Jews was not explicitly required in *Mein Kampf* or in other representative ideological documents, the implications were perfectly clear, as we know. In *Mein Kampf* Hitler states 'merely' that the Jews are devils, pernicious bacilli, a plague, vampires, parasites and irredeemable enemies of the human race; that they hate all culture and try to destroy everything sublime and beautiful; and that 'the Jews' instinct toward world domination' will die out only with them.*

In a speech in the Reichstag a few months before the beginning of the war (January 30, 1939), Hitler announced that if the Jews succeeded in provoking a war the outcome would be the annihilation of their entire race.† There was nothing equivocal in pronouncements of this kind, and yet they were not taken at face value at the time, or even later, when the massacre was already in progress: the reports from the Polish underground were simply not believed in the West, so that in Western countries, in spite of the information available, hardly anyone had a clear idea, before the end of war, of what was in fact going on under the Nazi occupation. And it was only much later that people started asking themselves why Hitler's threats had not been taken seriously.

The importance of this aspect of Nazism is brought into relief when it is confronted, as it often has been, with another ideology of a totalitarian state: with communism in its Stalinist period. Although analogies of this kind can often be convincing, one difference between Nazism and Stalinism is neither negligible nor secondary: in contrast to Nazism, Stalinism was all façade. It exploited – quite successfully – all the ideological instruments of the socialist, humanist, internationalist, universalist tradition. It never preached conquest, only liberation from oppression; it never extolled the state as a value in itself, only stressed the necessity of reinforcing the state as an indispensable lever to destroy the enemies of freedom; and it promised, in conformity with Marxist doctrine, the abolition of the state in the perfect world of communism. It preached equality, democracy, self-determination for all nations, brotherhood and peace.

---

* *Mein Kampf*, English translation (London, 1939), p. 539.
† *The Speeches of Adolf Hitler*, edited by N. M. Baynes, Vol. 1 (London, 1942), p. 741.

The presence or the absence of a powerful ideological façade may have been responsible for both the strengths and the weaknesses of each of these two orders. The fact that Stalinism was able to present itself as the legitimate heir of socialist dreams and values, as the embodiment of the old revolutionary humanism, was clearly its strength. Thanks to the skilful manipulation of words it was able – even when its oppressive and terrorist aspects were at their peak – to attract a large number of intellectuals and thus to enhance its worldwide influence. The fact that thousands of outstanding minds fell prey to Stalinist delusions and joined the cause of communism in good faith (whether briefly or for a long time) cannot be dismissed with melancholy comments on human naïvéte; it deserves attention as the most striking example of the power of ideology in our century. But that same power was vulnerable to internal dangers which were bound to become manifest in due course. Those who took the façade seriously – as very many did – and assimilated the art of seeing all events and facts, however inconsistent with the proclamations of the system, through the glass of ideology so that they were able to condone the horrors of Stalinism, sooner or later were caught up by the independent force of their beliefs and finally had to confront the doctrine with the reality. Time and again, in people's minds, the façade tore itself away from the reality, took on a sort of autonomous life and was turned against the reality. Time and again, communists used communist phraseology to attack the communist system. So it might be said that the ideology, mendacious though it was, carried the germs of its own self-destruction, and that communism, thanks to its ideological contradictions, was capable of producing its own critics.

Not so with Nazism. The high degree of convergence between its real and its avowed aspirations made it stronger in one sense and weaker in another – at least so it seems in retrospect. Because of its self-confessed genocidal ideology it had no chance of becoming an intellectual movement of any size or of producing cultural achievements of any value. Though it is true that the resistance of intellectuals to Nazism was astonishingly poor in Germany, their active involvement in building the new culture was very poor as well. In contrast to communism, which for a certain period proved fruitful in various domains of culture, Nazism was entirely sterile. It turned out to be pure cultural vandalism. In literature, art or philosophy it brought nothing but devastation, and what it left can today be counted as nothing but the decline of the human spirit.

It succeeded in attracting very few outstanding intellectuals, and the most famous of them, Martin Heidegger, adhered to the ideology for barely one year. Here was nothing remotely comparable to the ideological prowess of communism. And it naturally selected people according to 'characterological' criteria much different from those typical of communism when it was alive as a faith; the only virtues it was capable of mastering and of attracting were of a military nature: *Blut und Ehre*. On the other hand this spiritual poverty and the relative lack of a false façade was not without its advantages. It prevented Nazism, except for a few episodes at the beginning, from ideological splits: Nazism produced few heretics and seldom nurtured the germs of its own ideological dissolution.

It seems clear that the downfall of Nazism and its all-but-unanimous condemnation throughout the world greatly contributed to an important shift in the ideological aspect of post-war political struggles, and that we are still witnessing the impact of those events, including the way 'the Jewish problem' is approached and anti-Semitism articulated. This seems to me to be common sense, though I admit that it would be difficult to prove – as in all cases where we try to grasp the meaning and the causes of large-scale social phenomena. It is arguable that racial and national hatred in all parts of the world is more powerful and more threatening than it was before the Second World War, and that anti-Semitism is in quite good health. So is the cult of, and the need for, a 'strong state.' But this is probably not because of the continuing impact of Nazi ideology. On the contrary, this ideology, or rather the fact that it has been discredited, changed the way such hatreds and aspirations are expressed.

There are surely multiple reasons for the general growth of nationalism and for its particular form as state nationalism. Among them are the enormous growth of the economic role of the state under various political regimes and, at the same time, the emergence of a large number of new states with no tradition and no remotely homogeneous ethnic or cultural background. Alongside the nationalism of distinctive ethnic groups which affirm their right to build states of their own, we see the phenomenon of nationalism without a nation, or nationalism focused on a state that has no ethnic unity. But it is worth noting that national movements and political bodies, including those that accept the label of 'nationalism,' almost never phrase their grievances and claims in terms of a nation's right to dominate other people; they do not talk of natural superiority, of *Lebensraum* and the like. Not only are all national aspirations expressed in terms of an indisputable right to self-determination or of the right to regain possession of lost territories, but the very idea of conflict with another nation is very carefully avoided. Mussolini and Hitler were not afraid of revealing their imperial goals; they did not hesitate to admit that they were pursuing a policy of conquest, as they considered themselves entitled and called to do by virtue of the natural superiority of their peoples or by the laws of history. Hardly anyone does this today. Nationalist ideologies that expressly condemn the idea of human rights and praise war as the seminary of the highest human values, that preach the inequality of men, appeal to instincts that go against reason, and scoff at the concept of justice, are marginal phenomena in political life. (Mao Tse Tung was an exception in explicitly dismissing the concept of human rights.) Racial and national hatred, imperial aspirations, and totalitarian regimes and movements flourish under the cover of humanitarian, pacifist and internationalist slogans. The concepts of national sovereignty, progress and justice turned out to be useful in justifying all manner of internal repression and expansionist policies, including cases of what may properly be called genocide in post-war history (like the massacre of communists in Indonesia and the recent mass slaughter in Cambodia).

This applies to anti-Semitism as well. The patterns of anti-Semitism clearly changed after the horrors of Nazism. Explicitly anti-Jewish right-wing movements and ideologies, although they exist, are feeble and marginal. And apart from them, the concept of anti-Zionism is quite sufficient to absorb most of the traditional anti-Semitism. Of course, it would be very unfair to say that all those who oppose Zionism are anti-Semites. After all, there are Jews who are opposed to Zionism on political or religious grounds: old socialists who on principle reject all political ideas and movements based on national sentiments, and religious Jews who believe that Judaism is essentially a religious, not a political, idea. But while it is manifestly untrue that all anti-Zionists are anti-Semites, it is true, on the other hand, that virtually all anti-Semites call themselves anti-Zionists; one very seldom comes across people who define themselves as hostile to Jews as such, or who openly advocate their destruction. This has contributed to the erosion of the inherited political patterns and divisions.

Before the war Zionism in Europe was opposed most strongly by segments of the Jewish socialist movement; in various countries anti-Semites rather favoured the emigration of the Jews they wanted to get rid of. Today anti-Semitism has found a comfortable outlet in the form of anti-Zionism, and the latter has been adopted in the West both by communists and by various Leftist sects. Thus a good deal of the anti-Semitic tradition is on the side of the political spectrum that calls itself the Left. Again, it may not follow that all Leftist anti-Zionists are in fact anti-Semites, but to be an anti-Semite and to call oneself an anti-Zionist today will very likely mean being on the side of progress, freedom, equality and universal human happiness. Government-sponsored anti-Semitism – called anti-Zionism, of course, yet very poorly disguised – reappeared endemically throughout post-war history in European communist countries (in the Soviet Union, Poland, Czechoslovakia and Romania), It has been particularly virulent in the Soviet Union, and it led to the remarkable situation where being a Jew is compulsory and forbidden at the same time. It is compulsory in that if you had Jewish ancestors you have no right to define yourself as a Russian or a Ukrainian, and Jewish nationality is written in your internal passport by the police authorities whether you like it or not. And it is forbidden in that Jews have no right to cultivate their separate cultural tradition even in the miserably limited form allowed to other nationalities. In Poland the official Soviet anti-Semitism of the last years of Stalin's rule (the campaign against so-called 'cosmopolitans') was not followed on any significant scale, but in the turbulent years 1956–57 some factions in the ruling party started exploiting anti-Semitic slogans for their own purposes. But the great anti-Semitic campaign was launched by the Party leadership in 1967, after the Six-Day War, and again it had a background in the conflict of party cliques vying for power. Given the intensity and the omnipresence of anti-Semitic propaganda for quite a long period, the results must have appeared disappointing to its organizers, though the poison certainly was not harmless.

It may be said that, on the whole, the ideological effects of the Holocaust were not the same in East European communist countries as they were in the West. In Poland, where a good deal of the slaughter during the war actually took place, the Holocaust is mentioned in such a way as to efface or disregard the special character of what happened to the Jews. This was not the case in the first years after the war: then the Holocaust was discussed and depicted in many memoirs, novels, books and films. In recent years, however, official propaganda, while devoting a lot of effort to keeping the memory of Nazi atrocities alive, has stressed the universal character of genocide and – except for a few special and politically motivated occasions – avoided recalling the massacre of the Jews as a separate and unique story. The same rule is much more consistently and thoroughly observed in the Soviet Union, where specific references to Jews are hardly ever made when the horrors of war are mentioned. The general tendency is to induce people to forget that there was anything special about Jews in Nazi genocidal policy. It is true, of course, that millions of Poles and Russians were victims of the genocide, yet it is also true that the case of Jews was special, and the deliberate refusal to mention it is only one of many examples of how the history of the last war is being falsified in the official communist version.

Meanwhile, popular anti-Semitism in the Soviet Union, unceasingly encouraged and reinforced by state propaganda, displays features very similar to traditional anti-Semitic prejudices that can be traced back to the destruction of the Second Temple. Party leaders are paid back for their anti-Semitism with the familiar accusation that they are Jews themselves and that communist rule is in fact the oppression of the Russian people by the Jews. This tendency can be noticed to a certain extent in some factions of the Soviet nationalist underground movement, and it is expressed in the accusation that the Bolshevik Revolution was in fact the work of foreigners – Poles, Georgians, Latvians, and above all Jews. Thus the same patterns we know from the history of socialist anti-Semitism (Jews identified as bankers, usurers and capitalists, socialist ideas mixed with anti-Jewish stereotypes) return in popular discontent against the communist system: this time the communist power is identified with Jewishness. This characteristically incoherent search for national innocence recurs time and again. In Poland, during the anti-Semitic campaign of 1968, the Jews were accused simultaneously of undermining Soviet–Polish friendship and of having been responsible for the atrocities of Stalinism.

How is this deliberate verbal confusion, together with the impressive growth of Orwellian language and the above-noted changes in patterns of ideological struggle, to be assessed? Are racist and chauvinist tendencies more threatening or less once they are wrapped in universalist, humanitarian and pacifist phraseology? Do political slogans purposely designed to arouse national and racial hatred, anti-Semitism in particular, carry more or less danger when they are so transformed? This question may be put in a general way: is it as a whole better or worse if hatred is called love, slavery freedom, oppression equality?

The answer is not obvious. On the one hand, racism and anti-Semitism seem to be more vulnerable when they appear in full light, as in the Nazi movement, and better protected if their expressive forms are elusive and embellished with humanist ornaments. But the question can also be looked at from another angle. More hypocrisy in ideological expression generally displays more respect for those universalist values and thus attests to their increasing recognition. If movements more or less similar to Nazism cannot now openly employ the same ideology, this bears witness to the fact that the downfall of Nazism was more than military.

So it is not at all clear what sort of practical morals we can draw from the frightening experience of Nazism forty years later, and what is now the real meaning of the slogan 'never again' which resounded throughout all Europe after the fall of Hitler's Reich. Given the lavish use of political mimicry, and the trivial truth that history never repeats itself, the question of how we are to identify political and ideological phenomena which carry dangers similar to Nazism is bound to be controversial. The word 'fascism' has become a word of abuse devoid of content: who is not occasionally called 'fascist' by political enemies? Consequently the lessons we should learn from the Holocaust are by no means easy to set forth, though at first glance the opposite seems to be the case. Should we be wary of people wearing the swastika and worshipping Hitler? They are pathetic remnants of the past. Should we be alert to anti-Semitism? Yet anti-Semitism articulated as such is a marginal phenomenon, and anti-Zionism gives a respectable abode to the non-articulated kind. And it would be exaggerated to say that the Ku Klux Klan poses an enormous threat to humanity. Should we point out the perils of nationalism? But all of us, depending on our political allegiances, sympathize with some national movements and despise others. Throughout the world, ideologies and parties which define themselves as 'left' support nationalist movements and label them as 'progressive,' even the most extreme of them, if on an international plane they happen to be damaging to the United States, to any Western European country, or to Israel.

Thus there seem, regrettably, to be few clear and practical lessons we could learn from the history of Nazism – except, of course, the general recognition of democratic values and of human rights. Yet for this purpose the negative material we can collect from recent history is also only too abundant.

The Third Reich was an exquisite example of the ideological state, i.e., of a state supposed to be ruled by one *Weltanschauung*, the truth of which was guaranteed by the higher wisdom of those in a privileged cognitive position. Nazi philosophers were entirely right in terms of their doctrine when they concentrated their attacks on Descartes and the sceptical tradition. What they wanted to destroy was the belief in universal standards of cognition and the universal character of truth. Nazism had an 'epistemology' of its own, primitive though it may have been. It was based precisely on the abolition of universal criteria of truth and on the belief that some segments of mankind – the supreme race and its leaders – have a deeper insight which no arguments based on ordinary logical criteria could invalidate. The claim that absolute knowledge is stored in the better part of mankind and immune to the scrutiny of universal criteria of rationality – a claim that can justify anything – is obviously a prescription for despotism, no matter how this privileged part is identified – in racial, political, religious or class terms. And the reason Nazism was so shocking in the Western world was not that such claims had been made – they were not unusual, after all – but that they were applied with such consistency, in the very centre of Europe, in a country which in terms of technical, scientific and cultural achievements belonged to the most advanced part of civilization.

For years people kept repeating the same question: how was it possible that the same cultural setting which produced Thomas Mann and Einstein also produced Himmlers and Eichmanns? The shock came not just from Nazi atrocities but, more specifically, from the fact that they seemed to have emerged from the same civilization we all belonged to, which suggested that there was something essentially sick in the very foundation of this civilization. Marxists tried to argue that Nazism was a natural and inevitable product of capitalism – not a particularly strong claim when confronted with the liberating potential of Stalinism and with the fact that democratic institutions are so strongly and clearly connected with the market economy. Catholics, in their turn, devolved the main responsibility on the atheism of the National Socialist philosophy and argued that an attempt to forget God could not have failed to yield such results – again, a doubtful argument, considering that a clear positive correlation between a society's religious fervour and its respect for democratic values is by no means a well-proven sociological fact, to say the least. If it were so, some theocratic states of the past, or contemporary traditional Islamic states, should be models of democracy. Catholic critics are right, however, in pointing out that the cult of a nation, or of a state, or of a nation-state, as a supreme and absolute value carries a powerful totalitarian potential and, if consistently upheld, provides the justification for all imaginable violations of individual rights, including genocide if needed.

Many great Germans of the past were occasionally singled out as spiritual ancestors of Nazism, including Hegel, Fichte and Luther; and Lukács seemed to believe (in *Die Zerstörung der Vernuft*) that all of German philosophy from Schelling onwards, with the sole exception of Marxism, had been, as it were, teleologically propelled by an urge to pave the way for Hitler.

There is, however, something artificial in reconstructing such pedigrees. It seems safe to say that no ideology, and certainly no ideology with all-embracing claims, is immune to the danger of being used as an instrument of oppression and slavery, and this includes religious systems, socialist and anarchist ideals, national doctrines and all sorts of high-minded utopias. To be sure, some are better adapted to such use and some less so, and Nazism was obviously unusual in this respect. Yet if we judge various worldviews by their ostensible content alone, few seem less suited than Christianity to serve oppressive purposes, and yet Christianity turned out to be quite serviceable when needed. Evil can catch hold of any ideology, no matter how well designed, and turn it into its tool. Except for the virtue of tolerance, there are hardly any values which by force of their content, intrinsically, could not be employed for evil purposes, and the virtue of tolerance itself has been repeatedly attacked for protecting evil and lies from destruction and thus for being self-defeating. This is, as we know, a matter of persistent controversy: should tolerance be extended to people preaching and practising intolerance, in particular to racist and totalitarian movements? This is a question of the best strategy for defending democratic values, the absolute strategy – i.e., one that involves no cost – being impossible here or anywhere else. To suppress intolerant movements and ideas for the sake of tolerance is self-defeating, and not to suppress them is also self-defeating; this simply amounts to saying that as long as movements against tolerance exist, their very existence makes a state of perfect tolerance impossible – an apparently tautological assertion. A democratic order enjoying strong support and functioning with reasonable efficiency can survive while allowing intolerant movements, however abominable, to express themselves; the idea that it must stifle freedom of speech in order to maintain it can easily be expanded into a more general theory stating that we have to establish tyranny in order to prevent a tyranny from being established. After all, the saying 'we shall know freedom once more only when we have destroyed the foes of freedom'* is actually a quotation from Hitler.

Yet to tolerate totalitarian movements within a democratic society means just that: to tolerate them, and nothing more; it does not, or at least ought not to, imply that public institutions should treat them in the same way they treat movements and ideas within the democratic spectrum. In other words, a constitution which is committed to defending democratic values cannot at the same time pretend, without self-contradiction, to be indifferent to these values: it cannot treat ideologies and activities committed to their destruction on a par with all others. This is admittedly easier to state as a general rule than to convert into practical measures that would be sheltered from abuses. Nevertheless the self-protection of democracy is simply abandoned if its enemies enjoy the same kind of respect as its defenders. And if, on the other hand, totalitarian or racist movements are powerful enough to tear apart the legal fabric of a democratic society, this does not prove that democratic principles have lost their validity or turned out to be inconsistent. What it does prove is either that democracy was incapable of mobilizing its resources to defend itself, or that in some circumstances consistent nationalism and jingoism have enormous totalitarian potential. Once national values are declared supreme, there are no rights of individuals that could be defended if they happen to clash, or even just appear to clash, with the ideal of a strong nation, and there are no limits to mendacity and repression. Nazism was the most splendidly consistent example of national values exalted as the source and the measure of all others.

This last moral might appear trivial, but if we take it seriously it is perhaps less trivial than it appears. It cannot teach us which side

---

* *The Speeches of Adolf Hitler, op. cit.*, Vol. 1, p. 8.

we should take in today's conflicts, but it does at least teach us what kind of ideas, however adorned with humanist phrases, we should treat with the utmost suspicion. The history of the Holocaust is equally important viewed from both sides: the suffering of the victims and the depravity of the hangmen. The intensity of evil may not have been unique or unparalleled in history, or, for that matter, in our century, yet its ideological justification was apparently unique. Those who reject the content of this ideology – and there are very few who do not – must not avoid a question that reaches beyond Nazi doctrine: to what extent are they ready to justify evil for the sake of ideological values of any sort? Those who believe that such limits cannot be defined or who simply refuse to define them are in the proper sense the spiritual heirs of Hitler.

1997

The Marxist Roots of Stalinism

The Questions We Ask and the Questions We Don't

When we ask about the relation between Marxism and the Stalinist ideology and system of power, the main difficulty is in how to formulate the question. This can be done, and in fact has been done, in a number of ways. Some of the resulting questions are unanswerable or pointless; others are rhetorical, since the answers are obvious.

An example of a question that is both unanswerable and pointless: 'What would Marx have said had he lived to see his ideas embodied in the Soviet system?' If he had lived, he would inevitably have changed. If by some miracle he were resurrected now, his opinion about which practical interpretation of his philosophy is the best one would be just one opinion among others, and could easily be dismissed by saying that a philosopher is not necessarily infallible in recognizing the implications of his own ideas.

Examples of questions to which the answers are obvious and indisputable: 'Was the Stalinist system causally generated by Marxist theory? Do Marx's writings contain any implicit or explicit value judgments that conflict with the value system established in Stalinist societies?' The answer to the first question is obviously 'no': there has never been a society entirely begotten by an ideology or entirely explicable by the ideas of those who contributed to its origin. Anyone is Marxist enough to admit that. All societies reflect in their institutions their members' and makers' (mutually conflicting) ideas about how society ought to be, but no society has ever been produced from such ideas alone – from conceptions of it before its existence. To imagine that a society could ever spring up entirely from a utopia (or indeed from a *kakotopia*) would amount to believing that human communities are capable of doing away with their history. This is common sense – a platitude, and a purely negative one at that. Societies have always been moulded by what they thought about themselves, but this dependence has never been more than partial.

The answer to the second question is obviously 'yes,' and is irrelevant to our problem. It is easily established that Marx never wrote anything to the effect that the socialist kingdom of freedom would consist in one-party despotic rule; that he did not reject democratic forms of social life; that he expected socialism to lead to the abolition of economic coercion *in addition to*, and not *as opposed to*, political coercion; and so on. Nevertheless, his theory may logically imply consequences that are incompatible with his ostensible value judgments; or it may be that empirical circumstances prevented its being implemented in any other way. There is nothing odd in the fact that political and social programs, utopias and prophecies lead to outcomes not only very different from but significantly in conflict with the intentions of their authors; empirical connections previously unnoticed or neglected may make it impossible to implement one part of the utopia without abandoning some other ingredient. This, again, is common sense, and trivial. Most of what we learn in life is about which values are compatible and which mutually exclusive; and most utopians are simply incapable of learning that there *are* incompatible values. More often than not, this incompatibility is empirical, not logical, and this is why their utopias are not necessarily self-contradictory in logical terms, only impracticable, because of the way the world is.

Thus in discussing the relationship between Stalinism and Marxism I dismiss as irrelevant pronouncements like 'This would make Marx turn in his grave' or 'Marx was against censorship and in favor of free elections,' whether or not their truth could be decided with certainty (which is somewhat doubtful in the case of the former).

My own curiosity would be better expressed in another way: was (or is) the characteristically Stalinist ideology that was designed to justify the Stalinist system of societal organization a legitimate (even if not the only possible) interpretation of Marxist philosophy of history? This is the milder version of my question. The stronger version is: was every attempt to implement all the basic values of Marxist socialism likely to generate a political organization that would bear the unmistakable marks of Stalinism? I shall argue for an affirmative answer to both questions, while realizing that saying 'yes' to the first does not logically entail 'yes' to the second: it is logically consistent to maintain that Stalinism was one of several admissible variants of Marxism and to deny that the very content of Marxist philosophy favored this particular version more strongly than any other.

How Can 'Stalinism' be Identified?

It makes little difference whether we use the word 'Stalinism' to refer to a well-defined period of one-man despotism in the Soviet Union (i.e., roughly from 1930 to 1953) or to any system that clearly manifests similar features. Nevertheless, the question of the degree to which post-Stalinist Soviet and Soviet-style states are essentially extensions of that system is obviously not a terminological one. For a number of reasons, however, the second, less historical and more abstract definition, which stresses the continuity of the system, is more convenient.

'Stalinism' may be characterized as an (almost perfect) totalitarian society based on state ownership of the means of production. I use the word 'totalitarian' in its common sense of a political system where social ties have been entirely replaced by state-imposed organization and where, consequently, all groups and all individuals should be guided in their actions only by goals which are goals of the state, and which the state has defined as such. In other words, an ideal totalitarian system would entail the utter destruction of civil society: it would be a system in which the state and its organizational instruments were the only forms of social life, and where all forms of human activity – economic, intellectual, political, and cultural – were allowed and imposed (the distinction between what is allowed and what is imposed tending to disappear) only if they were at the service of state goals (again, as defined by the state). In such a system, every individual (including the rulers themselves) is considered the property of the state.

The concept so defined – and in so defining it I believe I do not differ from most authors who have dealt with the subject – calls for a few explanatory remarks.

First, it is clear that in order to achieve the perfect shape, a totalitarian principle of organization requires state control of the means of production. In other words, a state which leaves significant parts of productive activity and economic initiative in the hands of individuals, and in consequence permits segments of society to be economically independent of the state, cannot attain the ideal form. Therefore totalitarianism has the best chances of fulfilling this ideal within a socialist economy.

Second, it should be stressed that no absolutely perfect totalitarian system has ever existed. However, we do know some societies with a very strong, built-in, and constantly operative tendency to 'nationalize' all forms of individual and community life. Both Soviet and Chinese society are, or have been, in certain periods, very close to this ideal; so was Nazi Germany, even if it did not last long enough to develop itself fully, and even though it was satisfied with subordinating economic activity to state goals through coercion, without nationalizing everything. Other fascist states were (or are) far behind Germany on this path; nor have European socialist states ever achieved the Soviet level of totalitarianism, despite a permanent and undiminished determination to do so.

It is unlikely that the *entelechia* of totalitarianism could ever be realized in an ideal form. There are forms of life – among them familal, emotional, and sexual relationships – which stubbornly resist the pressure of the system; they have been subjected to all sorts of strong state pressure, but apparently never with complete success (at least not in the Soviet state; perhaps more was achieved in China). Similarly with individual and collective memory, which the totalitarian system constantly tries to annihilate by reshaping, rewriting, and falsifying history according to current political needs. Factories and labour are obviously easier to nationalize than feelings; and hopes easier than memories. Resistance to state ownership of the past is an important part of anti-totalitarian movements.

Third, the above definition implies that not every despotic system or reign of terror is necessarily totalitarian. Some, even the bloodiest, may have limited goals, and may not need to absorb all forms of human activity within them. The worst forms of colonial rule, in their worst periods, were usually not totalitarian; the goal was to exploit the subjugated countries economically, and many spheres of life which were neutral from this point of view could be left more of less untouched. Conversely, a totalitarian system does not need to use terror permanently as a means of oppression.

In its perfect form, totalitarianism is an extraordinary form of slavery: slavery without masters. It converts all people into slaves; because of this it bears certain marks of egalitarianism.

I realize that the concept of totalitarianism, applied in this way, has of late increasingly been dismissed as 'outdated' or 'discredited'; its validity has been questioned. Yet I know of no analysis, either conceptual or historical, that does discredit it, although I am acquainted with many earlier analyses which justify it. Indeed, the prediction that communism would mean state-ownership of persons appears in Proudhon; and so many well-known authors have pointed out (whether or not they used the word 'totalitarianism' in doing so) that this was what did in fact happen in Soviet society, and gone on to describe it, that it would be pointless pedantry to quote them here.

The Main Stages of Stalinist Totalitarianism

The Soviet variety of totalitarianism spent many years ripening before reaching its apogee. The main stages of its growth are well known, and need only to be briefly mentioned.

In the first stage, the basic forms of representative democracy –

parliament, elections, political parties, a free press – were done away with.

The second stage (which overlapped with the first) is known by the misleading name of 'war communism.' The name suggests that the policies of this period were conceived of as temporary and exceptional measures to cope with the monstrous difficulties imposed by civil war and intervention. In fact, it is clear from the relevant writings of the leaders – in particular Lenin, Trotsky, and Bukharin – that they all envisaged this economic policy (the abolition of free trade, coercive requisitioning of 'surplus' – i.e., whatever the local leadership considered to be surplus – from the peasants, universal rationing, forced labour) as a permanent achievement of the new society, and that it was eventually abandoned not because the war conditions which had made it necessary no longer existed, but as a result of the economic disaster it had caused. Both Trotsky and Bukharin were emphatic in their assurances that forced labour was an organic part of the new society.

Important elements of the totalitarian order that was set up in this period persisted and became permanent components of Soviet society. One such lasting achievement was the destruction of the working class as a political force: the abolition of the soviets as an independent expression of popular initiative and the end of independent trade unions and political parties. Another was the suppression – not yet definitive – of democracy within the party itself: the ban on factional activity. Throughout the NEP era the totalitarian traits of the system were extremely strong, despite the fact that free trade was accepted and that a large section of society – the peasants – enjoyed economic independence from the state. Both politically and culturally, the NEP meant mounting pressure of the party-owned state on all centers of initiative that were not yet, or not entirely, state-owned, although it was only in subsequent stages of development that full success was achieved in this respect.

The third stage was forced collectivization, which amounted to destroying the last social class not yet nationalized and gave the state full control over economic life. Which did not mean, of course, that it enabled the state to engage in real economic planning: it did not.

The fourth stage was to destroy the party itself, through purges; for it was still a potential, though no longer actual, non-nationalized force. Although no effective forces of rebellion survived within it, many of its members, especially the older ones, remained loyal to the traditional party ideology. Thus even if they were perfectly obedient, they were (rightly) suspected of dividing their loyalties between the actual leader and the inherited ideological value system – in other words, of being potentially disloyal to the leader. It had to be made clear to them that ideology was whatever the leader at any given moment said it was. The massacres successfully accomplished this task; they were the work of an ideological *Führer*, not a madman.

The Mature Face of Stalinism

Each stage of this process was deliberately decided and organized, although not all were planned in advance. The result was a fully state-owned society that came very close to the ideal of perfect unity, cemented by party and police. It was both perfectly integrated and perfectly fragmented, and for the same reason: integrated in that all forms of collective life were entirely subordinated to, and imposed by, one ruling center, and fragmented in that civil society had been to all intents and purposes destroyed, and each citizen, in all his relations with the state, faced the omnipotent apparatus alone, an isolated and powerless individual. Society was reduced to a thing like a 'sack of potatoes,' as Marx said of French peasants in the *Eighteenth Brumaire*.

This situation – a unified state organism facing atom-like individuals – defined the all-important features of the Stalinist system. They are well known and have been much-described, but it is worth briefly mentioning a few of the ones most relevant to our topic.

First, the abolition of law. Law persisted, to be sure, as a set of procedural rules governing public life. But as a set of rules which could infringe upon the state's omnipotence in its dealings with individuals it was entirely abolished. In other words, it could contain no rules which might restrict the principle that citizens are the property of the state. In its crucial points totalitarian law had to be vague, so that its application might hinge on the arbitrary and changing decisions of the executive authorities, and so that each citizen could be considered a criminal whenever these authorities chose so to consider him. The notable examples have always been political crimes as defined in penal codes; these are constructed in such a way that it is well-nigh impossible for a citizen not to commit crimes almost daily. Which of these crimes are actually prosecuted and how much terror is used depends on the political decisions of the rulers. In this respect nothing has changed in the post-Stalinist period: the law remains characteristically totalitarian, and neither the transition from mass to selective terror nor the better observance of procedural rules is relevant – as long as they do not limit the effective power of the state over individual lives – to its persistence. People may or may not be jailed for telling political jokes; their children may or may not be forcibly taken away from them if they fail in their legal duty to raise them in the communist spirit (whatever this means). Totalitarian lawlessness consists not in the actual application of extreme measures always and everywhere but in the fact that the law gives individuals no protection against whatever forms of repression the state wants to use at any given moment. The law as a mediator between the state and the people disappears, and is converted into an endlessly malleable instrument of the state. In this respect the Stalinist principle persists unchanged.

Second, one-person autocracy. This seems to have been a natural and 'logical' outcome of the perfect-unity principle which was the driving force in the development of the totalitarian state. In order to achieve its full shape, the state required one and only one leader, endowed with limitless power. This was implicit in the very foundations of the Leninist party (in accordance with Trotsky's often quoted prophesy of 1903, soon forgotten by the prophet himself). The whole progress of the Soviet system in the 1920s consisted in a step-by-step narrowing of the forum where conflicting interests, ideas, and political tendencies could be expressed. For a short period they continued to be articulated publicly in society, but their expression was gradually confined, in a narrowing upward movement: first to the party; then to the party apparatus; then to the Central Committee; and finally to the Politburo. But here, too, expressions of social conflict could be prevented, although the sources of conflict had not been eradicated. It was Stalin's well-grounded contention that even here, in this narrowest caucus, conflicting expressions of opinion, if allowed to continue, would convey the pressure of those conflicting interests which still survived within society. This is why the destruction of the civil society could not be fully accomplished so long as different tendencies or factions had room to express themselves, even in the supreme party organ.

The changes which occurred in the Soviet system after Stalin – the transition from personal tyranny to oligarchy – seem most salient here. They resulted from an incurable contradiction inherent in the system: perfect unity of leadership, required by the system and embodied in personal despotism, was incompatible with other leaders' need for a minimum of security. Under Stalin's rule they were demoted to the same precarious status as other people – the status of slaves. All their enormous privileges could not protect them against a sudden fall from grace, imprisonment and death. The oligarchical rule after Stalin was a sort of mutual security pact among the party apparatus. But such a contract, insofar as it is in fact applied, runs counter to the principle of unity. In this sense the decades after Stalin's death may properly be described as an ailing form of Stalinism.

Nevertheless, Soviet society, even in its worst periods, has never been ruled by the police. Stalin governed the country and the party with the aid of the police machine, but he governed as party leader, not as chief of police. The party, which for a quarter of a century was identical with Stalin, never lost its all-embracing sway.

Third, universal spying as the principle of government. People were encouraged – and compelled – to spy upon one another, but this was obviously not how the state defended itself against real dangers; rather, it was a way of pushing the principle of totalitarianism to its extreme. As citizens, people were supposed to live in a perfect unity of goals, desires, and thoughts – all expressed through the mouth of the leader. As individuals, however, they were expected to hate one another and to live in constant mutual hostility. Only thus could the isolation of individuals from one another achieve perfection. In fact, the unattainable ideal of the system seems to have been one where everyone is at the same time an inmate of a concentration camp and a secret police agent.

Fourth, the apparent omnipotence of ideology. This is a point on which, in all discussions of Stalinism, there is more confusion and disagreement than on any other. This is evident if we look at the exchange of views on the subject between Solzhenitsyn and Sakharov. The former says, roughly, that the whole Soviet state, in both its home and its foreign policy, in both economic and political matters, is subjugated to the overwhelming rule of Marxist ideology, and that it is this (false) ideology which is responsible for all the disasters that have struck both the state and the society. The latter replies that the official state ideology is dead and that no one any longer takes it seriously, so it is silly to imagine that it could be a real force in guiding and shaping practical policies.

It seems that both these observations are valid, within certain limits. The point is that the Soviet state has an ideology built into its very foundations, from the very beginning, as the only principle of its legitimacy. Certainly, the ideological banners under which the Bolshevik party seized power in Russia (peace and land for the peasants) had no specifically socialist, let alone Marxist, content. But it could only establish its monopoly rule on the Leninist ideological principle: as a party which by definition was the only legitimate mouthpiece of the working class and of all the 'toiling masses,' of their interests, goals, and desires (even if these were unknown to the masses themselves), and which owed its ability to 'express' the will of the masses to its 'correct' Marxist ideology. A party that wields despotic power cannot abandon the ideology which justifies this power and which remains, in the absence of free elections or an inherited royal charisma, the only basis of its legitimacy. In such a system of rule ideology is indispensable, no matter how few or many people believe it, who they are and how seriously they take it; and it remains indispensable even if – as is now the case in European socialist countries – there are virtually no more believers left, either among the rulers or among the ruled. The leaders clearly cannot afford to reveal the real and notorious principles of their policy without risking the utter collapse of the system of power. A state ideology believed by no one must be binding on all if the entire fabric of the state is not to crumble.

This does not mean that the ideological considerations appealed to in order to justify each step in practical policy are real, independent forces before which Stalin or other leaders bowed. But to a certain extent they do limit this policy. The Soviet system, both under and after Stalin, has always pursued the *Realpolitik* of a great empire, and its ideology had to be vague enough to sanctify any given policy: NEP and collectivization, friendship with the Nazis and war with the Nazis, friendship with China and the condemnation of China, support for Israel or support for Israel's foes, Cold War and détente, the tightening of the internal regime and its relaxation, the oriental cult of the satrap and the denunciation of that cult. And still this ideology preserves the Soviet state and holds it together.

It has often been pointed out that the Soviet totalitarian system is not intelligible unless we take into account the historical background of Russia, with its strongly pronounced totalitarian traits. The autonomy of the state and its overwhelming powers over civil society was stressed by Russian historians of the nineteenth century, and this view was endorsed, with some qualifications, by a number of Russian Marxists (such as Plekhanov, in his *History of Russian Social Thought*, and Trotsky in his *History of the Russian Revolution*). After the revolution this background was repeatedly referred to as the genuine source of Russian communism (Berdyaev). Many authors (Kucharzewski was one of the first) saw in Soviet Russia a direct extension of the czarist regime; they saw it in, among other things, her expansionist policy and her insatiable hunger for new territories, and also in the 'nationalization' of all citizens and the subordination of all forms of human activity to the state's goals. Several historians have published very convincing studies on the subject (most recently R. Pipes and T. Szamuely), and I do not question their conclusions. But this historical background does not explain the peculiar function of Marxist ideology in the Soviet order. Even if we go so far as to admit (with Amalrik) that the whole meaning of Marxism in Russia ultimately consisted in injecting a shaky ideological empire with flesh and blood that would allow it to survive for a time before definitively falling apart, the question of how Marxism fitted into this task still remains unanswered. How could the Marxist philosophy of history, with its ostensible hopes, aims, and values, supply the totalitarian, imperialist, and chauvinist state with an ideological weapon?

It could and it did; and it did not even need to be essentially distorted, merely interpreted in the appropriate way.

Stalinism as Marxism

In discussing this question I am assuming that Marx's thought from 1843 onwards was propelled by that same value-laden idea for which he was continually seeking a better form of expression. Thus I agree with those who emphasize the strong continuity of Marx's intellectual development; I do not believe that there was any significant, much less violent, break in the growth of his main ideas. But I will not argue here in favor of this controversial – although by no means original – view.

In Marx's eyes the original sin of man, his *felix culpa*, responsible both for great human achievements and for human misery, was the division of labour – and its inevitable result, the alienation of labour. The extreme form of alienated labour is exchange value, which dominates the entire process of production in industrial societies. It is not human needs but the endless accumulation of exchange value in the form of money that is the main driving force behind all human productive efforts. This has transformed human individuals, with their personal qualities and abilities, into commodities which are sold and bought according to the anonymous laws of the market, within a system of hired labour. It has generated the alienated institutional framework of modern political societies; and it has produced an inevitable split between people's personal, selfish, self-centered lives as members of civil society on the one hand and, on the other, the artificial and obscure community which they form as members of a political society. As a result, human consciousness was bound to suffer an ideological distortion: instead of affirming human life and its own function as an 'expression' of that life, it built a separate, illusory kingdom of its own, designed to perpetuate this split. With private property, the alienation of labour divided society into hostile classes struggling for the distribution of the surplus product; finally, it gave rise to the class in which all society's dehumanization was concentrated, and which was consequently destined both to demystify consciousness and to restore the lost unity of human existence. This revolutionary process starts with smashing the institutional mechanisms which protect existing labour conditions and ends with a society where, with all the basic sources of social conflict removed, the social process is subordinated to the collective will of the individuals associated in it. These latter will then be able to unfold all their individual potentialities not against society but for its enrichment; their labour will have been gradually reduced to the necessary minimum, and free time will be enjoyed in the pursuit of cultural creativity and high-quality entertainment. The full meaning of both history and present struggles is revealed only in the romantic vision of the perfectly united mankind of the future. Such unity implies no more need for the mediating mechanisms which separate individuals from the species as a whole. The revolutionary act that will close the 'pre-history' of mankind is both inevitable and directed by free will; the distinction between freedom and necessity will have disappeared in the consciousness of the proletariat as it becomes aware of its own historical destiny through the destruction of the old order.

I suspect it was both Marx's anticipation of man's perfect unity and his myth of the historically privileged proletarian consciousness that led to his theory's being turned into the ideology of the totalitarian movement; not because he conceived of it in such terms, but because its basic values could not be realized in any other way. It was not that Marx's theory lacked a vision of future society; it did not. But even his powerful imagination could not stretch so far as to envisage the transition from 'pre-history' to 'genuine history' and come up with the proper social technology for converting the former into the latter; this step had to be carried out by practical leaders. And that necessarily implied adding to the inherited body of doctrine and filling in the details.

In his dream of a perfectly unified humanity Marx was not, strictly speaking, a Rousseauist; Rousseau did not believe that the lost spontaneous identity of each individual with the community would ever be restored and the poison of civilization effaced from human memory. But this was precisely what Marx did believe: not because he believed that jettisoning civilization and returning to the primitive happiness of a savage state was possible or desirable, but because he believed that the irresistible progress of technology would ultimately overcome (dialectically) its own destructiveness and offer humanity a new unity – a unity based not on the suppression of needs but on freedom from wants. In this respect he shared the hopes of the St Simonists.

Marx's liberated mankind needs none of the machinery with which bourgeois society settles conflicts among individuals or between them and society: law, state, representative democracy, and negative freedom, as conceived and proclaimed in the Declaration of Human Rights. Such machinery is characteristic of societies ruled economically by the market and composed of isolated individuals with their conflicting interests; it is what they must rely on to maintain their stability. The state and its legal skeleton protect bourgeois property by coercion and impose rules on conflicts; their very existence presupposes a society where human activities and desires naturally clash with each other. The liberal concept of freedom implies that my freedom inevitably limits the freedom of my fellow men, and this is indeed the case if the scope of freedom coincides with the scale of ownership. Once the bourgeois order is replaced by a system of communal property, this machinery no longer has any purpose. Individual interests converge with universal ones, and there is no more need to shore up society's unstable equilibrium with regulations that define the limits of individual freedom. And it is not only the 'rational' instruments of liberal society that are then done away with: inherited tribal and national ties will also disappear. In this respect the capitalist order paves the way for communism: under the cosmopolitan power of capital and as a result of the internationalist consciousness of the proletariat, the old, irrational loyalties crumble away. The end of this process is a community where nothing is left except the individual and the human species as a whole, and where individuals will directly identify their own lives, abilities, and activities as social forces: they will have no need of political institutions or traditional national ties to mediate this experience of their identity.

How can this be achieved? Is there a technique for effecting such social transsubstantiation? Marx did not answer this question, and from his point of view it seems wrongly put: the point was not to find a technique of social engineering after drawing an arbitrary picture of a desirable society, but to identify and 'express' theoretically the social forces which are already at work to bring such a society about. And expressing them meant practically reinforcing their energy and providing them with the self-knowledge necessary for their conscious self-identification.

There were a number of possible practical interpretations of Marx's message, depending on which values one considered fundamental to the doctrine and which formulations one interpreted as basic clues to the whole. There seems nothing wrong with the interpretation which became the Leninist-Stalinist version of Marxism. It went as follows:

Marxism is a ready-made doctrinal body, identical with the class consciousness of the proletariat in its mature and theoretically elaborated form. Marxism is true both because it has 'scientific' value and because it articulates the aspirations of the 'most progressive' social class. The distinction between 'truth' in the genetic and the ordinary sense of the word has always been obscure in the doctrine; it was taken for granted that the 'proletariat,' by virtue of its historical mission, has a privileged cognitive position, and therefore that its vision of the social 'totality' has to be right. Thus the 'progressive' automatically becomes the 'true,' whether or not this truth could be confirmed by universally accepted scientific procedures.

This is a simplified version of the Marxist concept of class consciousness. Certainly, the party's claim to have a monopoly on truth did not automatically follow from it; the equation also required the specifically Leninist notion of the party. But there was nothing anti-Marxist in this notion. If Marx did not have a theory of the party, he did have a concept of a vanguard group which was supposed to articulate the latent consciousness of the working class, and he saw his own theory as an expression of that consciousness. The idea that a 'proper' working class revolutionary consciousness had to be instilled into the spontaneous workers' movement from without was one that Lenin took from Kautsky and supplemented with an important addition: that since only two basic ideologies can exist in a society torn by class struggle between the bourgeoisie and the proletariat, it follows that an ideology which is not proletarian – i.e., not identical with the ideology of the vanguard party – is necessarily bourgeois. Thus, since the workers are incapable of producing their own class ideology unaided, the ideology they will produce by their own efforts must be a bourgeois one. In other words, the empirical, 'spontaneous' consciousness of the workers can only generate what is essentially a bourgeois *Weltanschauung*. Consequently, the Marxist party, while being the only vehicle for truth, is also entirely independent of the empirical (and by definition bourgeois) consciousness of the workers (except that it sometimes has to make tactical concessions in order not to run too far ahead of the proletariat if it is canvassing for its support).

This remains true after the seizure of power. As the sole possessor of truth, the party may completely discard (except in a tactical sense) the (inevitably immature) empirical consciousness of the masses. Indeed it must do so: it cannot do otherwise without betraying its historical mission. It knows both the 'laws of historical development' and the proper connections between the 'base' and the 'superstructure,' and is therefore perfectly able to discern which elements of the real, empirical consciousness of the people deserve destruction as surviving remnants from a past historical epoch. Religious ideas clearly fall into this category, but so does everything that makes the minds of the people different in content from the minds of their leaders.

Within this conception of the proletarian consciousness, the dictatorship over minds is entirely justified: the party really does know better than society what society's genuine (as opposed to empirical) desires, interests, and thoughts are. And once the spirit of the party is incarnated in one leader (as the highest expression of society's unity), we have the ultimate equation: truth = proletarian consciousness = Marxism = the party's ideology = the party leaders' ideas = the chief's decisions. The theory which endows the proletariat with a sort of cognitive privilege culminates in the statement that Comrade Stalin is never wrong. And there is nothing un-Marxist in this equation.

The concept of the party as the sole possessor of truth was of course strongly reinforced by the expression 'the dictatorship of the proletariat,' which Marx used casually two or three times without explanation. Kautsky, Martov, and other Social Democrats could argue that what Marx meant by 'dictatorship' was the class content of government rather than its form, and that the term was not to be understood in opposition to a democratic state; but Marx did not specifically say anything of the sort in this context. And there was nothing obviously wrong in taking the word 'dictatorship' at its face value, to mean precisely what Lenin meant and expressly said: a reign based entirely on violence and not limited by law.

Beside the question of the party's 'historical right' to impose its despotism on all domains of life, there was the question of the content of this despotism. This was solved in a way that was basically in keeping with Marx's predictions. Liberated mankind was supposed to abolish the distinction between state and civil society, to eliminate all the mediating devices that had prevented individuals from achieving a perfect identity with the 'whole,' to destroy the bourgeois freedom that entailed conflicts of private interests, and to demolish the system of hired labor which compelled workers to sell themselves like commodities. Marx did not spell out exactly how this unity was to be achieved, except for one indisputable point: the expropriation of the expropriators – i.e., the elimination of the private ownership of the means of production. One could, and ought to, argue that once this historical act of expropriation has been performed, all remaining social conflicts are merely the expression of a backward (bourgeois) mentality left over from the old society. But the party knows what the content of the correct mentality corresponding to the new relations of productions should be, and it is naturally entitled to suppress all phenomena which are out of keeping with it.

What would, in fact, be the appropriate technique to reach this desirable unity? The economic foundations have been laid. One could argue that Marx did not mean for civil society to be suppressed or replaced by the state, but rather expected the state to wither away, leaving only the 'administration of things,' with political government becoming superfluous. But if the state is by definition an instrument of the working class on its road to communism, it cannot, by definition, use its power against the 'toiling masses,' only against the relics of capitalist society. And how could the 'administration of things,' or economic management, not involve the use and distribution of labour, i.e., of all working people? Hired labour – the free market of the labour force – was to be eliminated. This duly happened. But what if communist enthusiasm alone proves an insufficient incentive for people to work? Clearly, this means that they are imprisoned in bourgeois consciousness, which it is the task of the state to destroy. Consequently, the way to eliminate hired labour is to replace it by coercion. And how is the unity of civil and political society to be implemented if only the political society expresses the 'correct' will of the people? Here again, whatever opposes and resists that will is by definition a survival of the capitalist order; so once more the only way toward unity is through the destruction of civil society by the state.

Whoever argues that people should be educated to cooperate freely and without compulsion must answer the question: at what stage and by what means can such education be successful? It is certainly counter to Marx's theory to expect it to be possible in capitalist society, where the working people are weighed down by the overwhelming influence of bourgeois ideology. (Did not Marx say that the ideas of the ruling class are ruling ideas? Is it not pure utopia to hope for a moral transformation of society in a capitalist order?) And after the seizure of power, education is the task of the most enlightened vanguard of society; compulsion is used only against the 'survivals of capitalism.' So there is no need to distinguish between the production of the 'new man' of socialism and sheer coercion; in consequence, the distinction between liberation and slavery is inevitably blurred.

The question of freedom (in the 'bourgeois' sense) becomes irrelevant in the new society. Did not Engels say that genuine freedom should be defined as the extent to which people were capable of both subjugating their natural environment and consciously regulating social processes? On this definition, the more society is technologically advanced, the freer it is; and the more social life is submitted to a unified directing force, the freer it is. Engels did not mention that this regulation of society would necessarily involve free elections or any other bourgeois contrivances of the sort; and there is no reason to maintain that a society entirely regulated by one center of despotic power is not perfectly free in this sense.

One can find many quotations in Marx and Engels to the effect that throughout human history the 'superstructure' has been at the service of the corresponding relations of property in a given society, that the state is nothing but a tool for keeping intact the existing relations of production, and that the law cannot but be a weapon of class power. It is valid to conclude that the same situation continues in the new society, at least as long as communism in its absolute form has not entirely dominated the earth. In other words, the law is an instrument of the political power of the 'proletariat,' and since it is just a technique for wielding power (its main task being, more often than not, to cover up violence and deceive the people), it makes no difference whether the victorious class rules with the help of the law or without it. What matters is the class content of power, not its 'form.' Moreover, it also seems valid to conclude that the new 'superstructure' must serve the new 'base'; this means, among other things, that cultural life as a whole must be entirely subordinated to political 'tasks' as defined by the 'ruling class,' speaking through the mouth of its most conscious element. It is therefore arguable that universal servility as the guiding principle of cultural life in the Stalinist system was a proper deduction from the 'base-superstructure' theory. The same applies to the sciences: again, did not Engels say that the sciences should not be left to themselves, without theoretical philosophical guidance, lest they fall into all sorts of empiricist absurdities? And indeed this was how many Soviet philosophers and party leaders from the start justified the control of all the sciences (in their content as well as their scope of interest) by philosophy – i.e., by party ideology. In the 1920s Karl Korsch had already pointed out the obvious connection between philosophy's claim to supremacy and the Soviet system of ideological tyranny over the sciences.

Many critical Marxists considered this to be a caricature of Marxism. I would not deny this. I would add, however, that one can talk meaningfully of 'caricature' only if the caricature resembles the original – as in this case it does. Nor would I deny the obvious fact that Marx's thought was much richer, subtler, and more differentiated than it might seem from the few quotations which are endlessly repeated in Leninist-Stalinist ideology to justify the Soviet system of power. Still, I would argue that these quotations are not necessarily distortions: that the dry skeleton of Marxism adopted by Soviet ideology was a greatly simplified but not a falsified guide to building a new society.

The idea that the whole theory of communism may be summed up by the single phrase 'abolition of private property' was not invented by Stalin. Nor did he come up with the idea that wage labour cannot exist without capital, or that the state must have centralized control over the means of production, or that national hostilities will disappear together with class antagonisms. All these ideas are, as we know, clearly stated in the *Communist Manifesto*. Taken together, they do not merely suggest but logically imply that once the factories and the land are state-owned, as was to happen in Russia, society is basically liberated. This was precisely the claim made by Lenin, Trotsky, and Stalin.

The point is that Marx really did consistently believe that human society would not be 'liberated' without achieving unity. And there is no known technique apart from despotism whereby the unity of society can be achieved: no way of suppressing the tension between civil and political society except by the suppression of civil society;

no means of eliminating the conflicts between the individual and the 'whole' except by the destruction of the individual; no way toward a 'higher,' 'positive' freedom – as opposed to 'negative,' 'bourgeois' freedom – except through the suppression of the latter. And if the whole of human history is to be conceived in class terms – if all values, all political and legal institutions, ideas and moral norms, religious and philosophical beliefs, all forms of artistic creativity, etc., are nothing but instruments of 'real' class interests (and there are many passages to this effect in Marx's writings) – then it does follow that the new society must start by a violent break in cultural continuity from the old one. (In fact the continuity cannot be entirely broken, and in Soviet society a selective continuity was accepted from the beginning; the radical quest for 'proletarian culture' was only a short-lived extravagance sponsored by the leadership. The emphasis on selective continuity grew stronger with the development of the Soviet state, mostly as a result of its increasingly nationalist character.)

I suspect that utopias – visions of a perfectly unified society – are not simply impracticable but become counter-productive as soon as we try to create them by institutional means. This is because institutionalized unity and freedom are opposing notions. A society that is deprived of freedom can be unified only in the sense that the expression of conflicts is stifled: the conflicts themselves do not go away. Consequently, it is not unified at all.

I do not deny the importance of the changes that took place in the socialist countries after Stalin's death, although I maintain that the political constitution of these countries has remained intact. But the main point about them is that, however reluctantly it is done, allowing the market some limited impact on production and abandoning or even just loosening rigid ideological control in certain areas of life amounts to renouncing the Marxist vision of unity. What these changes reveal is the impracticability of that vision; they cannot be interpreted as symptoms of a return to 'genuine' Marxism – no matter what Marx 'would have said.'

An additional – although certainly not conclusive – argument in favour of the above interpretation lies in the history of the problem.

It would be utterly false to say that 'no one could have predicted' such an outcome of Marxist humanist socialism. Anarchist writers actually did predict it, long before the socialist revolution: they thought that a society based on Marx's ideological principles would produce slavery and despotism. Here, at least, mankind cannot complain that it was deceived by History and surprised by the unpredictable connections of things.

The question discussed here is one of 'genetic vs environmental' factors in social development. Even in genetic enquiry, when the properties under investigation are not precisely definable, or when they are mental rather than physical (like 'intelligence,' for example), it is very difficult to distinguish the respective roles of these factors; how much more difficult, then, to distinguish between the 'genetic' and the 'environmental' in our social inheritance – between an inherited ideology and the contingent conditions in which people try to implement it. It is common sense that both factors are at work in any particular case, and that we have no way of calculating their relative importance and expressing it in quantitative terms. To say that 'genes' (the inherited ideology) are entirely responsible for how the child turns out is just as silly as saying that the 'environment' (contingent historical events) can entirely account for it. (In the case of Stalinism, these two unacceptably extreme positions are expressed respectively as the view that Stalinism was in fact 'no more than' Marxism realized and as the view that it was 'no more than' a continuation of the czarist empire.) But although we cannot perform a calculation and assign each set of factors its 'fair share' of responsibility, we can still reasonably ask whether or not the mature form was anticipated by the 'genetic' conditions.

The continuity I have tried to trace back from Stalinism to Marxism appears in still sharper outline when we look at the transition from Leninism to Stalinism. The non-Bolshevik factions (the Mensheviks, not to mention the liberals) were aware of the general direction Bolshevism was taking, and predicted its outcome fairly accurately, just after 1917; moreover, the despotic character of the new system was soon attacked within the party itself (by the 'Workers' Opposition' and then the Left Opposition – e.g., Rakovsky) long before Stalinism was securely established. The Mensheviks saw all their predictions borne out in the 1930s, and Trotsky's belated rejoinder to their 'we told you so' is pathetically unconvincing. They may have predicted what would happen, he argued, but still they were quite wrong, for they believed that despotism would come as a result of Bolshevik rule; it has indeed come, he said, but as a result of a bureaucratic coup. *Qui vult decipi, decipiatur.*

My Correct Views on Everything

My Correct Views on Everything:
A Rejoinder to E. P. Thompson.

Dear Edward Thompson,

Why I am not very happy about this public correspondence is because your letter deals as much (at least) with personal attitudes as with ideas. However, I have no personal accounts to settle either with Communist ideology or with the year 1956; this was settled long ago. But if you insist,

Let us begin and carry up this corpse Singing together . . .

In a review of the last issue of *Socialist Register* by Raymond Williams, I read that your letter is one of the best pieces of Leftist writing in the last decade, which implies directly that all or nearly all the rest was worse. He knows better and I take his word. I should be proud to have occasioned, to a certain degree, this text, even if I happen to be its target. And so, my first reaction is one of gratitude.

My second reaction is of *embarras de richesses*. You will excuse me if I make a fair choice of topics in my reply to your 100 pages of Open Letter (not well segmented, as you will admit). I will try to take up the most controversial ones. I do not think I should comment on the autobiographical pages, interesting though they are. When you say, for example, that you do not go to Spain for holidays, that you never attend a conference of socialists without paying a part of the costs out of your own pocket, that you do not participate in meetings funded by the Ford Foundation, that you are like Quakers of old who refused to take off their hats before authorities, etc., I do not think it advisable to reply with a virtue-list of my own; this list would probably be less impressive. Neither am I going to exchange the story of your dismissal from the *New Left Review* for all the stories of my expulsions from different editorial committees of different journals; these stories would be rather trivial.

My third reaction is of sadness, and I mean it. Incompetent though I am in your field of studies, I know your reputation as a scholar and historian. I found it regrettable to see in your Letter so many leftist clichés which survive in speech and print owing to three devices. First, the refusal to analyse words and the use of verbal hybrids purposely designed to confound the issues. Second, the use of moral or sentimental standards in some cases and of political and historical standards in other similar cases. Third, the refusal to accept historical facts as they are. I will try to say more precisely what I mean.

Your letter contains some personal grievances and some arguments on general questions. I will start with a minor personal grievance. Oddly enough, you seem to feel offended by not having been invited to the Reading* conference and you state that if you had been invited you would have refused to attend anyway on serious moral grounds. I presume, consequently, that if you had been invited, you would have felt offended as well and so no way out of hurting you was open to the organizers. Now, the moral ground you cite is the fact that in the organizing committee you found the name of Robert Cecil. And what is sinister about Robert Cecil is that he once worked in the British diplomatic service. And so, your integrity does not allow you to sit at the same table with someone who used to work in British diplomacy. O blessed Innocence! You and I, we were both

* A conference held in May 1973 at the University of Reading, originally called 'What Is Wrong with the Socialist Idea?', but in the end entitled 'Is There Anything Wrong with the Socialist Idea?' The proceedings were published as *The Socialist Idea: A Reappraisal*, Basic Books, New York, 1974.

active in our respective communist parties in the '40s and '50s, which means that, whatever our noble intentions and our charming ignorance (or refusal to get rid of ignorance) were, we supported, within our modest means, a regime based on mass slave labour and police terror of the worst kind in human history. Do you think that there are many people who could refuse to sit at the same table with us on these grounds? No, you are innocent, while I do not feel, as you put it, the 'sense of the politics of those years' when so many Western intellectuals were converted to Stalinism.

From your casual comments on Stalinism, I gather that your 'sense of politics of those years' is obviously subtler and more differentiated than mine. First, you say that a part (a part, I do not omit that) of the responsibility for Stalinism lies with the Western powers. You say, second, that 'to a historian, fifty years is too short a time in which to judge a new social system, if such a system is arising.' Third, we know, as you say, 'times when communism has shown a most human face, between 1917 and the early 1920s and again from the battle of Stalingrad to 1946.'

Everything is right on some additional assumptions. Obviously, in the world in which we live, important events in one country are usually to be credited in part to what happened in other countries. You will certainly not deny that a part of the responsibility for German Nazism lay upon the Soviet Union. I wonder how this affects your judgment on German Nazism?

Your second comment is revealing, indeed. What is fifty years 'to a historian'? The same day as I am writing this, I happen to have read a book by Anatol Marchenko relating his experiences in Soviet prisons and concentration camps in the early 1960s (not 1930s). The book was published in Russian in Frankfurt in 1973. The author, a Russian worker, was caught when he tried to cross the Soviet border to Iran. He was lucky to have done this in Khrushchev's time when the regrettable errors of J. V. Stalin were over (yes, regrettable, let us face it, even if in part accounted for by the Western powers). And so he got only six years of hard labour in a concentration camp. One of his stories is about three Lithuanian prisoners who tried to escape from a convoy in a forest. Two of them were quickly caught, shot many times in the legs, ordered to get up (which they could not do), then kicked and trampled by guards. Finally, they were bitten and torn up by police dogs (such an amusement, survival of capitalism), and only then stabbed to death with bayonets. All this with witty remarks by the officer, of the kind 'Now, free Lithuania, crawl, you'll get your independence straight off!' The third prisoner was shot and, reputed to be dead, was thrown under corpses in the cart. Discovered later to be alive, he was not killed (de-Stalinization!) but left for several days in a dark cell with his festering wounds. He survived only because his arm was cut off.

This is one of thousands of stories you can read in many now available books. Such books are rather reluctantly read by the enlightened leftist elite. First, because they are largely irrelevant; second, they supply us only with small details (after all, we agree that some errors were committed) and because many of them have not been translated. (Did you notice that if you meet a Westerner who has learnt Russian you have at least 90% chance of meeting a bloody reactionary? Progressive people do not enjoy the painful effort of learning Russian. They know better anyway.)

And so, what is fifty years to a historian? Fifty years covering the life of an obscure Russian worker Marchenko or of a still more obscure Lithuanian student who has not even written a book? Let us not hurry to judge a 'new social system.' Certainly I could ask you how many years you needed to assess the merits of the new military regime in Chile or in Greece, but I know your answer: there is no analogy – Chile and Greece remain within capitalism (factories are privately owned) while Russia started a new 'alternative society' (factories are state owned, as is land, as are all its inhabitants). As genuine historians we can wait for another century and keep our slightly melancholic but cautiously optimistic historical wisdom.

Not so, of course, with 'that beast,' 'that old bitch, consumer capitalism' (your words). Wherever we look, our blood boils. Here we may afford to be ardent moralists again and we can prove – as you do – that the capitalist system has a 'logic' of its own that all reforms are unable to cancel. The national health service, you say, is impoverished by the existence of private practice, and equality in education is spoilt because people are trained for private industry etc. You do not say that reforms are doomed to failure; you only explain that as long as reforms do not destroy capitalism, capitalism is not destroyed, which is certainly true. And you propose 'a peaceful revolutionary transition to an alternative socialist logic.' You think apparently that this makes perfectly clear what you mean. I think, on the contrary, that it is perfectly obscure unless, again, you imagine that once the total state ownership of factories is granted, there remain only minor technical problems on the road to your utopia. But this is precisely what remains to be proved, and the *onus probandi* lies on those who maintain that these (insignificant 'to a historian') fifty years of experience may be discarded by the authors of the new blueprint for the socialist society. (In Russia there were 'exceptional circumstances,' weren't there? But there is nothing exceptional about Western Europe.)

Your way of interpreting these modest fifty years (fifty-seven now) of the new alternative society is also revealed in your occasional remarks about the 'most human face of communism' between 1917 and the early '20s and between Stalingrad and 1946. What do you mean by 'human face' in the first case? The attempt to rule the entire economy by the police and army, resulting in mass hunger with uncountable victims, in several hundred peasants' revolts, all drowned in blood (a total economic disaster, as Lenin would admit later, after having killed and imprisoned an indefinite number of Mensheviks and SRs [Socialist Revolutionaries] for predicting precisely that)? Or do you mean the armed invasion of seven non-Russian countries which had formed their independent governments, some socialist, some not (Georgia, Armenia, Azerbaijan, Ukraine, Lithuania, Latvia, Estonia; God knows where are all these curious tribes live)? Or do you mean the dispersion by soldiers of the only democratically elected Parliament in Russian history, before it could utter one single word? The suppression by violence of all political parties, including socialist ones, the abolition of the non-Bolshevik press and, above all, the replacement of law with the absolute power of the Party and its police in killing, torturing and imprisoning anybody they wanted? The mass repression of the

Church? The Kronstadt uprising? And what is the most human face in 1942–46? Do you mean the deportation of eight entire nationalities of the Soviet Union with hundreds of thousands of victims (let us say seven, not eight; one was deported shortly before Stalingrad)? Do you mean sending to concentration camps hundreds of thousands of Soviet prisoners of war handed over by the Allies? Do you mean the so-called 'collectivization' of the Baltic countries, if you have an idea about the reality behind this word?

I have three possible explanations for your statement. First, that you are simply ignorant of these facts. This I find incredible, considering your profession as a historian. Second, that you use the word 'human face' in a very Thompsonian sense which I do not grasp. Third, that you, like most communists, both orthodox and critical, believe that everything is all right in the communist system as long as the leaders of the party are not murdered. This is, in fact, the standard way communists become 'critical' – when they realize that the new alternative socialist logic does not spare the communists themselves and in particular party leaders. Did you notice that the only victims Khrushchev mentioned by name in his speech of 1956 (whose importance I am far from underestimating) were *pur sang* Stalinists like himself, most of them (like Postychev) hangmen of merit with uncountable crimes committed before they became victims themselves? Did you notice in memoirs or critical analyses written by many ex-communists (I will not quote names, excuse me) that their horror only suddenly emerged when they saw communists being slaughtered? They always are pleading the innocence of the victims by saying 'but these people were communists'! (Which, incidentally, is a self-defeating defence, for it suggests that there is nothing wrong in slaughtering non-communists. This implies that there is an authority to decide who is and who is not a communist, and this authority can be only the same rulers who keep the gun. Consequently, the slaughtered are by definition non-communists and everything is all right.)

Well, Thompson, I really do not attribute to you this way of thinking. Still I cannot help noticing your use of double standards of evaluation. And when I say 'double standards' I do not mean indulgence for the justifiable inexperience of the 'new society' in coping with new problems. I mean the use, alternately, of political or moral standards to similar situations. This I find unjustifiable. We must not be fervent moralists in some cases and *Real-politikers* or philosophers of world history in others, depending on political circumstances.

This is a point I would like to make clear to you if we are to understand each other. I will quote to you (from memory) a talk with a Latin-American revolutionary who told me about torture in Brazil. I asked: 'What is wrong with torture?' and he said: 'What do you mean? Do you suggest it is all right? Are you justifying torture?' And I said: 'On the contrary, I simply ask you if you think that torture is a morally inadmissible monstrosity.' 'Of course,' he replied. 'And so is torture in Cuba?' I asked. 'Well,' he answered, 'this is another thing. Cuba is a small country under the constant threat of American imperialists. They have to use all means of self-defence, however regrettable.' Then I said: 'Now, you cannot have it both ways. If you believe, as I do, that torture is abominable and inadmissible on moral grounds, it is such, by definition, in all circumstances. If however there are circumstances where it can be tolerated, you can condemn no regime for applying torture, since you assume that there is nothing essentially wrong with torture itself. Either you condemn torture in Cuba in exactly the same way you do for Brazil, or you refrain from condemning the Brazilian police for torturing people. In fact, you cannot condemn torture on political grounds, because in most cases it is perfectly efficient and the torturers get what they want. You can condemn it only on moral grounds and then, necessarily, everywhere in the same way, in Batista's Cuba, in Castro's Cuba, in North Vietnam and in South Vietnam.'

This is a banal but important point which I hope is clear to you. I simply refuse to join people whose hearts are bleeding to death when they hear about any, major or minor (and rightly condemnable), injustice in the US and suddenly become wise historiosophists or cool rationalists when told about worse horrors of the new alternative society.

This is one, but not the only, reason for the spontaneous and almost universal mistrust people from Eastern Europe nourish towards the Western New Left. By a strange coincidence the majority of these ungrateful people, once they come to settle in Western Europe or in the US, pass for reactionaries. These narrow empiricists and egoists extrapolate a poor few decades of their petty personal experience (logically inadmissible, as you rightly observe) and find in it pretexts to cast doubt on the radiant socialist future, elaborated on the best Marxist-Leninist grounds by ideologists of the New Left for the Western countries.

This is a topic I will pursue somewhat further. I assume that we do not differ in accepting facts as they are and that we do not get knowledge of existing societies by deducing from a general theory. Again, I will quote my talk with a Maoist from India. He said: 'The cultural revolution in China was a class struggle of poor peasants against kulaks.' I asked: 'How do you know that?' and he replied: 'From Marxist-Leninist theory.' I commented: 'Yes, that is what I guessed.' (He did not understand, but you do.) This is not enough, however, for, as you know, any properly vague ideology is always able to absorb (meaning: to discard) all facts without giving up any of its ingredients. And the trouble is that most people are not dedicated ideologists. Their shallow minds work in such a way as if they believed that nobody has ever seen capitalism or socialism but only sets of small facts they are incapable of interpreting theoretically. They simply notice that people in some countries are better off than in others, that in some of them production, distribution, and services are much more efficient than in others, that here people enjoy civil and human rights and freedom and there they do not. (I should rather say 'freedom' in quotation marks, as you do, to use the word when applied to Western Europe. I do realize that this is a part of the absolutely obligatory leftist spelling: what 'freedom,' indeed; enough to burst one's sides with laughter. And we, people without a sense of humour, do not laugh.)

I am not trying to make you believe that you live in paradise and we in hell. In my country, Poland, we do not suffer hunger, people are not being tortured in prisons, we have no concentration camps (in contrast to Russia), in the last couple of years we have had only a few political prisoners (in contrast to Russia), and many people go abroad relatively easily (again, in contrast to Russia). Still, we are a country deprived of sovereignty, and this not in the sense Mr Foot and Mr Powell fear that Britain could lose her sovereignty because of joining the Common Market, but in a sadly direct and palpable sense: in that all key sectors of our life, including the army, foreign policy, foreign trade, important industries, and ideology, are under the tight control of a foreign empire which exerts its power with considerable meticulousness (e.g., preventing specific books from being published or specific information from being divulged, not to speak of more serious matters). Still, we appreciate immensely our margins of freedom when we compare our position with that of entirely liberated countries like the Ukraine or Lithuania which, as far as the right to self-government is concerned, are in a much worse situation than the old colonies of the British empire were. And the point is that these margins, important though they are (we can still say and publish significantly more than people elsewhere in the 'ruble zone,' except for Hungary), are not supported by any legal guarantees at all and can be (as they used to be) cancelled every night by a decision taken by party rulers in Warsaw or in Moscow. And this is simply because we got rid of this fraudulent bourgeois device of division of powers and achieved the socialist dream of unity, which means that the same apparatus has legislative, executive and judicial power in addition to its power of controlling all means of production; the same people make law, interpret it and enforce it: king, Parliament, army chief, judge, prosecutor, policeman and (new socialist invention) owner of all national wealth and the only employer at one and the same desk – what better social unity can you imagine?

You are proud of not going to Spain for political reasons. Unprincipled that I am, I was there twice. It is unpleasant to say that this regime, oppressive and undemocratic though it is, gives its citizens more freedom than any socialist country (except, perhaps, for Yugoslavia). I am not saying this with *Schadenfreude*, but with shame, keeping in mind the pathos of the civil war. The Spanish frontiers are open (never mind the reason, which is, in this case, thirty million tourists each year), and no totalitarian system can work with open frontiers. They have censorship after, and not before, publication (my own book was published in Spain and then confiscated, but only after one thousand copies had been sold; we all should like to have the same conditions in Poland). You find in Spanish bookshops Marx, Trotsky, Freud, Marcuse, etc. Like us, they have no elections and no legal political parties, but, unlike us, they have many forms of organization which are independent of the state and the ruling party. They are sovereign as a state.

You will probably say that I am talking in vain because you clearly stated that you are far from seeing your ideal in the existing socialist states and that you were thinking in terms of democratic socialism. You did, indeed, and I am not accusing you of being an admirer of the socialist secret police. Still, what I am trying to say is very relevant to your article for two reasons. First, you consider the existing socialist states as (imperfect, to be sure) beginnings of a new and better social order, as transitional forms which went beyond capitalism and are heading towards utopia. I do not deny that this form is new, but I do deny that it is in any respect superior to the democratic countries of Europe. I defy you to prove the opposite, i.e., to show a point on which existing socialism may claim its superiority, except for the notorious advantages all despotic systems have over democratic ones (less trouble with people). The second, and equally important, point is that you pretend to know what democratic socialism means to you, yet you do not know. You write: 'My own utopia, two hundred years ahead, would not be like Morris's "epoch of rest." It would be a world (as D. H. Lawrence would have it) where the "money values" give way before the "life values," or (as Blake would have it) "corporeal" will give way to "mental" war. With sources of power easily available, some men and women might choose to live in unified communities, sited, like Cistercian monasteries, in centres of great natural beauty, where agricultural, industrial and intellectual pursuits might be combined. Others might prefer the variety and pace of an urban life which rediscovers *some* of the qualities of the city-state. Others will prefer a life of seclusion, and many will pass between all three. Scholars would follow the disputes of different schools, in Paris, Jakarta or Bogota.'

This is a very good sample of socialist writing. It amounts to saying that the world should be good, and not bad. I am entirely on your side on this issue. I share without restrictions your (and Marx's, and Shakespeare's, and many others') analysis to the effect that it is very deplorable that people's minds are occupied with the endless pursuit of money, that needs have a magic power of infinite growth and that the profit motive, not use value, rules production. Your superiority consists in that you know exactly how to get rid of all this and I do not.

Why the problems of the only existing communism, which left-ist ideologists put aside so easily ('all right, this was done in exceptional circumstances, we won't imitate these patterns, we will do better,' etc.), are crucial for socialist thought is because the experiences of the 'new alternative society' have shown very convincingly that the only universal medicine these people have for social evils (state ownership of the means of production) is not only perfectly compatible with all disasters of the capitalist world, with exploitation, imperialism, pollution, misery, economic waste, national hatred and national oppression, but adds to them a series of disasters of its own: inefficiency, lack of economic incentives and, above all, the unrestricted role of the omnipotent bureaucracy, a concentration of power never known before in human history. Just a stroke of bad luck? No, you do not say exactly so, you simply prefer to ignore the problem, and rightly so. All attempts to examine this experience lead us back not only to contingent historical circumstances but to the very idea of socialism and the discovery of incompatible demands hidden in this idea (or at least demands whose compatibility remains to be proved). We want a society of small communities with a large autonomy, do we not? And we want central planning in the economy. Let us try to think now how both work together. We want technical progress and we want perfect security for people; let us look closer how both could be combined. We want industrial democracy and we want efficient management: do they work well together? Of course they do, in the leftist heaven everything is compatible and everything settled, lamb and lion sleep in the same bed. Look at the horrors of the world and see how easily we can get rid of them once we make a peaceful revolution toward the new socialist logic. The Middle East war and Palestinian grievances? Of course, this is the result of capitalism; let us make the revolution and the question is settled. Pollution? Of course, no problem at all, just let the new proletarian state take over the factories and there will be no pollution. Traffic jams? This is because capitalists do not care a damn about human comfort; just give us power (in fact, this is a rather good point: in socialism we have far fewer cars and correspondingly fewer traffic jams). People die from hunger in India? Of course American imperialists eat their food. But once we make the revolution, etc. Northern Ireland? Demographic problems in Mexico? Racial hatred? Tribal wars? Inflation? Criminality? Corruption? Degradation of educational systems? There is such a simple answer to everything and, moreover, the same answer to everything!

This is not a caricature, not in the slightest. This is a standard pattern of thought of those who have overcome the miserable illusions of reformism and invented a beneficial device for solving all problems of mankind, and this device consists in a few words which, when repeated often enough, start looking as if they had content: revolution, alternative society, etc. And we have in addition a number of negative words to provoke horror, for instance 'anti-communism' or 'liberal.' You use these words as well, Edward, without explanation, aware though you must be their purpose is to mingle many different things and to produce vague negative associations. What is, in fact, the anti-communism you do not profess? Certainly, we know people who believe that there are no serious social problems in the Western world except for the communist danger, that all social conflicts here are to be explained by a communist plot, that the world would be a paradise if only sinister communist forces did not interfere, and that the most hideous military dictatorships deserve support if only they suppress communist movements. You are not anti-communist in that sense? Neither am I. But you will be called anti-communist if you do not strongly believe that the actual Soviet (or Chinese) system is the most perfect society the human mind has invented so far, or if you wrote a piece of purely scholarly work on the history of communism, without lies. And there is a great number of other possibilities in between. The convenience of the word 'anti-communism,' the bogey-man of leftist jargon, is precisely to put all of them in the same sack and never to explain the meaning of the word. The same with the word 'liberal.' Who is a 'liberal'? Perhaps a nineteenth-century free-trader who proclaimed that the state should forbear from interfering in the 'free contract' between workers and employers and that workers' unions were contrary to the free contract principle? Do you suggest that you are not 'liberal' in this sense? This is very much to your credit. But according to the unwritten revolutionary OED, you are 'liberal' if you imagine in general that freedom is better than slavery (I do not mean the genuine, profound freedom people enjoy in socialist countries, but the miserable formal freedom invented by the bourgeoisie to deceive the toiling masses). And the word 'liberal' has the easy task of amalgamating these and other things. And so, let us proclaim loudly that we spurn liberal illusions, but let us never explain exactly what we mean.

Should I go on with this progressive vocabulary? Just one more word which, I emphasize, you do not use in this sound sense: 'fascist' or 'fascism.' This is an ingenious discovery, with a fair range of applications. Sometimes a fascist is a person I disagree with but, because of my ignorance, I am unable to debate with, so I would do better to kick him. When I collect my experiences, I notice that a fascist is a person who holds one of the following beliefs (by way of example): 1) that people should wash themselves, rather than go dirty; 2) that freedom of the press in America is preferable to the ownership of the whole press by one ruling party; 3) that people should not be jailed for their opinions, communist or anti-communist; 4) that racial criteria, in favour of either whites or blacks, are inadvisable in admission to Universities; 5) that torture is condemnable, no matter who applies it. (Roughly speaking, 'fascist' is the same as 'liberal.') A fascist is, by definition, a person who happened to have been in jail in a communist country. The refugees from Czechoslovakia in 1968 were sometimes met in Germany by very progressive and absolutely revolutionary leftists with placards saying, 'fascism will not pass.'

And you blame me for making a caricature of the New Left. I wonder what such a caricature would be. Still, your irritation (this is one of the few points where your pen flares up) is understandable. You quote from an interview I gave to German Radio (and later translated from German into English and published in *Encounter*) two or three general sentences where I expressed my disgust with New Leftist movements, as I knew them in America and Germany, but – this is the point – I did not specify which movements I meant. I said instead vaguely 'some people' etc. This means that I did not specifically exclude the *New Left Review* in 1960–63 when you were associated with it or that I even tacitly included you in my statement. Here you got me. I did not specifically exclude the *New Left Review* in 1960–63 and, I admit, I did not even have it in mind when I was talking to the German journalist. I thought that to say 'some new leftists,' etc. is rather like saying, e.g., 'some British academics are drunkards.' Do you think that many academics would be offended by such a (admittedly not very ingenious) statement, and if so, which ones? My comfort is that if I happen to say publicly such things about the New Left, my socialist friends somehow never feel that they could be included even if they are not specifically excluded.

But I cannot delay any longer. I hereby solemnly declare that in an interview to German Radio in 1971, when I was talking about leftist obscurantism, I was not thinking of the *New Left Review* in 1960–63, with which Edward Thompson was involved. Will that be all right?

You are right, Edward, that we, people from Eastern Europe, have a tendency to underestimate the gravity of the social issues democratic societies face and we may be blamed for that. But we cannot be blamed for not taking seriously people who, unable though they are to remember correctly any single fact from our history or to say which barbaric dialect we speak, are perfectly able instead to teach us how liberated we are in the East. Neither can we take seriously those who have a rigorously scientific solution for humanity's illnesses, and this solution consists in repeating a few phrases we have heard for thirty years at each celebration on the 1st of May and read in any party propaganda brochure. (I am talking about the attitude of progressive radicals; the conservative attitude to the problem of the East is different and can be summarized briefly: 'This would be awful in our country, but for these tribes it is good enough.')

When I was leaving Poland at the end of 1968 (I had not been in any Western country for at least six years), I had a somewhat vague idea of what the radical student movement and different leftist groups or parties might be. What I saw and read I found pathetic and disgusting in nearly all (still, not all) cases. I do not shed tears for a few windows smashed in demonstrations. That old bitch, consumer capitalism, will survive it. Neither do I find scandalous the rather natural ignorance of young people. What impressed me was mental degradation of a kind I had never seen before in any leftist movement. I saw young people trying to 'reconstitute' universities and to liberate them from horrifying, savage, monstrous, fascist oppression. The list of demands, with variations, was very similar on campuses all over the world. These fascist pigs of the Establishment want us to pass examinations while we are making the revolution; let them give all of us A grades without examinations. Curiously enough, the anti-fascist warriors wanted to get their degrees and diplomas in such fields as mathematics, sociology or law, and not in such as carrying posters, distributing leaflets or destroying offices. And sometimes they got what they wanted. The fascist pigs of the Establishment gave them grades without examinations. Very often there were demands for abolishing altogether some subjects of teaching as irrelevant, e.g., foreign languages (these fascists want us, internationalist revolutionaries, to waste time in learning languages. Why? To prevent us from making world revolution). In one place revolutionary philosophers went on strike because they got a reading list including Plato, Descartes and other bourgeois idiots, instead of relevant great philosophers like Che Guevara and Mao. In another, revolutionary mathematicians passed a motion that the department should organize courses on the social tasks of mathematics and (this is the point) each student should be able to attend this course as many times as he wanted and each time get credit for it, which meant that he could get the diploma in mathematics exactly for nothing. In still another place, the noble martyrs of the world revolution demanded to be examined only by other students, whom they would choose themselves, and not by these old reactionary pseudo-scholars. Professors should be appointed (by students, of course) according to their political views and students admitted on the same grounds. In several cases in the US, the vanguard of the oppressed toiling masses set fire to university libraries (irrelevant pseudo-knowledge of the Establishment). Needless to say, you could hear that there is no difference, no difference at all, between life on a California campus and a Nazi concentration camp. And all were Marxists, of course, which meant they knew three or four sentences written by Marx or Lenin, in particular the sentence 'the philosophers have only interpreted the world, in various ways; the point, however, is to change it' (what Marx wanted to say in this sentence, it is obvious to them, was that it made no sense to learn).

I could carry on this list for pages but this may suffice. The patterns are always the same: the great socialist revolution consists, first of all, in giving us privileges, titles and power for our political opinions and in destroying the old reactionary academic values like knowledge and logical abilities (but these fascist pigs should give us money, money, money).

And what about the workers? There are two rival views. One (pseudo-Marcusian) says that these bastards were bribed by the bourgeoisie and one cannot expect anything more from them. Now the students are the most oppressed and the most revolutionary class of society. Another (Leninist) says that workers have a false consciousness and do not understand their alienation because the capitalists give them wrong papers to read, but we, revolutionaries, store in our heads the correct consciousness of the proletariat. We know what the workers should think and, in fact, do think without knowing it; consequently we deserve to take power (but not in this stupid electoral game which, as has been scientifically proved, is just for deceiving the people).

You say complacently 'revolutionary farce.' All right, it is. But to say this is not enough. This is not a farce capable of turning society upside down, but it is capable of destroying the university. This is a performance worth worrying about (some German universities already look like party schools).

Let us go back to the more general question we discussed earlier in private letters. You defend the movement I just described by saying '. . . but there was a Vietnam war.' Very much so, indeed, to put it elegantly. And many other things, no doubt. Traditional German universities had some intolerable features. Italian and French universities had others of their own. There are many things in any society and in any university to justify protest. And this is my point: you will find no political movement in the world which has no good and well-justified claims. If you look at mutual accusations of parties vying for power you always find some well-chosen and well-grounded points in their claims and attacks, and you do not take it as a reason to support all of them. Nobody is altogether wrong, and you are right, of course, in saying that those who joined the communist parties were not altogether wrong. When you look at Nazi propaganda again in the Weimar Republic, you will find a great number of well-justified points. They said that the Versailles Treaty was a shame, and it was; that democracy was corrupted, and it was; they attacked aristocracy, plutocracy, the power of bankers and, incidentally, pseudo-freedom, irrelevant to the real needs of the people and serving dirty Jewish newspapers. But this was not a good reason to say 'all right, they do not behave very decently and some points in their ideas are rather silly, but they are not wrong on many questions, so let us give them a qualified support.' At least, many people refused to say so. In fact, had the Nazis not had many good points in attacking the existing regime, they would not have won, and there would not have been such a phenomenon as the ranks of the *Rotfront* passing with unfurled banners over to the SA. This is the reason why, when I saw movements imitating the same patterns of behavior and imitating a part of the same ideology (viz. on all points concerning 'formal' freedom and all democratic institutions, tolerance, and academic values), I could not be strongly impressed by the observation: 'but there was a Vietnam war.'

You say that we should help the blind to recover their sight. I accept this advice with a slight restriction: it is difficult to apply when you have to do with people who are omniscient and all-seeing any-way. I do not remember having ever refused a discussion with people who were ready to have one. The trouble is that some were not ready, and this precisely because of their omniscience, which I lacked. True, I was almost omniscient (yet not entirely) when I was twenty years old, but, as you know, people grow stupid when they grow older. I was much less omniscient when I was twenty-eight and still less now. Nor am I capable of satisfying those who look for perfect certainty and for immediate global solutions to all the world's calamities and misery. Still, I believe that in approaching other people we should, as far as we are able, follow the Jesuit, rather than the Calvinist, method. To wit, we ought to presuppose that nobody is totally and hopelessly corrupted, that everybody, no matter how perverted and limited, has some good points and some good inten-tions. This is admittedly easier to say than to practise and I do not think that either of us is a perfect master in this maieutic art.

Your proposal to define yourself (and myself) by allegiance to the 'Marxist tradition' (as opposed to the system, the method, the herit-age) seems to me elusive and vague. I am not sure of the meaning you confer on this attachment unless you simply find it important to be called 'Marxist,' but you say you do not. Neither do I. I am not interested at all in being 'a Marxist' or in being so called. There are certainly only a few people working in the human sciences who would not acknowledge their debt to Marx. I am not one of them. I readily admit that without Marx our thinking about history would be different and in many respects worse than it is. To say this is rather trivial. Still, I think that many important tenets of Marx's doc-trine are either false or meaningless, or else true only in a very restricted sense. I think that the labour theory of value is a norma-tive device without any explanatory power whatsoever; that none of the well-known general formulae of historical materialism to be found in Marx's writings is admissible and that this doctrine is valid only in a strongly qualified sense; that his theory of class conscious-ness is false and that most of his predictions proved to be erroneous (this is admittedly a general description of what I feel, I am not trying to justify my conclusions here). If I admit nevertheless to still thinking, in historical (not in philosophical) matters, in terms inherited in part from the Marxist legacy, do I accept an allegiance to the Marxist tradition? Only in such a loose sense that the same statement would be equally true if I substituted for 'Marxist' – 'Christian,' 'sceptical,' 'empiricist.' Without belonging to any political party or sect, to any Church, to any philosophical school, I do not deny my debt to Marxism, to Christianity, to sceptical philosophy, to empiricist thought and to a few other traditions (more specifically Eastern European and less interesting to you). Neither do I share the horror of 'eclecticism' if the opposite of eclecticism is philosophical or political bigotry (as it usually is in the minds of those who terrify us with the label of eclecticism). In this poor sense, I admit to belonging to the Marxist tradition, among others. But you seem to imply more. You seem to imply the existence of a 'Marxist family' defined by spiritual descendance from Marx and to invite me to join it. Do you mean that all people who in one way or another call themselves Marxist form a family (never mind that they have been killing each other for half a century and still are) opposed as such to the rest of the world? And that this family is for you (and ought to be for me) a place of identification? If this is what you mean, I cannot even say that I refuse to join this family; it simply does not exist in a world where the great Apocalypse can most likely be triggered by a war between two empires both claiming to be perfect embodiments of Marxism.

In your letter there are several points which I should broach not because of their importance but because of the unpleasantly demagogic way you discuss them. I will take up two of them. You quote an article of mine containing a remark which I thought was a platitude: that exploited classes have not been allowed to participate in the development of spiritual culture. You appear as a spokesman of the excluded working class and you explain to me, with indignation, that the working class developed a sense of solidarity, loyalty, etc. In other words, I said this rather to deplore than to exalt the fact that the exploited were denied access to education and you show disgust at my alleged view that the working class has no morals. This is not a misreading but a sort of absurd *Hineinlesen*, which makes any discussion impossible. And then, when I stigmatized as obscurantist the idea of a new, socialist logic or science (again, a truism, as I saw it), you explain that the point is not to change logic but that Marx wanted to change property relations. Did he, really? Well, what can I say except that you opened my eyes? And if you think that the question of a 'new logic' or 'new science' as opposed to 'bourgeois logic' and 'bourgeois science' was not at issue, you are entirely wrong. This was not an extravagance but a standard pattern of thinking and talking among Marxist-Leninist-Stalinists. These patterns were inherited intact by the dozens of Lenins, Trotskys and Robespierres you could find on any American or German campus.

The second point is your comment on one sentence I uttered in the interview you quoted. It said that 'men have no fuller means of self-identification than through religious symbols' and that 'religious consciousness . . . is an irreplaceable part of human culture.' Here, you explode: 'By what right (you say), what study of its tradition and sensitivity, may you assume this as a universal in the heart of an ancient Protestant Island, doggedly resistant to the magic of religious symbolism . . .' I apologize for many reasons. First, that I gave my interview to a German journalist in the heart of the ancient Protestant Island instead of doing this on German soil. Second, that I failed to explain – because I assumed it, wrongly, to be known – that a 'religious symbol' is not necessarily, contrary to what you obviously believe, a picture, a sculpture, a rosary etc., but anything people believe gives them a way of communicating with the Supernatural or conveys its energy. (Jesus Christ himself is a symbol, not only a crucifix.) I did not invent this use of the word but, since I did not explain it in my interview, I offended your iconoclastic English tradition. Does this lexical explanation appease somewhat your Protestant conscience, hurt by a superstitious Ultramontanist? And you accuse me – that beats everything – of not justifying, in this interview, my belief in the permanence of the religious phenomenon. It was indeed thoughtless of me not to quote, in this interview, all the books and articles I have written on the subject to support this view. You had no reason whatsoever to read these books (one of them, over eight hundred dense pages, and dealing mostly with sectarian movements of the seventeenth century, is so boring that it would be inhuman to ask you to wade through it) – at least you had no such reason as long as you were not trying to criticize my views on the subject. Therefore your indignant 'By what right . . .' seems to be more appropriate when retorted to you.

Unfortunately, your article teems with instances when you shift the subject and try to make yourself believe that I said something you think I should have said, on the basis of some general beliefs you attribute to me. I am sure you do this unconsciously, according to a peculiar logic of beliefs which has always been very characteristic of dogmatic communist thinking, where the difference between those reasonings which are truth-functional and those which are not entirely disappears; however, even if it were true that A entails B, it would not follow that if someone believes A, he believes B. The wilful rejection of this rather unsophisticated distinction has always allowed the communist press to give its readers information constructed approximately in this way: 'The American President said that, in defiance of the protest of the whole of peace-loving mankind, he would carry on with the genocidal war in Vietnam' or 'Chinese leaders declare that their jingoist, anti-Leninist policy aims at the destruction of the socialist camp in order to help imperialists.' There is a consistency in this grotesque Wonderland logic and I rather dislike its echoes in your reasoning. But there is more than that. Since you think about society in categories or global 'systems' – capitalism or socialism – you believe that: 1) socialism, imperfect though it is, is essentially a higher stage of mankind's development, and this superiority of the 'system' is valid irrespective of whether or not it can be shown in any particular facts related to human life; 2) all negative facts to be found in the non-socialist world – apartheid in South Africa, torture in Brazil, hunger in Nigeria, or inadequate health service in Britain – are to be imputed to the 'system,' while similar facts occurring within the socialist world also have to be accounted for by the 'system', but by the same capitalist one (survival of the old society; impact of encirclement etc.), not by the socialist one), 3) whoever does not believe in the superiority or the socialist 'system' so conceived is bound to believe that 'capitalism' is in principle admirable and to justify or to conceal its monstrosities, i.e., to justify apartheid in South Africa, hunger in Nigeria etc. Hence your desperate attempts to force me to say something I have not said. (True, since you consider my case not entirely lost, you try to wake up my conscience and explain, for example, that there are spies and bugging devices in Western countries. Really? Are you not joking?) Needless to say, this peculiar way of reasoning is absolutely irrefutable because it is able to ignore all empirical facts as irrelevant (anything bad that happens within the 'capitalist system' is by definition the product of capitalism; anything bad that happens in 'the socialist system' is by the same definition the product of the same capitalism). Socialism is defined within this 'system-thinking' as total or nearly total state ownership of the means of production. You obviously cannot define socialism in terms of the abolition of hired labour, since you know that if empirical socialism differs in this respect from capitalism, it is only in restoring direct slave labour for prisoners, half-slave labour for workers (abolition of the freedom to change one's place of work) and the mediæval *glebae adscriptio* for peasants. So, within this construction it is consistent to believe that with the abolition of private ownership the roots of evil, if not all actual evil, on earth are eradicated. But these three statements I mentioned are nothing else but the expression of an ideological commitment, incapable of being either validated or disproved empirically. You say that to think in terms of a 'system' yields excellent results. I am quite sure it does, not only excellent but miraculous; it simply solves all the problems of mankind in one stroke. This is why people who have not reached this level of scientific consciousness (like myself) do not know this simple device for the salvation of the world, known to any sophomore in Berlin or Nebraska, viz. the socialist world revolution.

I have obviously not exhausted the topics of your text, which restores the dignity of the vanishing art of epistolography. But I believe I have touched on the most controversial ones. The gulf dividing us at the moment is unlikely to be bridged. You still seem to consider yourself a dissident communist or a sort of revisionist. I do not see myself this way, and have not for a very long time. You seem to define your position in terms of discussions from 1956, and I do not. This was an important year and its illusions were important, too. But they were crushed just after they appeared. You probably realize that what was labelled 'revisionism' in the people's democracies is virtually dead (possibly with the exception of Yugoslavia), which means that both young and old people in these countries have stopped thinking about their situation in terms of 'genuine social-ism,' 'genuine Marxism,' etc. They want (more often than not in a passive way) more national independence, more political and social freedom and better living conditions, but not because there is any-thing specifically socialist in these claims. The official state ideology is in a paradoxical position. It is absolutely indispensable, for it is the only way in which the ruling apparatus can legitimize its power; and it is believed by nobody – neither the rulers nor the ruled (both well aware of the unbelief of the others and of their own). In Western countries, virtually every intellectual who considers himself socialist (and even communist) will admit in private talk that the socialist idea is in deep crisis; few will admit this in print. Here buoyant jaun-tiness is obligatory and we must not sow doubt and confusion 'among the masses' or supply our foes with arguments. I am not sure if you agree that this is a self-defeating policy. I rather think you do not.

In the meantime some traditionally socialist institutions seem to have crept into capitalist societies in a rather unexpected way. Even the most short-sighted politicians realize now that not everything can be bought for money; that a moment might come when no amount of money will buy us clean air, clean water, more land or natural resources. And so, 'use value' comes back, slowly, into the economy. A paradoxical 'socialism' resulting from the fact that man-kind does not know what to do with garbage. The result is growing bureaucracy and the growing role of power centres. The only medicine communism has invented – centralized, uncontrolled, state ownership of national assets and one-party rule – is worse than the illnesses it is supposed to cure; it is less efficient economically and it makes the bureaucratic character of social relations an absolute principle. I appreciate your ideal of the decentralized society with a high degree of autonomy for small communities and I share your attachment to this tradition. But it is silly to deny the existence of powerful forces resulting from technological development, and not from private property, and leading toward greater and more powerful central bureaucracy. If you pretend to know a simple means to cope with this situation, if you imagine you have found the solution in saying, 'we will make a peaceful revolution and socialism will reverse this trend,' you delude yourself and fall victim to verbal magic. The more society depends on the complex technological network it created, the more problems have to be regulated by central powers, the more powerful state bureaucracy becomes, the more political democracy and 'formal' 'bourgeois' freedom are needed to restrain the ruling apparatus and to secure for individuals their shrinking rights to remain individuals. There has never been, and there cannot be, any economical or industrial democracy without political ('bourgeois') democracy, with everything it entails. We do not know how to harmonize the contradictory tasks contemporary society imposes upon us. We can only try to reach an uncertain balance between these tasks because we have no blueprint for a conflictless and secure society. I will repeat what I wrote once elsewhere: 'In private life there is the attitude of those who think about how to gain at one blow the capital that would allow them to spend the rest of their life without worries, in peace and security; and there is the attitude of those who must worry about how to survive until tomorrow. I think that human society as a whole will never be in the happy position of a pensioner, living on dividends and having the guarantee of secure life to the end, thanks to capital once acquired. Its position will be rather similar to that of a journeyman who must worry about how to survive until tomorrow. Utopians are people who dream about ensuring for mankind the position of pensioner and who are convinced that this position is so splendid that no sacrifices (in particular no moral sacrifices) are too great to achieve it.'

This does not mean that socialism is a dead option. I do not think it is. But I do think that this option was destroyed not only by the experience of socialist states, but because of the self-confidence of its adherents, by their inability to face both the limits of our efforts to change society and the incompatibility of the demands and values which made up their creed. In short, that the meaning of this option has to be revised entirely, from the very roots.

And when I say 'socialism' I do not mean a state of perfection but rather a movement trying to satisfy demands of equality, freedom and efficiency, a movement that is worth the trouble only as far as it is aware not only of the complexity of problems hidden in each of these values separately but also of the fact that they limit each other and can be implemented only through compromises. We make fools of ourselves and of others if we think (or pretend to think) otherwise. All institutional changes have to be treated entirely as a means at the service of these values and not as ends in themselves. They must be judged correspondingly, taking into account the price we pay in one value when we reinforce another. Attempts to consider any of these values as absolute and to implement them at all costs are not only bound to destroy the other two, but must lead to the destruction of the other one as well. Nota bene, this is a discovery of venerable antiquity. Absolute equality can be established only within a despotic system of rule which implies privileges, i.e., destroys equality; total freedom means anarchy and anarchy results in the domination of the physically strongest, i.e., total freedom turns into its opposite; efficiency as a supreme value calls again for despotism and despotism is economically inefficient above a certain level of technology. If I repeat these old truisms it is because they still seem to go unnoticed in utopian thinking; and this is why nothing in the world is easier than writing utopias. I wish we could agree on this point. If we do, we can agree on many others, even after exchanging a few caustic remarks, which, I hope, we will be generous enough to forgive each other. Such agreement will be much less likely if you keep believing that communism was in principle an excellent contrivance, somewhat spoilt in less than excellent application. I hope to have explained to you why, for many years, I have not expected anything from attempts to mend, to renovate, to clean up or to correct the communist idea. Alas, poor idea. I knew it, Edward. This skull will never smile again.

Yours in friendship,
Leszek Kołakowski
1974

II. *Religion, God and the Problem of Evil*

Jesus Christ – Prophet and Reformer

When a historian deals with Jesus, he is interested above all in what can reliably be said about this man, in what we know about him for sure. He also wants to know about the antecedents of his teachings in Jewish culture, and how the image of the Jewish God changed from the Pentateuch to the late prophets, and whether Jesus the prophet can be taken as a continuation or crowning of those changes. He is interested in the results of research on the Qumran manuscripts and the light they have shed on the problem. These are topics that can be profitably discussed only by specialists, and they are not what I want to discuss here.

A historian of ideas may also want to situate Jesus in the whole history of Christianity, exploring, in his research on this inexhaustible topic, the boundless area of thought and events which grew up around the myth of Christ. Indeed, it is difficult, when speaking about Jesus the man, to shake off the twenty centuries of events through which we see him. The figure of Jesus is enveloped in the shadow of theology and in the thicket of theological controversies that surrounds every word of the Gospels. How can we ignore the vast areas of ambiguity, real or ostensible, with which the history of Christianity has weighed down the teachings of its founder? But this, too, is not what concerns me here.

A historian of religion may treat Jesus as an element in a certain mythological structure, which he might compare with others in order to bring out cultural differences and similarities. He may, although this is difficult, try to ignore the extent to which the figure of Jesus is enveloped in the shadow of the contemporary world and the presence of Christianity in it; he may aspire to the same degree of disinterestedness and objectivity, the same scholarly and aesthetic distance, that we display toward Egyptian or Greek myths. But this is also not what I want to attempt here.

Finally, a biographer may try to unravel the psychology of Jesus and put together a consistent psychological profile of the whole person – if he can free himself from all ulterior motives, whether apologetic and Christian or blasphemous and anti-Christian. But this, too, is not what interests me here.

What interests me is the purely philosophical point of view: a view, in other words, that is neither historical nor psychological nor that of the historian of religion. My aim is to attain enough mental freedom to read the canonical and apocryphal texts of the Gospels without recalling the commentaries, or even the Epistles of St Paul; to read just the simple words, without reading any complex theological or philosophical speculations into them. I would like to summarize what the layman can discern in the figure and teaching of Jesus: the layman who professes no particular Christian faith, embraces no dogma and belongs to no church community, but who does feel himself to belong to the larger tradition of which Christianity is an essential part – the tradition of which Buddha, Socrates, Kant and Marx are also a part. I do not want to reconstruct the psychological profile of Jesus. I am interested in his place within the European tradition as a whole: in how, and in which of its aspects, the mission he ascribed to himself became a component of the intricately woven tapestry which makes up our cultural heritage. And I am interested in this tradition independently of the Christological dogmas around which the Christian religious consciousness has been shaped.

Philosophers and Jesus

Jesus Christ was not, as we know, a philosopher. Textbooks on religious philosophy, even Christian textbooks, do not mention him, and modern philosophers rarely deal with him. However, some philosophers have done so, and it is worth mentioning some of their views in order to outline the various types of philosophical approaches to this extraordinary figure.

Of the great philosophers, Pascal, Kierkegaard, Hegel, Nietzsche and Jaspers wrote about Jesus. For Hegel, he represented a phase of human historical self-knowledge; he was a concrete, sensory manifestation of that idea of God at which man arrives when he conceives of God as something in which he participates – something of which he himself is a manifestation, another form of being. Thus the person of Jesus is almost reduced to a stage of human self-consciousness in its relation to the absolute. This does not mean that Hegel makes Jesus unreal, stripping him of personhood and humanity; he acknowledges that Jesus is far more human than the Greek anthropomorphic gods. But he deprives Jesus of his peculiar extrahistorical uniqueness; of that quality – that timeless exceptionality, at once singular and enduring – which established Christianity, and which is embedded in the belief that here was something supranatural that irrupted into history from outside it.

Kierkegaard, on this issue as on others, developed his own view in opposition to Hegel, depicting Christ as always contemporary, and true for Christians only by virtue of this contemporaneousness. Christ, he said, is no more than a sterile item of historical information for us if we see him as the transmitter of a *past* revelation; he is the real Christian life for each individual only when that individual is able to make him *literally* contemporary, and thus to understand his invitation – 'Come unto me, all ye that labour and are heavy laden, and I will give you rest' – as addressed to him personally, always valid and spoken to him anew at every moment. For a Christian, Jesus is not just a messiah who appeared at a certain historical moment to teach dogmas or preach commandments in God's name. He is the personal embodiment of the permanence of Christianity in every individual Christian; an ever-vital counter-element of every existence; a presence in which each existence will seek the answer to its own frailty and its own wretchedness.

Pascal's attitude to Jesus, most evident in his attacks on deism and the 'philosophers' God,' was, despite all the differences, basically the same. For Pascal, the world manifests neither the complete absence nor the evident presence of a deity; it is not utterly abandoned by God, nor is it obviously under His protection. It manifests 'the presence of a God who is hidden.' This ambiguity of God's presence in the world is the ambiguity of our fate: the fate of those who are able to know God but who are permanently tainted by sin. It is through Jesus Christ that our knowledge of God becomes for us the knowledge of our own wretchedness, and we need this conjoined knowledge. We can learn each of these two truths – that God exists and that we are wretched – separately, but only the apprehension of Jesus as a person amalgamates them and contains them, necessarily, as one joint truth. By itself, our knowledge of our infirmity is a source of despair; by itself, our knowledge of God is merely speculative, theoretical, without value in our lives. But in the apprehension of Jesus we attain at once the full awareness of our fall and the hope of a possible cure; and it is this that constitutes Christian faith. Thus a purely philosophical Christianity, based on speculative proofs, is not possible. Nor is a purely historical one, based on what we know from the Bible. Jesus Christ appears to us not just in his dogmatic and his historical aspects, but as a real existence, a real redeemer; and it is through this presence, which is neither simply a fact nor simply a doctrine, that we become aware both of the darkness in which we live and of the way which leads out of that darkness.

Finally, Nietzsche's is also one of the 'great' philosophical interpretations of the figure of Christ. Nietzsche is the greatest of those very few who have dared to proclaim themselves not only enemies of Christianity but enemies of Christ. For him, Jesus was someone who wanted to annihilate all the important values of life, who glorified his own inability to resist and who raised this weakness to the rank of a virtue. He robbed all values of their reality by transferring them to man's spiritual 'interior,' and he codified a morality for those who cannot defend their own rights and who seek comfort in their own passivity, making it a cause for pride.

These attitudes, briefly sketched, are three ways in which philosophers have approached the person of Jesus. Nietzsche addresses him as one prophet to another; as a true prophet to a false one. Hegel's approach is that of a historian of the spirit toward a certain historical phase. Pascal and Kierkegaard approach him as Christians who seek the supra-natural realities of their faith in its most personal values.

In some limited sense, Pascal's and Kierkegaard's approach may also be acceptable to those who are not bound by the dogmatic content of Christianity. Not, of course, in the sense that they see Christ as a personal and historically unequivocal embodiment of the supra-natural world, to whom they could address their questions or worries, but in the sense that Jesus, like all great thinkers, prophets, reformers and philosophers, has that peculiar contemporaneous-ness which can be achieved where universal values spring from one unique source. A philosopher, if he wants to go beyond the purely historical or purely factual point of view, will not approach a philo-sophical or religious tradition as a fact that is simply there to be understood, nor as a line of thought which is simply to be agreed or disagreed with; he will not view a cultural tradition as a cumulation of 'truths,' nor as a sequence of historically neutralized facts. He will try, rather, to bring out those of its values which are universal and yet enduringly linked to their author, inextricably bound up with their personal source. This duality is one of the more difficult elements of the philosophical approach to tradition. Jesus, on this approach, is reducible neither to a set of events (a set that would also comprise the content of his teaching) nor to a set of abstract values that could be viewed and assessed quite independently of the cir-cumstances in which they came into being. We approach his teach-ing as, to use an ugly expression, 'essentialized fact,' or as a universal value whose content is linked to its historical origin.

Jesus's Main Prophecy

From a purely historical perspective, Jesus was a Jew from Galilee who believed in the Jewish God and believed that this God had entrusted him with a special mission of teaching. He was also someone of whom his disciples in turn believed that he could calm winds by his command, walk across a lake, draw fish into nets, resurrect the dead, heal lepers, make the blind see again, drive out demons from the possessed, talk with Moses and Elias, multiply bread for the poor, and turn water into wine and wine into blood; they also believed that he fulfilled the promises of the Old Testament about the Messiah and that his mission was attested to by his resurrection. This Jesus, although he accepted the tribute of his believers, did not consider himself to be God; indeed he denied that he could be so considered. When he was called good he said that only God is good; he acknowledged that he did not know when the promised day would come; he said, 'not what I will, but what thou wilt.' In this sense one cannot say that Jesus made Christianity, if the belief in his divinity is counted among Christianity's fundamental precepts. It was Paul who began the deification process, and in the end, in spite of the opposition which still persisted among the pre-Nicene Fathers, he prevailed; thus was the dominant understanding of Christianity definitively established, despite numerous 'Arian' relapses. This Jesus considered himself, we may assume, a Jewish reformer, charged with a supra-natural mission as God's anointed, that is, as Christ, who brought from God – the same God in whom he and his listeners believed – the news of the approaching end of the world and an appeal to all to prepare themselves immediately for the final cataclysm. He was convinced that the end of the world was imminent – so imminent that he sometimes told his listeners and disciples that many of them would see the coming of God's Kingdom on earth with their own eyes. This coming would be preceded by famines, pestilence, and earthquakes, by falling stars and the eclipse of the sun, and would end with the visible descent of God's son from the heavens, surrounded by angels playing trumpets. The failure of these prophecies to be fulfilled did not weaken the belief of the disciples, who explained them differently. But the expectation of imminent catastrophe imposed an entirely new perspective on things: from that moment on, all worldly concerns disappear in the shadow of the Apocalypse. Earthly realities, the whole multiplicity of things that are important in life, lose all meaning and all independent value. The material world is no longer important: it can still be, it still is, an object of duty, but it could not be an object of desire, for in its fragility it was approaching its end.

Jesus the Reformer

In this light, the precepts of the new teaching, and the extent to which it really was new, can be understood.

Readers of the Gospels have long been struck by certain inconsistencies in the personality of Jesus. He preaches peace, forgiveness, mercy and non-resistance to evil; but in his own behaviour he is quick to anger and easily irritated, even by small things. He warns that he will send away even those who perform miracles, prophesy, and exorcize demons in his name, and deny that he ever knew them, if they do not fulfil the will of God. He says that a terrible vengeance will befall cities which do not believe in him, and promises that on the Day of Judgment the fate of Tyre and Sidon will be more tolerable than that of Chorazin and Bethsaida, which disregarded his teachings in spite of his miracles. To Peter, when he expresses the hope that his Lord will not be killed, he says, 'Get thee behind me, Satan.' He curses a fig tree on which he finds no fruit and condemns it to wither away, although it is not the right time of year for figs. He drives out the money changers from the temple with a scourge. He proclaims that he brings not peace but a sword, that he will separate families and that because of him in every house fathers shall be set at variance against sons and daughters against mothers. His listeners say, 'These are hard sayings.' Opposition or scepticism rouse him to violent anger. He is unshakeably certain of his mission, and it is only at the very last moment, as he is dying in torment, that he seems to burst out with a cry of despair to the God who has forsaken him. But even that cry of despair is a quotation from the Psalmist.

It may seem that the impulsive character of Jesus does not quite fit his teaching; some of his behaviour seems to reveal the anger of the old Jewish God whose image he changes in his teaching (which was, in fact, in accordance with the intentions of earlier prophets).

And indeed it is difficult to sum up in one word Jesus's attitude toward the Old Testament – a difficulty testified to by the endless disputes on the matter in the history of Christianity (did he abolish the Law of the Old Testament? supplement it? amend it?). The Sermon on the Mount begins with the statement that he does not want to destroy the law but to fulfil it; but what follows is hard to reconcile with that passage. When Jesus broadens the commandment against killing to encompass mere anger, and the commandment against adultery to encompass mere lust, we may consider him to be supplementing the laws, in the same spirit that guides the whole of his teaching: it is not actions that matter but the spirit from which they spring, not behaviour but purity of heart and love of one's neighbour with no ulterior motive. But when he contrasts the principle of an eye for an eye with refraining from resistance to evil and turning the other cheek, he is no longer just supplementing the Old Testament: he is abolishing it, apparently without noticing. He certainly does not want to break the continuity of the Jewish creed; he wants to renew it and 'internalize' it. He disregards the Jewish laws of ritual; he does not observe the Sabbath, nor perform ritual ablutions; he does not pay taxes to the Jewish cult, which outrages the orthodox. He represents a continuity with the late prophets, but evokes the rigorous laws of Deuteronomy as if deliberately to stress the contrast between his own teaching and the old tradition (which by then was of course partly out of date). The break in the continuity was achieved by his disciples, mainly in the Jewish diaspora. But it was not just the news of his miraculous resurrection that created the break, but also his teaching, which can easily be formulated so that it no longer merely supplements the faith of Israel but transgresses it in a fundamental way. And indeed this is how St Paul views the matter.

This is a crucial point, and it means that Jesus does not, in fact, so much replace some laws by others, complete them or amend them, as teach that laws are not needed at all, for love entails the command, and thus makes it superfluous; it is, so to speak, spontaneously bound up with it. And only love is important. In other words, the contractual relation between man and God is not altered by a change in the content of the contract, but ceases to exist entirely, and is supplanted by a relation of love. This is how Paul understood Christ's teaching, and Augustine, and Luther. Only that which comes from love has true value, and whatever springs from love cannot be judged by laws nor measured by a paragraph in a decree. No action matters unless it springs from a desire to do God's will. We all have duties toward the world, but no rights: no claims on it and no right to expect anything from it. Never before in Mediterranean culture had the principle of this fundamental dichotomy been stated so starkly, and it was expressed with great force: the soul and the will to do good on the one hand, the rest of the world and the totality of existing things on the other. Only the soul matters. In view of the approaching catastrophe, only a blind man would take comfort from his temporal achievements. The kingdom of heaven is a priceless pearl for which we must abandon all we possess, all our goods. 'For what is a man profited, if he shall gain the whole world, and lose his own soul?'

The mission of Jesus Christ is to reveal the wretchedness of the temporal world. 'Freely ye have received, freely give. Provide neither gold, nor silver, nor brass in your purses, Nor scrip for your journey, neither two coats, neither shoes, nor yet staves.' All temporal bonds, all that links us to the physical world, is reduced to nothing before that single truly important bond: the bond with God. The rest is secondary – either indifferent or hostile. Jesus renounces his mother and brothers, saying that his disciples are his family; he demands that his followers abandon their fathers and mothers, wives and children, sisters and brothers, in his name. According to Luke he even demands that they hate their fathers, mothers, brothers, sisters and children.

In the world Jesus reveals there is no gradation between good and evil. It is divided into the chosen and the cast out, the sheep and the goats, the heirs of life and the victims of eternal fire, the sons of the kingdom and the sons of evil, good seeds and weeds. To him who has, will be given; from him who has not, even that which he has will be taken away. There is nothing in between. This division corresponds exactly to the division between the spirit of love and the spirit of lust. To be sure, Jesus speaks to everyone: he says that he has come to call sinners, not the righteous, to repentance; he asks that faults be forgiven up to seventy-seven times; he believes that the repentant heart will wash away sin. But at the same time he knows very well that he cannot break obdurate pride. He hates the proud, the powerful, the self-assured, the smug and self-satisfied with their privileges and power, the rich and the avaricious; to them he does not promise the kingdom. He embraces the despised and the wretched, prostitutes and tax collectors; they believe in him because they know that temporal life is misery and suffering, and this is what one must believe in order to accept and understand Jesus's teaching.

The dichotomy between the world and God's Kingdom is a radical one. It is also a complete reversal of all values: the despised are raised to glory, while the proud are cast out with contempt. This division is the second point which marks a crucial departure from the traditional Jewish view of the world. It is a universal division and uniquely important, unconnected to the division into the chosen people and the rest. Here, too, Jesus perhaps wanted to be only a renewer of the Judaic tradition, not its destroyer; here, too, he was building on foundations laid by the prophets. But in choosing its older and more radical form, he was opposing the tradition; by confronting his own teaching with classical Jewish law, he brought out the conflict between the two, and abolished the idea of the chosen people, introducing, in its place, a universal principle of division.

All these novelties were generalized, so to speak, by his disciples, above all by Paul. In his writings, law and faith are opposed; the principle of universalism is unequivocally formulated (for God 'there is neither Jew nor Greek'); the wretchedness of temporal life becomes an injunction to asceticism. At the same time, however, and in the very same epistles, the new division became established as a dogma: condemnations of heretics began to appear. The death of Jesus cemented the reform and produced a separatist community: Christianity as a community was founded not on the disciples' belief in the truth of Jesus's teaching, but on their belief in his resurrection, and later in his divinity. And although in the later history of Christianity the deification of Christ – which is not confirmed in the Gospels – was sometimes questioned, even the doubters acknowledged that the only common dogma of Christianity as such, Christianity without further specification, was the belief that Jesus is Christ, that he was a historical figure, a man born in Galilee and crucified in Jerusalem, and that he is God's anointed. This dogma was constitutive of Christianity even in its 'loosest' variants.

But Jesus remains alive in our culture not only for those who believe in his divinity or even just in his supra-natural mission. He is present in our culture not through the dogmas of this or that religious community but through the value of certain precepts which were genuinely new and which – crucially – remain vital not as abstract norms but as living principles, enduringly bound up with his name and his life as handed down by tradition and quite independently of that tradition's historical accuracy.

Jesus for Us

Let us summarize these new rules – rules which can stand independently of Jesus's apocalyptic prophecies and of the belief in the imminent end of the world, although we know that in his teaching they were a function of those prophecies. They may be summarized in five points:

1. *Abolishing law in favour of love*. Again, this must be stressed: *abolishing*, not supplementing. This idea entered European culture as the belief that *human* relations which are based on trust cancel or preclude contractual relations: if harmonious co-existence is based on mutual trust and love, there is no need for contractual claims and duties. When the God of the Pentateuch – a vengeful God, who demanded obedience, sometimes cruel obedience; a God who made the covenant with Abraham for the price of absolute submission, the readiness even to sacrifice one's only child – when this God was transformed into the God of mercy, a new way of

viewing human relations was opened. The opposition between contractual relations and relations of love has remained alive in our culture in innumerable varieties, as something that, while genetically connected with Christian beliefs, is not organically bound to them. What is the opposition between 'existential' and 'pragmatic' communication in contemporary philosophy but a recreation of this distinction? For it was not only Christian philosophies that continued to recreate this opposition. It is recreated anew in the philosophy of Rousseau, of Kierkegaard and of Jaspers. And when Marx contrasts the relations of interest that obtain in a society based on the exchange of goods with the relations of free association that obtain between people who are voluntarily bound by mutual solidarity, he, too, is recreating the same idea, taking it up, in turn, from the old socialists. It is an idea which is rooted in Jesus, but which in modern Christianity appears most often in heresies and most rarely in the Church. Even Nietzsche, when he says that whatever flows from love is beyond good and evil, is repeating, unbeknownst to himself, the idea of the enemy. All utopias which want to abolish contractual and legal bonds in favour of voluntary and genuinely experienced solidarity, in short all utopias of universal brotherhood, flower from the same root, however indifferent they may be to their own remote origins.

2. *The hope of eliminating violence from human relations.* This is a hope that often seems to us to be particularly utopian and naive. Indeed, we can say with no hesitation that we have never seen a Christian who took his Christianity literally and really turned the other cheek. But this injunction is one thing when taken literally and something rather different in its restricted version, which demands the elimination of the sources of violence. No one expects Christians literally to fulfil the commandments of the Gospels; it is expected only that they take seriously the simple and elementary rules of tolerance laid out therein, and refrain from violence. But even this expectation is often considered wildly extravagant. People who like to pride themselves on their realism – as if this word meant anything, or as if any concrete directives could flow from its acceptance – consider the idea of abolishing

violence a laughable one. But who is being naive here? Those who think, despite all the evidence of human history, that it is possible to diminish the part violence plays in human relations, that much has been already been achieved toward this end, and that more can be peacefully achieved? Or those who imagine that nothing can be accomplished without the use of force, and in particular conversely: that with it everything can be accomplished? No opponent of Christianity can deny that Christianity achieved without the use of force a position in which it could use force against others, and use the name of Jesus as an instrument of torture. It is also true that some forms of practical action based on the principle of applying pressure without violence (for instance, the strategy of Gandhi) have been quite successful. The principle of refraining from violence in international relations is verbally accepted almost universally. Yes, verbally, someone may say; so what? Well, plenty, I would reply. Those values which are verbally accepted and violated in practice are verbally accepted only because of the pressure of universal opinion, which forces agreement. There is no need to despair over hypocrisy; we should, rather, accept that hypocrisy is the testimony to the real social power of those values behind which it hides – the homage that vice pays to virtue, as La Rochefoucauld put it. Until quite recently heads of state did not hesitate openly to announce policies of expansion by war and conquest; but such announcements are now very rare; the idea of a world without violence has been accepted. This being so, the *hope* for a world without violence is not a ludicrous fancy. It is not those who believe that use of force can decline, and who strive to bring about this decline, who are naive, but those who believe that force can resolve everything. This belief is like a kind of infantile fixation. The use of force toward children is unavoidable up to a certain age, but generally decreases with age; sometimes, however, parents extend the use of force for too long and beyond what is necessary. A person brought up in this way generally acquires the conviction that nothing except force can possibly regulate human relations. He builds an infantile view of the world from his own infantile experiences, promoting them to the status of a primitive philosophy of history, which he proudly calls 'realistic,' 'without illusions,' etc. In fact, the belief in the omnipotence of force is not only naive but also, in the long run, self-defeating: we know that collectivities which rely only on force and childishly believe in its universal effectiveness are doomed; they cannot survive, precisely because they cannot cope in situations where force is useless. On the other hand, people who are persistent and resolute often achieve their aims without the use of force, but rather by courage joined with intelligence. Renouncing force need not mean resigned passivity or cowed submission: Christ renounced force, but fought relentlessly for his own point of view; and in dying he broke the resistance of those who wielded power and were in a position to use force. The idea of life without force is neither stupid nor utopian. It calls only for courage – a virtue which is most lacking in those who worship force as a universal method, for they are prepared to fight only when they are in a position to use force against those who are weaker, never otherwise.

3. *Man shall not live by bread alone.* Christ quotes this sentence from Deuteronomy, a text he contradicts so often. But he gives it a broader sense: like the lilies and ravens, we should not worry about life and food. Is this, too, a product of pious naiveté? No. For centuries, people have battled for the recognition of values that are not reducible to physical needs and material satisfaction, for the acknowledgment that such values exist, and that they exist independently of all others; and these efforts persist throughout European culture. Such acknowledgment must seem trivial; it does not strike one with its originality. But after the passage of centuries, everything Jesus preached, if it has endured in our culture, comes to seem banal – and it is thanks to him that it has become so. What can be more banal than saying that man does not only clothe himself and eat? And yet the acceptance of this banality sometimes turned out to require a lengthy battle: for instance, a lot of persistent persuasion has gone into arguing that creative works of the human spirit cannot be assessed according to the dubious advantages they might bring to material production. Let us be grateful, then, to the man who reminded us that we do not live by bread alone, while at the same time being aware that the injunction to live

like the lilies and ravens cannot be taken literally.

4. *The abolition of the idea of a chosen people.* Jesus opened up God for everyone. Or perhaps he simply completed the opening process begun before him by the Jewish prophets. His God does not forbid his people to marry the daughters of unbelievers, nor does He require them to destroy other nations; he says that all the righteous are his people; he promises that many will come from east and west, from north and south, to be in God's Kingdom with Abraham, Isaac and Jacob. Jesus's God was filled with love for the world; He so loved it, according to John the Apostle, that He gave His only begotten son for its salvation. There was neither Jew nor Greek for Him among His people. These, too, are banalities, of course, but they were not banalities when they first entered European culture: they were great causes; problems which, once posed, were irrevocable; values steeped in the blood of those who battled for their recognition. In the realm of theoretical reflection there is no proposal more modest and none that, when taken seriously, has provoked more dramatic conflicts, than the idea that there are no chosen nations, no people beloved above all others by God or by History and entitled thereby to impose their leadership over others in the name of any cause. It was thanks to the teaching of Jesus that this idea – the idea that fundamental human values are the common property of all, and that humanity is one people – became an inalienable part of our spiritual world.

5. *The essential wretchedness of the temporal world.* It does not matter, for these purposes, to what extent the image of the human world as incurably sick is 'right.' What matters is that this image became an invariable element in the spiritual development of Europe. It is a constantly recurring theme in every variety of philosophical reflection, by no means limited to Christian thought or to thought directly inspired by Christianity. Jesus told people that they were wretched and that they were concealing their wretchedness from themselves. Pascal, when he embraced this belief, made it central to spiritual life. It is true that this idea has sometimes served to check people's desire to improve their temporal lot, to justify a spirit of resignation to their fate, and to extort an acceptance of things as they were; that it

was used to quash the protests of the deprived and oppressed when they rebelled against their exploitation; that it was interpreted in a way which made a virtue of discrediting the possibility of any real improvement in the world. It is also true that the chorus of the well-fed and well-satisfied sometimes clothed itself in the glorious robes of this idea in order to lecture the hungry and deprived about the worthlessness of earthly goods and the pointlessness of worrying about their temporal lot. The history of Christianity so teems with these interpretations that we have almost ceased to notice how revolting they are.

But, despite all this, there is another interpretation; an interpretation that need not entail approval of the privileged and well-satisfied. The vileness of this approval was exposed a long time ago and Christianity, as we can see, is slowly renouncing it. The belief in the essential wretchedness of human existence does contain something that can be, and has been, a topic of philosophical reflection, quite independently of the base uses to which it has been put. It is something that has always been an important subject for philosophers; it can be reflected upon regardless of whether or not one believes in an afterlife; and it does not suggest the conclusion that, in view of the structural infirmity of our existence, all efforts to repair what can be repaired are vain and sterile. For one can try to change for the better all that can be changed in the conditions of human existence, one can battle for it relentlessly, while being aware that the absolute is unattainable, and that the essential frailty of human existence is irreparable, because it is a fundamental part of that existence, and arises from human finiteness itself. This topic will not cease to be of interest to philosophers.

Returning Jesus to Culture

This is the list – incomplete and selective, but not arbitrarily selective – of the values which, thanks to the teaching of Jesus, found an enduring place in the spiritual substance of Europe and of the world, in a way that was not essentially bound to Christian dogma. But the abstraction of these values, in their non-Christian form, from their personal roots, is a sort of cultural impoverishment. It is connected with the way Jesus has been monopolized by dogmatic Christian communities and with the decline of his presence as a person in other areas of the spiritual world. This poses the risk that all the symptoms of Christianity's decline will, unavoidably, also erode the historical meaning of the existence of Jesus. This is what we want to avoid.

It is true that many of the above-mentioned points could evoke the response, 'we've heard all this all before'; it is not without justification that we look for similar themes in the religions of Asia. But in Mediterranean culture, the culture of our birth, these values are bound up with the teaching of Jesus and with his name; they are the spiritual fund which he introduced and to which he gave momentum. Hence any attempt to 'invalidate Jesus,' to eliminate him from our culture on the pretext that we do not believe in the God in whom he believed, is absurd and fruitless. Such attempts are made only by those primitive enough to imagine that crude atheism not only suffices as a view of the world, but can also justify trimming the cultural tradition as one sees fit, according to one's own doctrinal fancies, hacking away an essential part of it and depriving it of its most vital source.

Finally, if – as we uncertainly hope – the Christian world proves capable of real improvement and change, it will draw its reparative strength only from its own source (non-Christian critics can weaken Christianity, but they cannot repair it). Consequently, it can maintain its ability for self-repair only by constantly concentrating its attention on that spiritual fund which is bound to the name of Jesus.

Regardless of this hope, however, the person and the teaching of Jesus Christ cannot be invalidated or removed from our culture if that culture is to continue to exist and to create itself. The figure of this man, who for centuries was not just a teacher but the model of the highest human values, cannot fall into oblivion without a fundamental break in the continuity of spiritual life. For he incarnated, in his person, the ability to express one's own truth fully and loudly, to defend it to the end with no evasion, and to resist to the end the pressure of the established reality which rejected him. He taught how we can confront the world and ourselves without resorting to violence. He was a model of that radical authenticity in which, uniquely, every human being can give true life to his own values.

1956

Leibniz and Job:
The Metaphysics of Evil and the
Experience of Evil

To review human reflection about evil is to review the entire history of theology, philosophy, religion and literature, from the Rig Veda to Plato to Dostoyevsky to Wittgenstein. And to consider the effective operations of evil in human life is to consider the whole history of mankind, from paleolithic tribes to twentieth-century man.

There are two ways – each of them with a number of variants – that philosophers, theologians, scholars, scientists and ordinary people have tried, throughout the centuries, to cope with the so-called problem of evil. As with all important human issues, we can try either to solve the 'problem' or to get rid of it altogether by declaring it invalid: by denying that the problem exists. Among those who have tried to tackle the problem we find adherents of two fundamentally opposed (or so it seems) metaphysics: Manichaeans and Christians. Among those who have denied the validity of the problem – though not all of them for the same reason – there are some mystics, some pantheists, all Marxists and communists, most other utopians, and most advocates of a naturalistic worldview, like Nietzscheans, Nazis and philosophical Darwinists.

It is trivially true that the concept of evil as pure negativity is a simple deduction from the belief in a creator who is both unique and infinitely good, so that whatever is, is good necessarily, and existence as such is good. This, to repeat, is a logical deduction, not a matter of experience. But it is mostly through such arguments that Christian theodicy has made its enormous, indeed heroic, efforts to respond to the most common experience of ordinary people – the experience of evil. When St Augustine says that the very presence of evil must be good because if it were not, God would not have allowed evil to appear, he is stating something that is obvious in Christian terms. This, again, is a logical deduction from the concept of God; it implies that God could, if He wanted, prevent evil from appearing, but for reasons best known to Himself preferred to let it stay.

Leibniz is more specific in explaining what those reasons may have been. He, too, does so by deduction. Having proved the necessary existence of God and, separately, His supreme goodness, Leibniz inferred from these that God must have created the best world that is logically conceivable, and that this is the world we inhabit; any other world would be worse.

Voltaire's famous derision of this idea is too easy. Leibniz was well aware of the horrors of life. Nevertheless, belief in the supreme goodness of creation is irresistible given such an idea of the divine being. And it implies that God, in His all-embracing wisdom, must have solved, as it were, an equation in an infinitely complex higher calculus in order to calculate which world would produce the maximum goodness. Christian tradition has always stressed, after Plato, the distinction between moral evil and suffering: moral evil – *malum culpae* – is the inevitable result of human (and angelic) free will, and Leibniz's creator reckoned that a universe populated by rational creatures endowed with free will, and thus capable of doing evil, would generate more good than a world whose dwellers would, in effect, be automata, programmed never to do evil (and presumably, though Leibniz does not say so explicitly, never to do good either, if by a good action we mean, as we commonly do, an action done out of choice, not from compulsion).

As for non-man-made suffering – *malum poenae* in the Christian idiom – there are two possible answers. One says that such suffering is the work of malevolent spirits whose work is permitted by God because it serves to punish, correct or warn us. The other, in the Leibnizian spirit, says that it results from the workings of the laws of nature, and that God is not omnipotent in the sense of being able to combine everything with anything and impose on the physical universe an order where things would not move according to strict regularities, would stop interfering and colliding with each other. Those Christian thinkers who believed (like some fourteenth-century nominalists and, among contemporary thinkers, Shestov) that God is omnipotent in the absolute sense – i.e., that He can change the past and establish moral commandments and the laws of mathematics by *fiat* – left themselves more vulnerable to the traditional Epicurean criticism: if God could do these things, then – since there is evil in the world – He must be either evil or powerless. This criticism does not affect Leibnizian theodicy, where God cannot alter the rules of logic or mathematics. But His inability to do so is not a limitation of His omnipotence, for those rules, valid in themselves, are not imposed on Him from outside, like some alien law: they are identical with Him. Therefore we should not complain and ask God why He failed to make our universe a paradise without suffering. Besides, God never promised that He would suspend the laws of nature for our benefit and use miracles to prevent people from harming one another; He did not promise a world without wars, torture, Auschwitz or Gulags.

All this is trivial and well known. Not surprisingly, however, many people have found that this theological structure fails to give them a satisfactory explanation of the evil they face, experience, and do. It is not convincing, and seems contrary to common sense, to be told that evil is pure privation, a purely negative phenomenon; that the devil is a good thing insofar as he exists; and that human suffering and pain are elements of the best arrangement God could have devised for the world. The common-sensical mind is much more inclined to echo Voltaire's famous ironic question after the Lisbon earthquake: would the world be worse without it? It would seem that, according to this theological explanation, the world would be worse if there had been no Auschwitz and no Gulags, or, for that matter, if I had not broken my finger.

But here, again, Leibniz, or any other Christian theologian, would say that this is the wrong way of looking at the question. They do not claim, they would say, to be able to apply a divine algorithm and demonstrate that particular instances of suffering, however horrifying, turn out, on closer inspection, to be good – in the infinite global balance sheet, because each prevents a greater evil from occurring or makes a greater good possible. The balance sheet is known only to God; we cannot try to reproduce it, and it would be hopeless to try. Besides, we have no idea how to measure and quantitatively compare various evils and goods in their infinite variety. The proper attitude is to trust God's plan in advance, without calculation or complaint; to accept it, and with it to accept all human misery and the indifferent destructiveness of nature. The idea (present in St Augustine and in Hegel) that evil is needed for aesthetic reasons – because it adorns the world by the contrasts and variety it creates – sounds even more preposterous.

It is understandable that in the face of so many tormenting riddles the human mind came up with another solution, which we usually, rightly or not, call Manichaean. It goes back to old Iranian mythology, and it seems convincing and in accordance with our everyday experience. It says that there are two powers, or twin gods, good and evil, which fight each other, and that the evil we know from experience – i.e., suffering – is simply the work of the evil god. In contrast to its Zoroastrian source, Manichaean theology, like its various gnostic relatives and unlike Christian doctrine, saw matter as the creation of the evil power. The Manichaean worldview has been a constant temptation for Christians, and for the European mind in general. The thought that Satanic powers, whatever their origin, are hard at work trying to upset God's benevolent blueprint, quite often successfully, seems more natural and in accordance with common sense than many other explanations of evil. Manichaeism is absorbed by our minds, so to speak, with minimal resistance. Even Judaism, which has the reputation of being the one-God religion *par excellence*, the model of monotheistic thinking, is not free of this temptation. Gershom Sholem, one of the most distinguished scholars of the history of Kabbala and Jewish mysticism, tells us that the book of Zohar often presents evil as something real, or positive, not just as privation. God's powers make a good harmonious whole, His judgments are good, His right hand distributes love and mercy and His left hand is the organ of His wrath – but it is when the latter operates independently of the former that radical evil appears: the kingdom of Satan. We do not know whether Jacob Boehme was familiar with Kabbalistic writings, but his theosophy contains a similar idea: evil is the negative principle of divine wrath; it is independent of human will and is somehow embedded in the structure of the world.

Some ancient Platonists (e.g., Plutarch of Cheroneia or Numenius) also succumbed to this belief in two independent powers, good and evil. But for Plotinus evil is simply the absolutely inevitable bottom rung on the ladder of being; the absolute goodness of the One could not prevent the natural descent of reality into matter. Nevertheless, we must still abhor the gnostic doctrine that the Creator of the world is himself evil.

Even in the dogmas of the Roman Church we find remnants of this 'dualistic' theology. Matter itself cannot be evil, of course; and, conversely, the Church also condemned, in 1347, the theory of Nicholas of Autrecourt, who wrote that the world is absolutely perfect, both as a whole and in each of its parts (*'universum est perfectissimum secundum se et secundum omnes partes suas'*) – presumably because such a daring statement seemed to suggest that there simply is no evil in the world: no sinful will of corrupted creatures, human or satanic. But the Catholic belief in the eternity of hell and the irreversible fate of the fallen angels implies that some evil, indeed huge swathes of it, is indestructible, irredeemable, incurable; that the world will forever be split into two realms, morally opposed to each other. Not surprisingly, some of the Greek Fathers, and some later theologians, were unable to stomach these dogmas or to reconcile them with the image of an absolutely good, loving, and merciful Creator.

Dogmatic pronouncements of the Church have often assured us that moral evil, while permitted by God, can never be caused by Him; that human misery and pain, if it cannot be attributed to the malicious will of other people, serves a good purpose – i.e., that it is not really evil. Priests and theologians may have tried to explain the suffering of individuals, particular calamities and atrocities, as parts of a shrewd divine plan, but the Church avoided official comments of this kind; it only advised us to be satisfied with global, unconditional trust.

In fact, we all know that pain and catastrophes are – on the face of it – distributed at random and cannot be interpreted in terms of merit and sin, reward and punishment. Job knew this as well. Job does not try to construct a theodicy. He has been a just man all his life and God knows that his misery is not retribution for his crimes. He suffers horribly for no reason, but he is able to say: 'Though he slay me, yet will I trust in him' (Job 13:15). He accepts that God alone is the source of wisdom and that His ways are inscrutable. God Himself is angry at Job's advisers, theologians, presumably because they argue that Job's sufferings are the proper punishment for his sins. The whole of the book of Job seems to refute the theory of pain as just retribution.

This is what God said to Job and his wife many centuries later in Robert Frost's play 'A Masque of Reason':

I've had you on my mind a thousand years

To thank you someday for the way you helped me
Establish once for all the principle
There's no connection man can reason out
Between his just deserts and what he gets.
Virtue may fail and wickedness succeed . . .
Too long I've owed you this apology
For the apparently unmeaning sorrow
You were afflicted with in those old days.
But it was of the essence of the trial
You shouldn't understand it at the time.
I had to seem unmeaning to have meaning . . .
My thanks are to you for releasing me
From moral bondage to the human race.
The only free will there at first was man's,
Who could do good or evil as he chose.
I had no choice but I must follow him

With forfeits and rewards he understood . . .
I had to prosper good and punish evil.
You changed all that. You set me free to reign.
You are the Emancipator of your God.

We see the horror of this: supreme goodness is incompatible with free will as we understand it. In every situation it has only one option: to maximize good. And Job's story changes that: it frees God. He can support the wicked and torment the just, according to His wish or whim. If so, no theodicy is possible or needed. Perhaps a consistent theodicy has never been written?

In various mythologies evil is explained in various ways; gods often share good and evil qualities, ambiguously. It is beyond the scope of this essay to plunge into the complexities of Hindu and Buddhist theories of evil. Nietzsche said that Buddhism is beyond good and evil. This might be true of some varieties of Buddhism, purified of later mythological imagery. To some Buddhist sages, and presumably to Gautama himself, the world we know from experience is nothing but misery and suffering; there is no liberation, no salvation except through abandoning it. This idea is in fact not alien to many European thinkers. We all remember the immortal words of the dying Socrates: 'Crito, I owe a cock to Asclepius.' This amounts to saying: here ends the sickness called life.

But this is not a universal belief. Some pantheists and some mystics live lives so immersed in the divine environment that evil is unnoticeable in their universe. The light of God penetrates everything; there is no reason to complain and no point in complaining, for the world is full of joy and 'whatever is of God, is God,' as Eckhart says. Or, in the words of the seventeenth-century French mystic Louis Chardon, 'God in the sky is more my sky than the sky itself; in the sun He is more my light than the sun, in the air He is more the air than the air I breathe.'

It may well seem less than obvious why the same word should be used for both suffering and moral wickedness. Many thinkers, Christian and non-Christian, identified evil with moral evil. Epictetus says that there is no good or evil in things that do not depend on our will;

that the blows of fate we cannot avoid cannot be evil; that we should seek good and evil in ourselves; and that a wise man can turn every-thing into good – illness, death, misery. The only thing in the world that is contrary to God is sin – so says the Cambridge Platonist Ralph Cudworth – and sin is a nonentity: nothing. God Himself said to Catherine of Siena that no suffering can redeem our guilt, only repentance. And He added that the worst sin is the refusal or mis-trust of divine mercy: the despair of Judas was a greater sin and a worse insult to God than his betrayal of Jesus.

All these considerations suggest that suffering in itself is morally indifferent: only our will, our intentions, our deeds can be morally assessed. It is evil to maliciously inflict pain on other people, but suffering pain is not an evil.

However, if I decide that the word 'evil' can be used to describe my intentions but not my suffering, I am thereby suggesting that what other people do is of no interest to me. If they make me suffer, the evil done is not *my* evil, but an evil caused by them. Should I say that my problem is only my own saintliness and not the evil that exists in the world, or the problem of how to make the world better? This might be in keeping with Stoic moral doctrine, but not with common sense, which tells me to condemn not only my own evil but all evil, throughout the human world.

But in that case we might need another restriction. If we limit the word 'evil' to what is caused by human will, then its meaning cannot be extended to encompass all suffering: suffering caused by natural forces, or even by human actions if their harmful or painful effects were not intended but happened by accident. And since the word 'evil' in this sense clearly has a moral association, if we do apply it to earthquakes, plagues, or deaths from lightning, we seem to be implying that such events are intentionally produced: that nothing in nature happens simply as a result of the blind operation of natural laws, that everything happens by design. Such an interpretation is, of course, part of the religious view of the universe, and does not necessarily contradict the belief in the laws of nature. According to many theologians, God, in His omniscience, included natural events in the moral order of the cosmos: they happen by natural necessity, but at the same time they have a moral purpose; they are not miracles that break the chain of cause and effect. Such a view is, in fact, close to the Leibnizian position. And – as Malebranche said – even if natural events are caused directly by God, and the world is thus an infinite series of miracles, the regularity in the natural order of things remains undisturbed.

As for those who implicitly or explicitly invalidate the 'question of evil' for religious reasons, they, of course, believe in good: they believe that good permeates the entire material and spiritual cosmos.

Then there are those who are at the opposite end of both the theological and the anti-theological spectrum, who believe that both 'good' and 'evil' are no more than mythical inventions. Pleasure and pain exist, of course, and can be explained within the natural order; but in themselves they have no moral qualities. Nothing is good or evil in itself; something can be pleasant or unpleasant, harmful or beneficial, to particular people – to you, to me, to him – and without this qualifier even the words 'pleasant' and 'unpleasant,' not to speak of the words 'good' and 'evil,' are meaningless. This is what Hobbes, Hume, and even Spinoza believed (although in the case of Spinoza things are more complicated). Nietzsche says that we do not need the word 'evil,' for the world is 'bad' enough as it is. But what is 'bad'? Something that produces undesirable effects or does not fit the purposes we have in mind. The same idea is suggested by the very title of Konrad Lorenz's book on aggression, *Das sogenannte Böse*.

Within the naturalistic or materialistic view of reality the qualities of 'good' and 'evil' are inadmissible, or useless and misleading, for they suggest that something can possess these qualities in itself, unconditionally and independently of the circumstances, and this suggestion can be suspected of having a religious provenance.

This view is clearly visible in the Marxist or communist *Weltanschauung*. Let us take an example from literature.

A character in Solzhenitsyn's novel *The Cancer Ward* visits the zoo and sees an empty cage with a notice on it; the notice says that the monkey which used to live in that cage was blinded as a result of the mindless cruelty of a visitor: an *evil man* threw tobacco in its eyes.

Reading this notice is a tremendous shock for the visitor. How can it be? An evil man? Not an agent of American imperialism but simply an evil man? What sort of description is that?

The visitor's shock and amazement were genuine and quite understandable. The adjective 'evil' (and no less so the noun) as the description of a moral quality was absent from the ideological jargon of the totalitarian Soviet world. There were, of course, criminals, monsters, traitors, foreign agents; but no one who was simply 'evil.' This was not only because the quality of being evil might easily have suggested the religious tradition. It also suggested an inherent, lasting property of a person or an act, independent of the political context. Whereas it is obvious to anyone who thinks dialectically that actions which are ostensibly the same kinds of actions can be right or wrong depending on the circumstances – or rather, on the cause in the name of which they are performed. Both Lenin and Trotsky were quite explicit on this point. Is there, for instance, something inherently wrong in slaughtering children? – No. It was right, Trotsky argues, to slaughter the children of the Russian czar because it was politically expedient. (Presumably it was not right to kill Trotsky's sons, however, because Stalin did not represent the historical interests of the proletariat; Trotsky, as far as I know, did not deal with this question directly, but such an answer would be perfectly in keeping with his fanatical mentality.) If we reject the principle that the end justifies the means, we can only appeal to higher, politically irrelevant moral criteria; and this, Trotsky says, amounts to believing in God.

This is not properly speaking a relativist doctrine. We normally reserve that label for the belief that an act can be good or evil depending on the circumstances; but this is not what the person who thinks dialectically says. The person who thinks dialectically says that when we talk about an action being right or wrong according to the circumstances, we are never talking about the same action; the similarity is only ostensible, merely superficial. In one case, by eliminating potential enemies of the proletariat, we are performing an act that is politically right; in the other, we are committing a crime against the mission of the proletariat. Similarly, an act that is an act of liberation of another country from capitalist oppression must not be called an 'invasion'; Nazi concentration camps must not be compared with the educational system of a socialist state. And so on. We have scientific knowledge of the progress of history, and thus we know that once everything – including human beings – becomes state property, the way is open to universal rejoicing. And we know what is right and wrong, politically correct and incorrect; we have no need of superstitious descriptions like 'evil.' There is no point in dwelling on this primitive 'dialectics' and mendacious language; it is well known.

What has happened to our question? Need we appeal to the idea of evil at all? May we not be satisfied with the distinction between 'pleasant' and 'unpleasant' (always relative to person, time and place)? But who would be bold and dogmatically rigid enough to claim that 'good' and 'evil' are not empirical qualities; that there is no perception of moral qualities, including the intuition of evil; that centuries of human experience, from the indescribable cruelties of ancient Rome to the monstrosities of the twentieth century, are irrelevant to the 'question of evil' and may be dismissed as no more than a series of unpleasant impressions (and no one is denying that unpleasant things do happen to people)? I will end with a remark by a French Catholic theologian whose name escapes me; he said that he can understand people who do not believe in God, but the fact that there are people who do not believe in the devil is beyond his comprehension.

2002

Erasmus and his God

When Luther was still an unknown monk tormented by religious anxieties, Erasmus was already enjoying European fame. In 1517 he had under his belt, among other works, *In Praise of Folly*, the *Enchiridion* and the *Adages*, as well as the *Novum Instrumentum*, a revised Latin text of the New Testament side by side with the Greek. Each of these four works reveal a different facet of his character, but the direction of his spiritual evolution is the same in all of them. All four were among the most vital texts of the century: never before had the invention of printing played such a pivotal role in Europe's cultural life and its spiritual transformations.

Writer and satirist, Christian moralist, philologist and ardent propagator of ancient literature – here, looking at it schematically, are four facets of Erasmus which found expression in those four texts. Not all of his writings are as readable today as these; indeed very few can be read without the aid of a commentary. Only *In Praise of Folly* and perhaps, in part, the *Colloquia* will be easily understood by the modern reader; the rest need explanation if they are to be read with profit. But they become easily comprehensible once we identify the object of their attack and the model of Christianity they were advocating. The reason for the extraordinary excitement to which the *Enchiridion* gave rise, and continued to provoke for decades, is not immediately apparent from a reading of the text, which at first glance might seem to consist of no more than the standard platitudes of Christian moralizing. But if Erasmus's thought continues to attract the attention of historians and interest in his writing shows no sign of abating, indeed seems to be increasing, the explanation lies in the relevance of his work to the Christian world today.

All genuinely ecumenical currents within Catholicism, all attempts to find a way of freeing Christianity, at least to some degree, from its confessional exclusivity, are a continuation of Erasmus's thought, and all are to some degree conscious of this.

It is well known that when Luther's efforts became widely talked of and more successful than he himself would ever have dreamt, the conviction that Luther's and Erasmus's ideas were tending in more or less the same direction was a fairly general one. Luther himself counted on Erasmus's support. With hindsight we can – or think we can – see both the basis for those hopes and beliefs and the reasons for which they were respectively misplaced and mistaken.

The state of the Catholic Church in the years preceding Luther's rebellion is well known and has been too often described to justify dealing with it here at any length. These were times of what one might call the perfect disintegration of the papacy – a disintegration milked for all it was worth in anticlerical historiography, but even Catholic historians have for a long time now been hard pressed to find excuses for it. Erasmus was born during the pontificate of Paul II – a pope who knew no Latin. He was brought up and educated during the papacy of Sextus IV, the proverbial pope of nepotism, who liberally bestowed cardinal's hats on all his relatives, sold Church benefices left and right, and – as his service to the faith – named Torquemada inquisitioner. The last stages of Erasmus's education took place under Innocent VIII, who publicly celebrated the marriage of his illegitimate son in the Vatican; another of his claims to fame was to have issued a bull about witches. Erasmus's writings and his growing fame fell in the infamous age of the bloody Alexander VI, who was made a bishop at a young age without the formality of ordination, sold off Church benefices only to murder the buyers shortly afterwards in order to sell them again to someone else, organized ballets of Roman courtesans in the Vatican, and in general did not neglect to indulge in a single one of the sins and vices mentioned in all the catechisms of all the religions of the world. The great Julius II got his hands on the Holy See through bribes to cardinals. His successor, Leo X, a Medici and the son of Lorenzo the Magnificent, was made a cardinal at the age of fourteen thanks to his sister, who married Innocent VIII.

In the last decades of the fifteenth century the need for reform in the Church was so general and so strongly felt among Christian intellectuals, the corruption so glaring and extreme, that the divergence of aims and programmes among those who called for reforms was hard to discern; it was fully revealed only when the Protestant schism had clearly become an organized movement.

Erasmus's ideas for reform were simple. Theologically they were an extension of that religion of Grace which, grounded in the Gospels and the Epistles of St Paul, undergoes a regular renaissance in Christianity whenever the weight of bureaucracy and creeping secularisation in the organized Church become intolerable for some part of the Christian world. Christianity as Erasmus understood it was defined above all through its opposition to the religion of the Old Testament – a religion of Law, where the relation between God and the faithful is a sort of business contract. On this legalistic reading, God entrusted man with a certain number of duties and promised suitable payment if they were conscientiously performed. No wonder, then, that one can buy one's way out of certain duties and replace them by others, seek to outwit the other party by interpreting the contract in a way most advantageous to oneself, exploiting its loopholes and ambiguities, and in general barter with God, viewing relations with Him in terms of precisely calculated accounts to be settled. The Christian religion as St. Paul understood it was distinguished above all by the abolition of this legalistic order. The relation with God is one of love, involving no calculation; the Covenant with God is not a system of mutual claims and obligations but a free and unconstrained personal relationship – and thus essentially an irrational one, involving no justifications or claims. It is a relationship based on trust rather than control, on genuine good faith rather than demonstrative displays of obligations fulfilled; in short, a relationship based on faith, not on 'works'. However, a hierarchically constructed Church clearly could not survive within the confines of such a religion. The Church is a system of binding relations which impose certain duties on the faithful with the promise, made in

God's name, of certain rewards in return. Its role as mediator would be unthinkable without a code of duties, and such a code, though it may insist verbally on the idea of divine love as the condition for good works, has only those 'works' as an effective measure of human deeds. The invisible and unverifiable bond of the faithful with a personal God cannot be sufficient justification for the existence of an organized Church. But the tradition of the religion of Grace has always found strong support in canonical texts, so that anti-Church currents which find expression in subjectivist and irrational interpretations of faith inevitably invoke it, making use of those same 'basic' or 'core' sources of Christianity to bolster their arguments against the Church.

In this respect the young Luther's main preoccupation does indeed coincide with Erasmus's ideals. Abolishing the 'religion of works' means, in practice, abolishing the Church – a Church trading in Christian values and corroded from within by simony and corruption. And this can be accomplished only by returning to the ideals of the Gospels: to the idea of justification through faith alone. Faith not in the sense of orthodox beliefs, however, but rather in the sense, found in the Pauline Epistles, of *pistis*: trust. Faith, in other words, as the feeling of filial love and devotion towards God, who despite our offences wants to acknowledge us as His children if that is what we truly feel ourselves to be. Setting aside all the theological complications involved in the doctrine of justification by faith, there is no doubt that this doctrine, in its constitutive intention, is present both in Erasmus's thought and in Luther's early writings.

In Erasmus's writings all roads led towards the same goal: the restitution of Christianity as the effective readiness to fulfil the dictates of morality – dictates grounded in trust in God but also, if fulfilled without calculation and with a truly willing heart, encompassing all that is important in Christianity on Earth. These dictates are simple and can be understood by everyone; they do not require superhuman heroism or extraordinary talents; they are cut to fit human beings and are addressed to all. The rest is of no importance. In particular, the ritual and ceremonial aspects of Christianity, the whole system of Church organization, the dogmatic subtleties, the fine distinctions of speculative theology – none of these have any weight in light of the main goal. Christianity means being good to others, but it also means humility, doing good without flaunting one's goodness, and crediting one's good deeds to God, not to oneself. This, ultimately, reduced to its original and essential intention, is the principle whereby divine Grace, rather than works, justifies us before God.

But the opposition between Luther's intentions and Erasmus's efforts at renewing the Church became apparent as soon as the outline of a new, separatist church community began to emerge from the undifferentiated momentum for reform. If Erasmus did not join the Reformation, it was not only because of his natural caution, his prudence, his conformist streak, his dislike of irrevocable solutions – in short, those character traits so often described by historians. The conflict between Christian humanism and the Reformation was a real one, encompassing a set of utterly irreconcilable basic values. For Erasmus, Christianity was not a violation of human nature; it was an ennobling of that nature, a growth stimulus for at least some of its innate tendencies. Man was not, for him, a creature corroded through and through by original sin, a vessel of evil that must be smashed before human nature, miserable and corrupt, can give way to the sanctifying power of God's gratuitous Grace. Despite the human propensity to sin and crime, divine Grace can gain a foothold, so to speak, on those innate seeds of goodness which survived the calamity of original sin; thanks to divine Grace we can pull ourselves up out of the mire of our wretchedness. Grace does not kill human nature; it purifies and elevates it. Christianity is the continuation of the good aspects of man's nature, not the triumphant conquest of nature by super-nature.

This belief is the foundation of what was traditionally called Renaissance Christian humanism. The word 'humanism' is used in so many different ways, so laden with ideology and overgrown with associations, that one should not really use it without explaining precisely what one means. There is certainly some justification for insisting that it should only be used in its original sense, to refer to those 'paganized' philosophers and writers for whom in principle the only values that exist in the universe are those produced by human effort and employed in the service of human needs. But there is no reason not to use the word in another sense as well, namely to refer to that current in Renaissance culture which, while accepting the fundamental Christian values and recognizing them to have been created beyond man and without his contribution, nevertheless believes that human nature is capable, by and of itself, of glorious moral and intellectual achievements. The difference between Christian humanism in this sense and the ideas of the Reformation, of both the Lutheran and the socially radical variety, emerges with striking clarity in attitudes towards the heritage of antiquity. Christian humanists were engaged in a vast enterprise to make the spiritual and intellectual riches of ancient culture available to the Christian world; they did so with no sense of unease or internal conflict, for they believed that paganism – in other words, the 'forces of nature' themselves, not yet sanctified by the blessings of incarnation – could achieve splendid things in all areas of culture. They popularized the stereotype of Plato as a Christian unbeknownst to himself (thus Ficino and other Florentine Platonists) and made Socrates into something approaching a Christian martyr (thus Erasmus). Secular culture was not suspect in their eyes just because it was secular; they did not believe that nature and natural talents were entirely in the grip of Satan. Man, although corrupt through his own fault, was created by God; a nature created by God, and all the achievements of that nature, could not be simply evil.

The conviction that faith in the infinite power of Grace can be reconciled with faith in the 'naturalness' of Christianity was perhaps the most distinctive feature of Erasmus's thought. It allowed him to ridicule scholastic wordplay while at the same time propagating the literature of antiquity. He could expose the immorality of the Church and the clergy, the monastic orders above all, while at the same time defending his own idea of genuine Christianity – a Christianity defined by the moral qualities of every individual Christian.

This is why Erasmus's moral writings were – as they clearly were – the 'third power' of the Christian world in the sixteenth century. They stood in opposition both to Luther's hope that benefits would automatically flow from the dismantling of the organized Church and to his contempt for all 'natural' human effort and achievements. At the same time Erasmus proposed a model of Christian life which, in contrast to the idea of morality traditionally imposed by the Church, did not increase in value through multiplying ceremonies, rites, scholastic learning or ritual 'good works', but could be almost entirely reduced to a practical morality in which good intentions and good deeds were linked as essential conditions. In other words, the hope that salvation can be bought by multiplying good deeds (let alone through the power of money) was no less alien to Erasmus's idea of Christianity than the assumption of mystics that purity of heart alone, unverifiable and invisible in one's relations with one's fellow men, can justify us at the Last Judgement.

It must be stressed that Erasmus's thought was grounded in two fundamental principles. The first was the belief in the innate goodness and value of human nature (including natural reason); the second attributed salvation to Grace as the efficient cause and enjoined us to put our trust in God instead of trying to gain favour with Him. The first was later adopted by the Jesuits in their moral teaching, which is why Catholic historiography gives them a place in the history of Christian humanism. But if, in the face of these disputes, the word 'humanism' is to have any meaning at all, it must mean upholding *both* these principles, as Erasmus did. Later doctrinal vicissitudes of Christianity showed that the first principle taken alone, unyoked from the second, leads back to a legalistic religion of works – in other words, to a system in which moral values become items to be totted up in an accounts ledger. While the second, when unyoked from the first, can easily produce a feeling that one is not responsible for one's own life, coupled with a carefree reliance on God's unfathomable verdicts – verdicts of which we know only that they are entirely unconnected to any good works we might do to find favour in His eyes. On this principle, taken alone, one trusts in God the way one trusts in one's luck, with no thought of doing anything to contribute to one's own salvation. These two principles are perfect models of, respectively, Jesuit and Calvinist morality as presented by their opponents. One could go on endlessly demonstrating that the

Calvinist principle does not in fact entail that we can go through life blithely leaving everything to God and His decrees without taking any responsibility for what we do, just as the Jesuit theory of Grace does not in fact entail that our salvation is guaranteed if we only make sure to perform certain small formalities. Indeed, in both cases the most important doctrinal texts take precautions to guard against just such interpretations. The fact remains, however, that there is a doctrinal inertia that is independent of the intention of the doctrine-makers, and that the Calvinist critique of Jesuitism had as many arguments and examples to support it as did the Jesuit critique of Calvinism.

It is here that the strength of the Erasmian doctrine lies: in the attempt to find a model of Christianity safeguarded on both sides against interpretations which could serve as convenient excuses for moral sloth; a model that, in other words, would exclude both the unconstraining religiosity of ritual and the convenient religiosity of irresistible Grace. However, although polemically clear and power-ful, this attempt is much weaker, and also extremely risky, as a theo-logical doctrine, for it involves the simultaneous acceptance of two principles which in the conceptual heaven of pure theology seem at first glance to be incompatible. The ostensible simplicity of the Eras-mian position is misleading, as is the ostensible facility of its adop-tion. For it tells Christians to behave as if everything depended on their own efforts while at the same time telling them that nothing does. This contradiction becomes less glaring if we treat it as a par-ticular instance of the difficulty inherent in any doctrine which views genuine human effort as the unique source of moral value while at the same time refusing to acknowledge any human contri-bution to the results of that effort, or indeed to the very capacity to make it. It is a difficulty which besets Stoic no less than Christian moral doctrine.

In later years, when Europe was riven by religious conflict, with new sects multiplying and religious life increasingly dominated by confessional controversies, it was thanks to his conception of Chris-tianity in moral and individual rather than dogmatic or ritualistic terms that Erasmus's thought became the foundation for all attempts to formulate non-confessional models of Christian life. Erasmus was invoked by the first dissidents from Lutheranism, the German spiritualists; Spanish anti-Church mystics were nourished by his principles; Anti-Trinitarians sought their arguments in his work. All those who, in the age of religious wars and confessional disputes, sought a return to the mythical simplicity of the Gospels and wanted to free Christianity from creeds and catechisms, leaving just its moral content, constantly went back to Erasmus and drew on his thought. Erasmus became a symbol of Christianity as a moral stance, a Christianity which refused to recognize the value of an organized Church. He was a source of inspiration for that religiosity which, while rejecting any compromise with the morals of the world, neither sought to escape from the world nor proclaimed its contempt for life, but trusted in natural human capacities. Later this position was itself to develop divisions and offshoots, revealing a wealth of concealed potential. But this is not the place to follow the tortuous paths of Erasmianism in European thought. It is enough to mention the main questions which are essential for an understanding of the *Enchiridion* – one of the most important texts of Renaissance Christianity. Erasmus's position as the force seeking a supra-confessional Christianity, a purely moral Christianity without dogma or ritual, explains the condemnations and bans that rained down on his work, especially after his death, when the practical fruit of his efforts became visible in the religious life of every European country.

But – another caveat worth repeating – followers of Erasmus were not rebels trying to provoke divisions within the Church. The most illustrious of those who in the sixteenth century were influenced by his ideas did not ostentatiously break with the Church of Rome or join Reformist communities. Neither Coornhert nor Modrzewski joined the Reformation as a new ecclesiastical organism. The last thing they wanted was to construct separatist churches with their own rites and observances, their own system of dogmas and – as was shortly to become apparent – their own intolerance. Erasmus's ideas influenced those who dreamt of a reform of Christian life as a whole, not of new churches which would go on to cultivate their own sanctity, infallibility and exclusivity outside the mother Church. They saw the Church disintegrating and had no intention of playing down its corruption; but they also trusted that the collective efforts of 'true' Christians, who understood the foundations of genuine, hidden Christian values, unknown to popes and Vatican dignitaries, would result in a reform of the Church despite the Curia. So they preferred not to ally themselves with any of the new churches, which, like all newly formed organisms, promised, if anything, even greater confessional exclusivity rather than attempting any genuine renewal of religious life. For Erasmus the Church was not a goal in itself, to which all other values must be subordinated; on the contrary, it was an instrument, useful only in so far as it was able to transmit the pure and undistorted values of the Gospels to the faithful. Religiosity focused on what was beneficial to the Church, conceived as an organization and a system of power, was entirely alien to him. It was not his aim to destroy the Church; he wanted only to deprive it of the ideological instruments which allowed it to maintain its system of power. He could, accordingly, speak of his loyalty to Christian ideals, declare that he wanted only 'to build, not to destroy', go on repeating that he was not a rebel and wished only to teach the wisdom of the Gospels. But for his opponents the destructive influence of his gentle moral teaching was clear. There was no escaping the fact that his ideas, if followed to their logical conclusion, ultimately compelled a choice: either Christianity or the Church; either the Gospels or organized religion. Erasmus himself never spelled out this alternative and perhaps was not entirely conscious of its unavoidability; perhaps he really did believe in the possibility of reforming the Church in the spirit of the Gospels. But later generations of reformers knew that such an alternative was unavoidable and that it was Erasmus who implicitly formulated it.

Erasmus's work was not fruitless, although it might, on the face of it, appear so: after all, his ideal of Christianity remained unrealized, one of the many utopias which have appeared and then vanished throughout the history of the Church, leaving no visible mark on the Church system. Of course his propaganda did not destroy the system which was its target. But it did have an effect: it put certain basic principles of the Christian faith back into circulation, with the result that they were incorporated into the language of the Church, becoming a natural part of it; and this made it difficult to violate them too blatantly. All internal criticism of the Catholic Church made since Erasmus's time, all attempts to reform it from within, have relied on the same sources and drawn, more or less consciously, on his work. Everything that has been done to repair, even in part, its ossified rigidity, was inspired by those ideas – ideas which go through a regular cycle of being condemned by the orthodox and then, after a time, taken up again, in a weaker and simplified form. Modern attempts at repairing and renewing the Church are also part of the Erasmian heritage; whatever succeeds in loosening its rigid exclusivity and weakening the system of intolerance is a continuation of Erasmus's ideas. For these reasons his work merits the attention not just of Christians but of all those who, although not Christians themselves, cannot view the fate of Christianity with indifference; for Christianity belongs to the culture and the history of which we are all a part.

1965

Anxiety About God in an Ostensibly Godless Age

If someone were to ask, 'Where are we on the God question?', many of us would be inclined to respond by asking: what God question? Is there such a question?

Of course not, scientists and extreme rationalists will reply. For them there is indeed no such question. They believe it is simply not possible to make sense of the idea of God: it cannot be made into an intelligible and contradiction-free intellectual construction. Their argument goes like this: before we formulate a statement or ask a question, we have to know what it is about. Which means that before we can even ask whether God exists, or consider statements like 'God exists' or 'God does not exist', we must already have a clear idea of God. But this is supposed to be impossible: by definition, every abstract statement about God is supposed to be either self-contradictory or unintelligible, for there is no way of referring God to empirical reality. The question is therefore meaningless, an empty question.

For some believers, too, there is no God question: namely those (if indeed any such exist) whose inherited faith is firm and unshakeable as a rock, and who have not the slightest doubt that they live in a world directed by God. And for those few chosen souls who have been blessed with mystical experience, the very word 'faith' may be inappropriate, for we can speak of faith only when there is a distance between perceiver and perceived whose dimness might give rise to uncertainty. But in mystical experience all distance is removed. For such people the God question obviously does not exist.

Then there are the convinced atheists (if indeed any such exist);

for them, too, there is no God question. They have not the slightest doubt that science has definitively driven God from the world; in their view, the idea of God is merely a vestige of old superstitions and past ignorance, or a psychological defence mechanism, or an expression of social conflict.

But the world in which we live is not one of people serene in their certainty, unshaken in their belief or unbelief. We live in an age of exiles and refugees, the banished and the expelled, 'eternally wandering Jews' searching for their lost (physical or spiritual) homeland. In this nomadic life nothing is certain or guaranteed or established for all time; nothing, except the wandering itself, is unquestionably given.

The God who once guaranteed a stable order of values and social relations, rules of reasoning and mechanisms of the physical world, and who functioned as the culmination of that order, no longer exists, for that order no longer exists. While people were still able to trust in its permanence, it was an order in which non-believers, too, had their place (in all these remarks I have in mind only European, Christian civilization). They may have been seen as errant sheep, madmen or emissaries from hell, but they were none the less part of the accepted order of things. And while they may have been persecuted, punished and condemned to death, they were none the less, in some sense, happy: certain in their unbelief and spiritually serene. For them there was no God, and thus neither heaven nor hell, and with this they were content. But even this state of affairs belongs to the past.

As the certainty of faith collapsed, so did the certainty of unbelief. Today's godless world – unlike the cosy world of Enlightenment atheism, protected by a friendly and benevolent Nature – is perceived as a dark abyss of eternal chaos, with no meaning or direction, no structure or signposts to show the way. Thus spoke Zarathustra. Ever since Nietzsche proclaimed the death of God a hundred years ago, there have been no more happy atheists. The world in which people relied on their own powers and considered themselves unconstrained legislators on questions of good and evil, the world where, freed at last from the chains of divine bondage, they could hope to recover their lost dignity – that world was transformed into a place of endless anxiety and suffering. The absence of God became a permanently festering wound in the European spirit, even if it could be forgotten with the aid of artificial painkillers. Compare the godless world of Diderot, Helvétius and Feuerbach with the godless world of Kafka, Camus and Sartre. The collapse of Christianity so eagerly awaited and so joyfully greeted by the Enlightenment turned out – to the extent that it really occurred – to be almost simultaneous with the collapse of the Enlightenment. The new, radiant anthropocentric order that was to arise and supplant God once He had been deposed never appeared. What happened? How did the fate of atheism become so singularly bound with the fate of Christianity that the two enemies came to share the same misfortune and uncertainty?

Of course, the history of Christianity, too, provides some splendid testimony of spiritual unease, from a variety of periods: the writings of the young Augustine, Pascal or Kierkegaard. But unease as an essential quality of the spirit is a distinctive feature of our time and culture – a culture which, though still alive and hurtling forward on its creative momentum, we nevertheless perceive as sick, even if we cannot agree on the diagnosis. Is the place abandoned by God the source of its sickness? Was Kierkegaard right when he said that all despair about temporal things is really despair about things eternal, whether or not we realize it? There is of course no way of proving this; we can only suspect it.

This unease is not limited to intellectuals, philosophers and poets; it has crept into the European spirit, haunting its everyday life. It afflicts and destroys the active poles of religious culture: militant Christianity and militant godlessness. But it can also be found lurking just beneath the surface of the widespread indifference which is the chief form of spiritual life today. Even at the very heart of what is ostensibly indifference there is a disquieting void, impossible to conceal; we cannot entirely silence all echoes of what we have, in part deliberately, forgotten. From somewhere beyond all our achievements and experiences emerges, unfailingly, the apocalyptic warning: 'Because thou sayest, I am rich, and increased with goods, and have need of nothing; and knowest not that thou art wretched, and miserable, and poor, and blind, and naked.' (Revelation 3:17)

Of the spiritual factors which in modern times, and especially in recent decades, have most contributed to the process of what we call secularization, two in particular are often mentioned, regardless of whether we view secularization as a calamity or as a form of liberation. They are, first, the progress of science, whose role in all areas of our lives has grown so spectacularly that it has left no room for God; and, second, the inability of Christianity, and in particular of the Catholic Church, to confront the great social problems to which industrialization gave rise in the twentieth century. On this view, Christianity has proven insensitive to new social conflicts and needs because its eyes are always raised upwards towards heaven and God while the world, forgotten, has had to fend for itself.

It may be worth explaining why neither aspect of this widespread belief appears credible to me.

As to the first: it is of course true that the existence of God is not and never will be an empirical hypothesis subject to scientific proof. This predicament is a permanent and inescapable one; it is not merely a question of insufficient knowledge. There is no logically valid way of getting from empirical knowledge, however great its scope, to infinity – let alone to a personal Providence whose actions are goal-directed. From the seventeenth century, when the natural sciences broke apart from theology and religious worship and basic scientific methodology was codified, the 'God question' has been entirely irrelevant both to the content of scientific statements and to the methods of justifying them. The codification of scientific method was supposed to make scientific discoveries into predictive tools and thereby to bring natural phenomena under human control.

But it is utterly implausible to suppose that this was how God was driven from the world, unless we confuse science with scientistic rationalism. And this latter – that is, the principle whereby the value of knowledge depends on the rigorous application of scientific method – is an arbitrary epistemological doctrine devised by philosophers precisely to undermine religious belief. Scientism is neither a logical nor – it can plausibly be maintained – a social consequence of science. If the two evolved in parallel, it was not because science gave rise to scientism in any causal sense. This is not, of course, to say that the link between them was merely accidental. Scientistic rationalism is a normative principle which expresses a specific hierarchy of values; in that hierarchy temporal goods, whose manufacture is the chief function of empirical science as a social institution, are the value *par excellence*. God is naturally excluded from the scientistic conception of the world, as is everything that is of no use in the human pursuit of domination over nature. But from this point of view He would be of equally little use within the Christian view of the world, for if the way He rules the world were subject to immutable laws with predictive power, it would mean that the laws of the physical world had ceased to function.

In fact, both Christian theology and its popular interpretations bear some responsibility for the confusion between knowledge and faith, for both promoted the view that divine justice can be discovered in the world by empirical means and God Himself magically harnessed to the service of our passions and desires. Yet this view, fundamentally anti-Christian, is precisely what we call superstition – superstition being a conception of God as a sort of machine which, if we apply the right technique, will produce the desired effects. Thus prayer, for instance, is seen as a technical procedure which, if carried out with proper care, will infallibly produce the results it was intended to achieve. To the extent that Christian teaching encouraged such superstitious beliefs, it contributed to its own demise. This still applies to those theologians who claim to do 'scientific theology'. When faith tries to compete with science and to apply its criteria, it inevitably becomes a pseudo-science; its efforts will always be futile and its claims disproved at every step. But the more widespread the confusion of faith with secular knowledge became, the more people, especially educated people, felt compelled to reject faith together with superstition. The Christian worldview remains a profound and clear-sighted view of the human condition. 'Scientific theology', on the other hand, is superstition.

One can say that scientistic rationalism also had a beneficial effect on culture, for it helped purge Christianity of superstition and allowed it to gain a better understanding of its calling. Atheism and scientism are mutually supporting; that much is obvious. But – to repeat – neither is in any sense the product of science. The origin of both should rather be sought in cultural phenomena, in our tendency to disregard anything that does not seem useful in our pursuit of domination and control. The present crisis of trust in science and technology, brought about by an awareness of their dangers, may weaken the ideologies of scientistic rationalism, but it is irrelevant to the validity of scientific methods and norms.

So it seems to me astonishingly naive to say that Christianity has suffered the decline it has because it is not 'scientific' enough. On the contrary: when Christianity tries to lay claim to 'scientific' validity, it produces only useless pseudo-science. The humiliations it suffered in its conflicts with science were the consequence of its pretensions to scientific status rather than its failure to be sufficiently 'scientific'. It was precisely Christianity's fear of defining itself in clear opposition to rationalism and continuing to be what it had always been – God's Word translated into human language – that led both to the erosion of faith and to the futile attempts to attack science. For the very idea of a conflict between science and faith was predicated on a concept of faith as a kind of profane knowledge – thus entailing its profanation in the proper sense of the word.

Similarly with the second charge – the charge that Christianity, its attention concentrated on spiritual values to the exclusion of everything else, has neglected its duties towards the human community and failed to seek (and therefore also to find) answers to the urgent social problems of modern times. In this, too, it supposedly conspired in its own downfall. But there would seem to be far better grounds for arguing precisely the contrary: that the Church erred in tying its moral teaching exclusively to one specific social doctrine, for in doing so it laid itself open to the charge of allowing the fusion of its eternal values with facts in the world – allowing, in other words, the confusion of the sacred and the profane. There was a good deal of justice, in my view, in the attacks levelled against the

Church hierarchy by nineteenth-century socialists; the Church's attitude to social change and the fate of the poor and exploited could indeed justifiably be criticized. But it is a gross distortion of any justifiable criticism that might be made to say that the Church thought only about the other world or devoted too much attention to 'religion' when it should have been concentrating on the world here and now, on temporal life and suffering. It would be far more accurate to argue the contrary: that the Church was too much a prisoner of existing social structures and often contrived to suggest that these structures were founded upon immutable Christian values.

This is still a danger facing Christianity, though it now comes in two opposing forms; for the temptation today is not so much to forget about the temporal world as such but to forget about the inevitable relativity of temporal values. Both variants further godlessness by appearing to blur, or even to abolish, the boundary between the sacred and the profane. But there is no temporal cause, no social or intellectual end, whose defence Christianity could ever be better equipped to undertake than the secular powers in whose province such matters lie. Christianity can engage in politics and social conflicts, but if it is to escape self-destruction, it must perceive all temporal goods as relative. Since one cannot, in today's world, be entirely apolitical in good faith, the Church, too, insofar as it is part of culture, should assume its political responsibilities; but this does not mean that it should identify itself with any existing political organization or movement, or treat political values and goals as ends in themselves. The Church's past links with ossified social orders which harked back to the previous century are no less dangerous for the cause of Christianity than new attempts to link Christian ideas to the political ideologies of revolutionary messianism. Neither of these tendencies encourages the hope of a resurgent vitality of the Christian message; in both, one can sense the temptation to subordinate this message to temporal ends – to transform God into a tool, a potential object of human manipulation. The theocratic tendency – that vain and disastrous hope, enfeebled but still breathing, that humanity can be dragged to redemption by force – and the ostensibly opposing tendency – the attempt to embed Christian values in the framework of this or that revolutionary ideology – share one fundamental feature: both transform God into an instrument for attaining ends which from a Christian perspective, whether or not they are justified, should never be seen as ultimate ends. Both run the risk of transforming the Christian community into a political party. Thus both are symptoms of the inner corrosion of Christianity. As so often throughout history, the greatest danger today comes from the enemy within the gates.

Described in such general terms, this state of affairs does not, of course, strike one as particularly new. The entire history of Christian doctrine, however entangled with social conflicts, indeed to some extent dependent on and emerging from them, can be seen as a constant struggle to maintain the boundary between the sacred and the profane. The great spiritual upheavals, radical shifts and moments of awakening which were, so to speak, ruptures in this history, were usually attempts to halt the process of profanation, to lead Christianity back to its original calling and to weaken its domination by secular concerns. But they always came at a price, and they were never entirely successful. There was ultimately no escaping the danger inherent in the nature of Christianity itself: the constant tension between its temporal and its sacred self-interpretation. The Church sees itself as the repository of divine Grace, but it exists in the world, embedded in it, a culturally determined and historically changeable organism which uses temporal means to achieve its ends.

The Gospels proclaim solidarity with the poor, the defenceless, the unfortunate and the oppressed; but we have no Gospel that promises a world without evil, suffering or conflict. The Gospels condemn those who enjoy lives of comfort and ease if they are deaf to the suffering and hunger of the disinherited; but we have no Gospel that preaches social equality or inequality, or contains a recipe for the ideal social system, in which all desires and aspirations are fulfilled and all obstacles to happiness removed. The Gospels denounce tyrants and persecutors; but we have no Gospel that substitutes one tyranny for another in the name of chiliastic delusions. A Christianity which tacitly accepts that God is an instrument for us to use in the furtherance of some cause, doctrine, ideology or political party is godlessness in disguise.

In this sense one can say that both the traditional theocratic tendency within Christianity and Christian 'progressivism' have encouraged dechristianization – not because they adopted any particular political position, but because they are responsible for the secularization of Christian values. What people seek in religion is – *mirabile dictu* – God, not the justification of a political ideology or a 'scientific' explanation of the world. A Christianity that bows before intellectual and political fashions in pursuit of transient success participates in its own destruction. It can never surpass science by applying scientific criteria to Christian doctrine. And it can never surpass political ideologies by promising earthly happiness. When it attempts to do so, it inevitably reveals its impotence and irrelevance. Christianity views the human condition in light of the Gospels and the book of Job, not in terms formulated by theocratic, technocratic or revolutionary utopias.

Perhaps – and this is of course only speculation – dechristianization, insofar as it accompanied the decline of the temporal power of the Church, will prove beneficial, or indeed salutary, to the cause of Christianity. Perhaps it is not really such a terrible thing for that cause, if we take it seriously, that the Christianity which was once identified with power politics and diplomatic intrigue on the one hand, and with fanaticism and raw clericalism on the other, is coming to an end. Perhaps all the vicissitudes of its profane history will act as a sort of purgatory, a cleansing which will allow it to emerge renewed and true to its spirit. Perhaps.

It can be said with justice that Christianity must adapt itself and the language of its teaching to changes in our civilization. It has done so more than once, though not without overcoming huge difficulties. But there is always a risk in this process of accommodation: the risk that in the search for new forms the content will be forgotten. It does seem to be true that modern Europeans are mostly deaf to the conventional language of theology; Thomism, though of immense importance in the history of our culture, is not a conceptual framework that can encompass the modern world. But the problem is not, as many claim, that traditional Christian teaching has become 'incomprehensible' to people. There is no reason to believe that we have suddenly become so stupid that what was easily understood by people in the Middle Ages has become inaccessible to us. The problem is rather one of distance – the distance between our everyday experiences and traditional theological idiom. The search for meaning in the world must start from the state of our present civilization, in all its dimensions; but it must also constantly keep in mind those aspects of the sufferings, concerns and anxieties specific to that civilization which express the permanent presence of evil in the world. Couched in such general terms, the problem is not hard to articulate. But the search for a new idiom for Christian doctrine will be long, and its success is uncertain.

We begged God to leave the world, and He has, at our request. A gaping hole remains. We continue to pray to that hole – to Nothingness. There is no answer. We are angry and disappointed. Is this proof of the non-existence of God?

But what is there that is new in our experience? Evil? Evil has always been with us; it was born with us and through us. Is there really more of it now than there was before? People ask: where was God in Auschwitz? Where was He in Kolyma, and in all the genocides, wars and atrocities we have witnessed? Why did He do nothing? But this is the wrong question. Leaving aside the fact people have done monstrous things to one another down the centuries, that genocide, bloodbaths and torture have always occurred and that evil – the evil in us – has never ceased in its work, putting the question this way smuggles in an idea of God as a being whose duty it is to protect the human race, through miracles, from the evil it does and to ensure its happiness despite its self-inflicted wounds. But this god – a god who functions as a magical power in the service of our immediate needs – was never the god of the Christian faith, nor of any other great faith, despite his frequent appearances in folk religion. If he were, we should have expected the early Christian martyrs to lose their faith once they saw that their God did not intend to provide miraculous assistance to liberate them from their executioners. Of course, people have always believed in miracles; but they were also warned never to rely on them.

No, Auschwitz and Kolyma are not the cause of godlessness. There is a temptation to think that, because such atrocities were the work of godless people, they should be used to defend the cause of God. It is a temptation to which many succumb, but it is a dangerous one; history provides too many examples of cruelty inflicted by the pious.

People today do not lose their faith because of the evil they see around them. Unbelievers perceive evil in a way that is already determined by their unbelief; the two are mutually supporting. The same holds true of the faithful: they perceive evil in light of their faith, which is consequently affirmed rather than weakened by what they see. So there seem to be no good grounds for saying that the evil of our time casts doubt on the presence of God; there is no compelling logical or psychological connection.

Similarly with science: Pascal was terrified by the 'eternal silence' of infinite Cartesian space; but both this silence and the voice of God are in the ear of the listener. God's presence or absence lies in belief or unbelief, and each of these attitudes, once adopted, will be confirmed by everything we see around us.

The meaning of the godless Enlightenment has not yet become apparent, because the breakdown of the old faith and the collapse of the Enlightenment are taking place simultaneously, both before our eyes and in our hearts. Are we in a 'period of transition'? The expression is almost tautological, for history consists exclusively of periods of transition. But if we are, where are we transitioning to? This we cannot know. One can plausibly claim that the Enlightenment, with its godlessness, was the condition of all the intellectual and technical achievements of modernity. And yet the Enlightenment is increasingly a source of unease. Was Jung right when he said that in mythological archetypes God's death is always followed by His resurrection? Are we, then, living in the dreadful time between Friday and Sunday, when the Redeemer, dead but not yet resurrected, visits hell? This, too, we cannot know. We can be sure only of our own uncertainty.

Finally, as an example, a history lesson. Consider the following well-known facts, some important, some less so:

In 490 B.C. the Persian army, as expected, defeated the much weaker Athenian infantry at Marathon.

In 44 B.C. the fifty-six-year-old Julius Caesar followed the advice of the seer Spurinna and did not go to the Senate.

In A.D. 33, in answer to Pontius Pilate's question of who should be released, the mob in Jerusalem cried: 'Jesus!'

In 1836 the eighty-year-old Wolfgang Amadeus Mozart died in Vienna.

On December 22, 1849, in St Petersburg, a young Russian named Fyodor Mikhail Dostoyevsky was executed by firing squad for his revolutionary activities.

On August 30, 1918, Fanya Kaplan shot and killed Vladimir Ilyich Lenin.

In August 1920 Marshal Piłsudski made a small mistake, and the Red Army occupied first Warsaw, then Poland and Germany.

In 1938 Adolf Hitler died of a heart attack.

In 1963 Joseph Stalin died.

What is the world like now, after these events? That is something only God knows. Is that tantamount to saying that no one knows? And what does any of this have to do with God?

People have always known, unless they were wilfully blind, that history is a series of accidents; its fabric is woven from tiny chance events. This means that if there is any plan or reason in it, it can only be God's plan and God's reason. None of us knows what they are; we can only believe in them.

Once we realize that this succession of accidents which is history conceals nothing but emptiness, it becomes our own internal emptiness. Is all this just a series of truisms and banalities? Certainly. The question of belief and unbelief is banal, because it is ubiquitous.

Our age is marked by disquiet and uncertainty about God's presence or absence. The faithful worry about God, but their worries are really disguised worries about the world. Unbelievers worry about the world, but their worries are really disguised worries about God. Since the dispute is about ultimate questions, it cannot be resolved by the means considered by each side to be infallible and definitive. But for both the world abandoned by God is clearly a source of unease.

This unease also shows that the triumph of the godless and self-satisfied Enlightenment could never be entirely secure. In its victory it proved so unsure and divided, and its successes have brought so much new uncertainty, that our age can be described as only ostensibly godless: it is too intensely aware of God's absence. Hence the prominence of the 'return of the sacred' as a topic of discussion. Godlessness tried desperately to replace the departed God with something else. Enlightenment humanism proposed a religion of humanity. Nietzsche already saw through the futility of such artificial substitutes. The twentieth-century followers of Comte and Feuerbach, such as Erich Fromm or Julian Huxley, are the least convincing of the godless. God can of course be rejected as morally dangerous, denied as unacceptable to reason, cursed as the enemy of humanity or excommunicated as a source of bondage. But the Absolute could be replaced by something finite and non-absolute only if it were really forgotten. And if this were possible, there would no longer be any need to replace it. So the object could be attained only once there was no need for it. But the Absolute can never be forgotten. And the fact that we cannot forget about God means that He is present even in our rejection of Him.

1981

An Invitation from God to a Feast

It is not hard to see why the seventeenth century was an attractive time for philosophy, and for intellectual pursuits in general. We think of it as the golden age of philosophy and perhaps that is what it was. It was still possible then to believe in the eventual discovery of all-encompassing, ultimate, universal constructions which would, within one conceptual framework and without invoking divine revelation, solve all philosophical, religious, moral, scientific and theological questions; it was possible to believe that nothing was fundamentally unsolvable. Leibniz was said to have been the last man in Europe who knew everything, and he really did know everything: he carried in his head the sum of the accumulated scientific, philosophical, theological and even historical knowledge of the time. That kind of omniscience soon became culturally impossible.

In philosophy and in theology as well as in science, the great minds of the age tried to apply rigorous rules of consistency, sometimes borrowing or adapting them from mathematics. Even scepticism aimed at perfect consistency. The Enlightenment in the first stages of its blossoming harboured almost divine ambitions – unlike the later, mature Enlightenment, which, at least in its most refined form, argued for the self-limitation of Reason and with various degrees of radicalism rejected the idea of rational theology.

Jansenist thought, too, although not usually sympathetic to the idea of rational theology – that is, to a theology whose content is entirely subordinated to the rules of human reason, in all its miserable inadequacy – was imbued with the spirit of consistency. 'God does what He likes,' the Jansenists might say, 'not what you would like Him to do. Does He not? This is something you accept; and from a Christian point of view its acceptance seems easy enough. Very well. But you also accept, do you not, that *He* judges *you*, not the other way round? If so, then how can you say He is unjust? You say it is unjust that unbaptized infants should roast in the fires of hell, not for a thousand years and not for a million, but for all eternity? Or that God should dispense His Grace arbitrarily, with no regard for supposed human merit, and abandon the great majority of human beings to the clutches of the Devil? And that none of those few who are saved should be able to resist His Grace? But if you say this is unjust, you are in fact saying that you know better than God what is just and what is not.' In Jansenist theology everything is grounded in the same perfectly consistent order; all the horrifying sides of that theology (as humanists saw them) are justified if we really believe that God knows better than we do what is just. And who would dare deny this?

Pascal accepted this whole Jansenist horror without a murmur. Or so it appeared. He claimed to understand it and to be happy with that understanding. He felt no need of theodicy – of a theoretical demonstration of God's justice and goodness in spite of all the evil in the world. In any case it would be absurd to try to justify God.

Or so it appeared. But somewhere in the thought of probably every great philosopher there is a rent, a hidden tear in the fabric, painful and irreparable. He may be only partly or dimly aware of it, but it torments him even as he tries to ignore it or deny its existence. And Pascal's was here.

Let us now imagine a conversation between Pascal and a Christian humanist, perhaps a Jesuit, perhaps a follower of Erasmus, who challenges Pascal's image of God:

Humanist: Pascal, according to you I may not say that a God who dispenses His Grace according to His whim, regardless of our merits, past or future, and who deliberately abandons most of us to the eternal abyss of hell while compelling others to be good – I may not say that such a God would be an unjust despot. Why?
Pascal: I told you: because your complaint presupposes that you know better than God what is just. Calling God unjust is like calling

a circle square. Whatever God does is just, simply because He does it.

Humanist: I am not saying that God is unjust. I am saying He would be unjust if He behaved in the way you describe.

Pascal: Well, there you are. You know in advance what God can do; what He may and may not do according to the dictates of morality. You invent an idea of justice and then say that God should conform to it.

Humanist: It is not my invention. God tells us how we should act to be just.

Pascal: But He does not say how *He* should act to be just. And with good reason, because He is necessarily just; He is just by definition.

Humanist: So do you understand how and why God is just when He does something that is entirely contrary to justice as we know and understand it?

Pascal: Of course I understand how and why God is just.

Humanist: Well, explain it to me, then.

Pascal: I can't, because you wouldn't understand it.

Humanist: Why not? Am I too dense?

Pascal: Not at all. You could be a great mathematician, a great historian, an eminent philosopher, even a great theologian, and still you couldn't understand it, because you have no faith.

Humanist: How can you say such a thing! I'm a good Catholic, I'm pious, I'm obedient, I believe in God and accept without qualification every word of the creed. And you say I have no faith?

Pascal: Yes. And your questions confirm it. Faith is not an intellectual act; it does not consist in accepting a certain number of theological propositions. You do not acquire faith by saying: Yes, it is true that God is an omnipotent Creator, that His son Jesus Christ was born of the Virgin Mary, etc. Faith is another reality, quite different from the reality most people inhabit. The rules of the secular world no longer apply in it. It encompasses every aspect of the lives of those happy few who inhabit it; it is suffused with divine goodness and mercy. When you are in it, all the things about the world that seem absurd and incomprehensible when viewed from within that world, from the secular point of view, at once become perfectly clear and comprehensible.

Humanist: And how do you enter this reality?

Pascal: Only on God's invitation. And it is an invitation you cannot decline.

Humanist: And how could I procure such an invitation?

Pascal: There is nothing you can do to procure it. God gives it to whomever He likes.

Humanist: And that is just, according to you?

Pascal: Perfectly just. When you inhabit this spiritual realm of faith, you can see clearly that it is just. But there is no way of explaining this to someone from outside.

Humanist: So there is no way of understanding faith if you are standing outside the door of this realm, and the door is closed?

Pascal: No. There is no way. And yes, the door is closed.

Humanist: But you want this door to open for me?

Pascal: Yes, with all my heart. I want you to be saved.

Humanist: But what can I do to make that happen? And what can you do?

Pascal: I can try to convince you to stop resisting God's will.

Humanist: But surely, according to you, it is impossible successfully to resist God's gratuitous Grace?

Pascal: Yes, it is.

Humanist: Well, then?

Pascal weeps.

Ultimately, all the stratagems elaborated by Pascal to make his apologetics clear and convincing came to nothing, smashed to pieces against the wall of his theology. He never explained this rent in his thought and never repaired it. But, who knows, perhaps it is to this that we owe that extraordinary work which is his *Pensées*, of necessity unfinished and to all appearances inexhaustible: every reading throws up something new and astonishing. There is no end to its interpretation.

Seen from our privileged perspective, Pascal is the polar opposite of the Enlightenment, for in his thought the gap between the realm of faith and the 'world' in the pejorative Christian sense is unbridgeable; there is no point, moral, intellectual or ontological, at which these two realities meet (though Pascal himself would not of course have agreed with this way of putting it). There is no universal language which could encompass both. Obviously, the radical separation of the religious from the secular is not in itself necessarily anti-Enlightenment – it was, after all, insisted on by Kant, who was the Enlightenment personified – but in the Pascalian version it is. In the end, the only conclusion we can supply to Pascal's thought must be this: that nothing in life is of any importance save those things which are so deeply hidden that there is nothing we can do to find them. Nothing at all.

2002

Why a Calf? Idolatry and the Death of God

Strictly speaking, if God is dead – though I do not believe that to be the case – there can be no such thing as idolatry. At least not for His assassins. Idolatry is by definition the worship of something other than God as if it were divine; it is veneration voluntarily displaced. Since only God is the proper object of worship, all other forms of veneration are not only illegitimate but sinful; indeed, according to St Thomas Aquinas, idolatry is the worst sin of all (*Summa Theologica* II, II a–e, q.94). As to the question of why God, as Christian civilization conceives of Him, is worthy of worship, it is a pointless question – a non-question. It seems reasonable to say that if God, the infinite, omnipotent and infinitely good Creator of heaven and earth, does not deserve our worship, then nothing does. Without God the concept of idolatry makes no sense.

According to Duns Scotus, the first two commandments could not be revoked even by God Himself. Worship, obedience and reverence for His name are part of the very idea of God insofar as that idea encompasses His relations with the world of His creation, and in particular with His children, the inhabitants of that world. Most Christian thinkers agree that God can be known only through His creatures; enclosed in His hidden nature, He is not accessible to us except as He is reflected in them: *posuit in tenebris latibulum suum*. To the extent that He reveals Himself to us, we perceive Him in acts of worship. Thus whenever we break the commandments, as of course we often do, we also commit the sin of idolatry, for in violating them we are, as it were, violating infinity; we are sacrificing God on the altar of our own selfish interests, as if we were worshipping ourselves instead of Him. This is why St Paul – oddly, it might at first seem – counts fornication, covetousness and greed as sins of idolatry. Indeed, in Christian terms every sin could be considered idolatrous, in that sin always involves contempt for God: to sin is to reject God in favour of other goods which we value more highly.

All this might seem perfectly simple, obvious and uncontroversial. But as with everything that seems simple and uncontroversial, it turns out, on closer analysis, that the matter is more complicated and less certain than we thought.

What does it mean to worship someone or something? Does the act of worship satisfy some natural need? Is it part of our innate spiritual make-up? The extraordinary and disturbing story of the golden calf in Exodus might incline us to think so. The story is extraordinary because the initial idolatrous act was performed by Aaron at the request of the Jews, who demanded that he make gods for them; the creation of this new 'god' seems therefore to have been the result of the Jews' need to worship someone or something, even if it had no connection to their faith or their tradition. But why a calf? And why golden? How did the Jews come to embrace this extraordinary cult, and how could they really have believed that this piece of metal was divine? What spiritual benefit did they derive from it?

A god or person whom one worships is not the same thing as an authority. I can rationally regard as an authority someone who simply possesses certain skills or knowledge that I do not have: the doctor who examines my heart, the electrician who repairs my lamp, the translator from a language I do not know, and so on. They are authorities for me because I accept their verdict. I know they are not infallible; my reliance on their advice is based on empirical premises and can be withdrawn if it proves ill-founded. God or other objects of worship are not authorities in this sense. Whatever God does is good by definition, by virtue of His nature, not because He happens to possess certain skills. However atrocious His ways of governing the world might seem to unbelievers, in the eyes of the faithful they are the best they could possibly be. Similarly, a 'charismatic' political leader, for instance, is right whatever he does: those who believe in him give him their assent in advance. There is nothing empirical in their worship, just as there is nothing empirical in the worship of God. Hitler and Stalin were not worshipped because they were right; they were right because they were worshipped. Similarly, too, with romantic love – earthly Eros. The beloved person is right because she is what she is; her words, her eyes or her hands deserve worship because they are hers, and it would be absurd to ask the lover: 'Why do you love her?' There is no possible answer, for no one, strictly speaking, deserves the love of another; love is freely given and freely withdrawn. These two kinds of worship – worship of a political leader and worship of a beloved person – could be considered instances of idolatry par excellence; they come closest to divine worship in the sense that adoration, when it is very intense, seems to fill the whole person of the worshipper, as it is supposed to in religious worship. The worshipper expresses his thanks to God for His very existence; love for a person involves a similar kind of emotion. Other kinds of idolatry – the worship of money, nature, reason, science, the State and other abstract things – generally do not attain this level of intensity; in such cases we tend to speak of obsession rather than worship. They are, nevertheless, cases of idolatry, and indeed they are sometimes called that, for the God of the Bible is a jealous God and demands a monopoly on worship.

This requirement, however, is observed with various degrees of rigour or laxity. On its most rigorous interpretation, we should not love other people, not even our children or parents, our friends or lovers, other than through God or by reference to Him. In other words, if I love someone, it should be either because God commanded us to love our neighbour or because that person's very existence is owing to God's Grace, His wisdom and His will. Warnings and admonitions about this often appear in the writings, speculative or lyrical, of mystics, and in the works of adherents of some of the stricter currents of Christianity, like the Jansenists or militant Protestant groups. But loving people because God commands it seems a peculiar and probably impossible feat; how can love arise from obedience? Unless it is an odd form of love that is not felt but only expressed through one's behaviour – but this surely bears very little relation to what we normally mean by the word. Loving other people through or by reference to God also seems to bear little resemblance to what we usually mean when we speak of love; a secondary, derivative form of worship, offered because something belongs to God or was created by Him or is somehow connected to Him, seems artificial, devoid of true affection and devotion. In any case, it is by no means certain that God, the Father of Jesus, did in fact forbid us to love our fellow men except through or by reference to Him. To the Pharisees' question about the most important commandments, Jesus replied that there were two: to love God and to love one's neighbour. Two separate commandments, then; not one. In other words, we may, and indeed should, treat our neighbour as an end in himself, a separate object of our love and care, independently of God, and this is not idolatrous. Without this separate Commandment Christianity would be a dismal and rather sinister sort of religion, condemning as idolatry our every feeling and expression of disinterested love and affection towards others, even towards our children or parents – unless we immediately corrected ourselves and directed our feelings towards the Almighty before directing them again, this time in an act of obedience, towards those others. Happily this dry, lifeless, bureaucratic version of Christianity has not been imposed on us in the name of doctrinal purity.

The concept of idolatry is necessary, indeed indispensable, to any religious cult. But to say that we should worship God above all else, and must sacrifice anything that conflicts with the reverence due to Him and His commandments, is quite different from saying: 'Thou shalt not love nor honour nor bestow affection upon anything except God and that which can be honoured by reference to Him; nothing deserves love or reverence in itself, nothing has value in itself.' According to the first version, God should always take first place in the hierarchy of our interests, feelings and goals, as He is indeed first in the hierarchy of being; but there is nothing to prevent us from honouring and loving other things for themselves, providing that God always comes first in our thoughts and emotions. Nothing must take precedence over Him or be given equal place with Him. The second version, however, not only establishes God's priority but also reiterates the demand for an absolute monopoly. One of its dangers is the ease with which it can be transformed into an obscurantist and anti-cultural slogan. Indeed it is hard to see how, assuming a minimum of consistency, such a transformation could be avoided, for this version in one fell swoop condemns the entire sphere of cultural activity as a sinister den of vice and godlessness. Happily, contemporary Christianity seldom makes appeal to it.

Some Church Fathers and later theologians also emphatically condemned the hideous sin of curiosity – and no wonder, as it was curiosity that led our progenitors to taste the forbidden fruit of the tree of knowledge, thus bringing about the greatest calamity in human history. But without that sin there would be no knowledge, no science, no art and no technical progress. One could argue that contempt for all the things of this world is quite in conformity with Jesus's teachings and therefore part of the core of Christianity: that we should see ourselves as pilgrims journeying through life, putting their trust in God and expecting no recompense or reward here on earth for the suffering and hardship they encounter on the way. Jesus taught that the Day of Judgement was imminent, and all mundane concerns were naturally overshadowed by this prospect; in the shadow of the Apocalypse this world seemed of little importance. But Jesus himself admitted that he did not know the date of the second coming, and since then mankind has survived for two millennia. We condemn human curiosity in vain; God clearly created us with an instinct for exploration and it seems hard to imagine that this instinct is punishable or that it inevitably leads to idolatry.

The most visible and spectacular form of idolatry emerged, of course, in the controversy about iconoclasm. The story is an interesting one in itself, independently of its social and political context. Theologically the matter seems clear. The biblical prohibition against images is not explained in the Bible, but then God is not in the habit of explaining His commands (indeed, certain rabbis emphatically warned against demanding explanations from Him or attempting to supply them). Perhaps God simply anticipated that if images were permitted, artists would not limit themselves to secular objects but would eventually want to depict various

Is God Happy?

things holy and divine as well, and this could easily lead to false cults. So painting was relegated to the sphere of goyish amusements. The Church finally yielded on the question, but issued a number of warnings (among others at the Council of Trent) against abuses: the veneration of religious images and saints' relics should not be directed towards those objects themselves, but only towards God. Predictably, the warnings had little effect. The faithful worshipped icons and relics as sources of magical powers and expected them to produce miraculous effects through supernatural mechanisms. The cult of images is natural; an omnipresent but invisible God the Father is an elusive abstraction, and people find it easier to concentrate their prayers and religious feelings on visible figures. Mystics used paintings as simple tools to aid concentration, although they cautioned that images should not be contemplated or enjoyed for their aesthetic value; accordingly they used paintings devoid of any aesthetic value. The most intense focus of the cult of images is, understandably enough, on the Virgin Mary, who for the mass of the Catholic faithful is an unfailing source of consolation and the ultimate refuge from life's problems and hardships; this suffices to explain her prominent presence in popular Catholicism. The mass popular devotion in centres of the Marian cult shows that God is not dead, academic verdicts notwithstanding. The Virgin Mary even seems to lead a number of different lives in the many sanctuaries where she is worshipped: there is a Virgin Mary of Guadeloupe, of Fatima, of Częstochowa, of Lourdes, and so on, all differing somewhat in the efficacy of their interventions and services. Protestants have always condemned the Marian cult as a blatant example of Papist idolatry, or even as an attempt to make the Holy Trinity into an unholy quadrinity by sneaking in an extra figure, and of the female sex to boot. In some countries European art suffered enormously from Protestant iconoclastic vandalism. It is hard to deny, however, that the Christian theological tradition provides some justification for the vandalism. '*Hi tres unum sunt*', the famous apocryphal *Comma Johanneum*, gave rise to a sufficient number of impossible puzzles and conundrums to keep the priests and scholars of Christian Europe busy for cen-

206

turies. Perhaps we should not multiply our theological problems.

Iconoclastic urges have certainly not died out; Alain Besançon, in his book *L'image interdite*, even finds them among the sources of twentieth-century European abstract art.

Both in theological terms and for the religious sensibility, idolatry is the opposite of sacrilege. To commit sacrilege is to touch the untouchable, to defile something sacred by treating it as a secular object, or to ignore holiness and deny it the respect due to it. To commit idolatry is to ascribe holiness to what is not holy: to extend the sphere of the sacred to things which are not sacred. It is the religious worship of secular objects. But both idolatry and sacrilege presuppose the existence of a sphere of the sacred; they involve the assumption that there *is* something that is sacred and worthy of worship. In a hypothetical entirely secular society, a society where nothing is sacred, nothing can be idolatrous or sacrilegious; for people with no religious sensibility whatsoever, both concepts lose their meaning. But for religious people both idolatry and sacrilege are omnipresent in our secular societies. When the things people worship are not God, their every act of worship is necessarily idolatrous; and since people are at best indifferent to the sacred, they constantly commit sacrilege, though they may not be aware of it. It is sacrilege, for instance, to visit a church only in order to admire its architecture and art, perhaps even to listen to sacred music for its aesthetic value alone, to read the Bible because it is a great work of literature, and so on. In a godless society the word 'idolatry' is still used, but its meaning has become, like everything else, trivialized and vague; people sometimes use it to refer to reverence for things which in their view are not worthy of reverence. Thus from the standpoint of a liberal ideology one might condemn the cult of a nation or a Führer as idolatry. This is not, however, because such a cult is not the worship of God, but because it is the worship of something other than, say, freedom, which for a liberal is the supreme value. In other words, in an age of universal relativism the category of idolatry is sometimes used to condemn those who do not share our hierarchy of goods. In such contexts 'idolatry' is no more than a meaningless insult.

But there is a mass phenomenon today which really does seem to deserve the name, and it plays a significant role in people's lives. It is the worship of celebrities: rock stars, actresses, sportsmen. This is more than merely collective worship: it draws in huge numbers of people, who through participating in it are able to experience a strange feeling of collective identity. The spectacle is indeed a strange one for those observing it from the outside, for what kind of identity can be attained through the worship of a football player? What values are created through the hysterical euphoria of a crowd of young people at a concert? How are great goddesses of the screen produced, like Marilyn Monroe, Marlene Dietrich or Greta Garbo? Quite recently we were able to witness an extraordinary event in the history of idolatry, namely the funeral of Princess Diana. Here was a woman of no education, who devoted her brief life mostly to building her 'image', to (extraordinarily successful) self-publicity and the creation of her own cult, and who at the moment of her death became a genuine source of identity for countless millions of people. Millions thought of this young woman, who probably never in her life wore the same dress twice and travelled only by private jet or, more modestly, first class, as 'one of us'. Instead of envy and resentment she provoked a sort of dream-feeling of identity. Television created her, but television creates many famous people and few of them become genuine idols.

Manifestations of pseudo-religious worship are omnipresent in our culture, and their ubiquity naturally prompts questions about their source. What kind of deep, innate human need explains the phenomenon of modern idolatry? If God is dead, if we expelled Him from our world and forced Him to hide in His impenetrable solitude, why do we go on manufacturing imitations, or rather caricatures, of past forms of religious worship? There is a strong temptation to suspect that this is a modern form of the hypothetical anthropological invariant, and we are not sure how to define it.

Why a calf? The most visible difference between religious worship and modern forms of idolatry, apart from the lack of reference to God, is the absence of any beliefs – the absence of a creed. Modern cults require no doctrinal expression, only an ill-defined and uncodified form of ritual. Religion, on the other hand, in the forms in which we know it, is never pure ritual: it requires at least a set of beliefs which explain the meaning of the ritual. So if there really is such an invariant, it involves no claims to truth. The similarity to religious worship lies elsewhere. Collective idolatry is simply a projection of shared emotions, an emotional quasi-reality which generates the feeling of identity we seem to need so much. It seems reasonable to suppose that everyone feels the need for such collective participation in an emotion-laden world; both true religious cults and their modern, idolatrous pastiche forms, as well as politics, sport and popular art, can generate this feeling of belonging. Cases of individual idolatry, such as intense love or irresistible fascination, are of course a different matter, but they display the same fundamental characteristics: our life seems absorbed by something better than ourselves, and we feel somehow ennobled, part of a higher reality. The act of worship elevates the worshipper.

Idolatry is unlikely to disappear even from societies where true religion is still vital, since modern technology makes communication – and thus also the emergence of collective realities – so easy. And people have always felt a longing for forms of worship that allow them some kind of sensory or visual contact with the divine, or with supernatural powers. Today various sects satisfy this need better than great Churches, which would indicate that cults and sects will continue to proliferate. In the eyes of traditional religions such sects are idolatrous; but traditional religions in the Christian world have largely lost their missionary zeal and live in fear of accusations of intolerance. They need a new language, and so far they have not found one. Miracles are quite frequent, but they generally happen among poor and uneducated people, and the Church of Rome is reluctant to confirm them. This, too, must weaken its influence and facilitate the spread of sectarian movements.

But religion, too, is unlikely to disappear, even if we do live in an age of idolatry in the sense that secular substitutes are so much more powerful than what the Church can offer. The cult of small, transient, temporal divinities which inevitably soon disappear, to be replaced with other idols, cannot satisfy the needs which religion answers: the everlasting need to live in a universe that is not devoid of meaning, a purpose-endowing universe itself endowed with purpose. Moreover, there is a hidden desperation that seeps out from the pseudo-prayers and pseudo-rituals centred on idols. Religious needs may not always be experienced as such by everyone, but there is reason to suppose that they are indeed an anthropological invariant and cannot be supplanted by scientific theories. If they were ever really extinguished, it would mean that the human race had ceased to be what it is and something else had taken its place – something we know nothing about.

1998

Is God Happy?

The first biography of Siddhartha, the future Buddha, reveals that for a long time he was entirely unaware of the wretchedness of the human condition. A royal son, he spent his youth in pleasure and luxury, surrounded by music and worldly delights. He was already married by the time the gods decided to enlighten him. One day he saw a decrepit old man; then the suffering of a very sick man; then a corpse. It was only then that the existence of old age, suffering and death – all the painful aspects of life to which he had been oblivious – was brought home to him. Upon seeing them he decided to withdraw from the world to become a monk and seek the path to Nirvana.

We may suppose, then, that he was happy as long as the grim realities of life were unknown to him; and that at the end of his life, after a long and arduous journey, he attained the genuine happiness that lies beyond the earthly condition.

Can Nirvana be described as a state of happiness? Those who, like the present author, cannot read the early Buddhist scriptures in the original, cannot be certain; the word 'happiness' does not occur in the translations. It is also hard to be sure whether the meaning of words like 'consciousness' or 'self' corresponds to their meaning in modern languages. We are told that Nirvana entails the abandonment of the self. This might be taken to suggest that there can be, as the Polish philosopher Elzenberg claims, happiness without a subject – just happiness, unrelated to anyone's being happy. Which seems absurd. But our language is never adequate to describe absolute realities.

Some theologians have argued that we can speak of God only by negation: by saying what He is not. Similarly, perhaps we cannot know what Nirvana is and can only say what it is not. Yet it is hard to be satisfied with mere negation; we would like to say something more. And assuming that we are allowed to say something about what it is to be in the state of Nirvana, the hardest question is this: is a person in this state aware of the world around him? If not – if he is completely detached from life on earth – what kind of reality is he a part of? And if he is aware of the world of our experience, he must also be aware of evil, and of suffering. But is it possible to be aware of evil and suffering and still be perfectly happy?

The same question arises with regard to the happy residents of the Christian heaven. Do they live in total isolation from our world? If not – if they are aware of the wretchedness of earthly existence, of the dreadful things that happen in the world, its diabolical sides, its evil and pain and suffering – how can they be happy in any recognizable sense of the word?

(I should make it clear that I am not using the word 'happy' here in the sense in which it might mean no more than 'content' or 'satisfied', as in 'Are you happy with this seat in the aeroplane?' or 'I am quite happy with this sandwich'. The word for happiness has a broad range of meaning in English; in other European languages its meaning is more restricted, hence the German saying '*I am happy, aber glücklich bin ich nicht*'.)

Both Buddhism and Christianity suggest that the ultimate liberation of the soul is also perfect serenity: total peace of the spirit. And perfect serenity is tantamount to perfect immutability. But if my spirit is in a state of immutability, so that nothing can influence it, my happiness will be like the happiness of a stone. Do we really want to say that a stone is the perfect embodiment of salvation and Nirvana?

Since being truly human involves the ability to feel compassion, to participate in the pain and joy of others, the young Siddhartha could have been happy, or rather could have enjoyed his illusion of happiness, only as a result of his ignorance. In our world that kind of happiness is possible only for children, and then only for some children: for a child under five, say, in a loving family, with no experience of great pain or death among those close to him. Perhaps such a child can be happy in the sense which I am considering here. Above the age of five we are probably too old for happiness. We can, of course, experience transient pleasure, moments of wonderment and great enchantment, even ecstatic feelings of unity with God and the Universe; we can know love and joy. But happiness as an immutable condition is not accessible to us, except perhaps in the very rare cases of true mystics.

That is the human condition. But can we attribute happiness to the divine being? Is God happy?

The question is not absurd. Our conventional view of happiness is as an emotional state of mind. But is God subject to emotion? Certainly, we are told that God loves His creatures, and love, at least in the human world, is an emotion. But love is a source of happiness when it is reciprocated, and God's love is reciprocated only by some of His subjects, by no means all: some do not believe that He exists, some do not care whether He exists or not, and others hate Him, accusing Him of indifference in the face of human pain and misery. If He is not indifferent, but subject to emotion like us, He must live in a constant state of sorrow when He witnesses human suffering. He did not cause it or want it, but He is helpless in the face of all the misery, the horrors and atrocities that nature brings down on people or people inflict on each other.

If, on the other hand, He is perfectly immutable, He cannot be perturbed by our misery; he must therefore be indifferent. But if he is indifferent, how can He be a loving father? And if He is not immutable, then He takes part in our suffering, and feels sorrow. In either case, God is not happy in any sense we can understand.

We are forced to admit that we cannot understand the divine being – omnipotent, omniscient, knowing everything in Himself and through Himself, not as something external to Him, and unaffected by pain and evil.

The true God of the Christians, Jesus Christ, was not happy in any recognizable sense. He was embodied and suffered pain, he shared the suffering of his fellow men, and he died on the cross.

In short, the word 'happiness' does not seem applicable to divine life. But nor is it applicable to human beings. This is not just because we experience suffering. It is also because, even if we are not suffering at a given moment, even if we are able to experience physical and spiritual pleasure and moments beyond time, in the 'eternal present' of love, we can never forget the existence of evil and the misery of the human condition. We participate in the suffering of others; we cannot eliminate the anticipation of death or the sorrows of life.

Must we, then, accept Schopenhauer's dismal doctrine that all pleasant feelings are purely negative, namely the absence of pain? Not necessarily. There is no reason to maintain that the things we experience as good – aesthetic delight, erotic bliss, physical and intellectual pleasure of all kinds, enriching conversation and the love of friends – must all be seen as pure negation. Such experiences strengthen us; they make us spiritually healthier. But they cannot do anything about either *malum culpae* or *malum poenae* – evil or suffering.

There are, of course, people who consider themselves happy because they are successful: healthy and rich, lacking nothing, respected (or feared) by their neighbours. Such people might believe that their life is what happiness is. But this is merely self-deception; and even they, from time to time at least, realize the truth. And the truth is that they are failures like the rest of us.

An objection could be raised here. If we have absorbed true wisdom of the higher sort, we might believe, like Alexander Pope, that whatever is, is right; or, like Leibniz, that we dwell in the best of all logically possible worlds. And if in addition to accepting something like this intellectually, in addition, that is, to simply believing that all must be right with the world because it is under the constant guidance of God, we also feel in our hearts that this is so, and experience the splendour, goodness and beauty of the Universe in our daily life, then can we not be said to be happy? The answer is: no, we cannot.

Happiness is something we can imagine but not experience. If we imagine that hell and purgatory are no longer in operation and that all human beings, every single one without exception, have been saved by God and are now enjoying celestial bliss, lacking nothing, perfectly satisfied, without pain or death, then we can imagine that their happiness is real and that the sorrows and suffering of the past have been forgotten. Such a condition can be imagined, but it has never been seen. It has never been seen.

2006

III. *Modernity, Truth, the Past and Some Other Things*

In Praise of Unpunctuality

Unpunctuality is the ingrained habit of regularly failing to fulfil people's expectations regarding the specific time at which certain of our actions will take place, these expectations being the result of assurances on our part, tacit or explicit, regarding that specific time.

It is not hard to see that the above definition involves a contradiction. When people expect that I will behave in a specified way (for instance, come to the café or finish some work) at a specified time, they do so on the basis of certain premises which justify their indulging in such predictions; but my assurances alone cannot constitute such a premise. For in promising that I will behave in a specified way at a specified time (for instance, that I will meet you in the café at ten) I am merely making a prediction about certain future facts. These facts in turn can be considered dependent on my free will or independent of it. If they are independent of it, my assurances clearly cannot be taken seriously, for how could any human action, an occurrence determined by so immense a number and variety of factors, be predicted to the minute? And if they are dependent on it, my prediction concerns my own freely willed behaviour. But in this latter case there are two possibilities: either my present behaviour is merely a prediction of my future decision in the matter, but is not in itself a decision, nor does it imply a decision; or it is the result of a decision I have already taken, or can even be identified with that decision. The first case must be rejected as impossible, for if I were merely making a promise about my future behaviour but had not yet decided what it would be, in other words if I considered myself still at liberty to choose (whether or not I would come to the café at ten) at some point in the future, then there are two possibilities:

either my promise is false or it must have been expressed in the form: 'I will come or not, depending on what I decide,' in which case it would not have been a promise at all. We are left, then, with the second possibility: that in making my promise I also make my decision, thereby depriving myself of the freedom to choose between the two possibilities before me (to come or not to come to the café at ten) at some future time, in consequence of which my future behaviour ceases to be dependent on my free choice, for it is determined by certain facts in the past (namely, the fact of my having made my decision). But then my promise becomes an attempt to describe my state of consciousness (namely, the act of deciding) through a description of certain non-existent external events (namely, my future behaviour). And this is surely odd.

But let us suppose that it is not in the least odd, and that it is indeed possible to describe one's state of consciousness by describing non-existent facts which are to take place in the future. If my interlocutor is to take my declaration seriously, he must have some knowledge of the rules which govern the connection between my states of consciousness and my future behaviour – for we are assuming that he is treating my declaration as a description of my states of consciousness, but my declaration itself is not *about* those states: its content makes no reference to them. Now this knowledge cannot be *a priori* knowledge, for there are no *a priori* rules that determine the connections between my private experiences and my behaviour. Nor can it be deduced from any universal laws of physics, chemistry, psychology or sociology, for if it could be so deduced, then everyone's behaviour as regards the phenomena encompassed by the word 'punctuality' would be identical, which, as we know, is not the case. My interlocutor must therefore have some empirical knowledge – not about universal laws, but about the connections that obtain between the behaviour of this concrete person, namely myself, and his state of consciousness, as expressed by the description of his future behaviour. In other words, the interlocutor must, if he is to have any grounds for his expectations concerning my future behaviour, have some knowledge about my behaviour in the past, and in particular he must know that there are certain empirical rules which predict that, after my description of my state of consciousness through the description of certain non-existent events, those events will in fact always occur; in other words, my interlocutor must know that I am a punctual person in the ordinary sense of the word. His expectations will be rational only if he knows that I am punctual; only then can one say of me that I failed to fulfil expectations.

Thus, assuming the rationality of all the agents involved, only the person who notoriously fulfils the expectations of others as to his punctuality can fail to fulfil those expectations; only someone who is notoriously punctual can turn out to be unpunctual. To say of someone that he is 'notoriously unpunctual' is therefore absurd. The initial definition given above therefore characterizes an empty set, for it is self-contradictory; an 'ingrained regular habit of failing to fulfil people's expectations' etc is an impossible phenomenon. In other words, notorious unpunctuality is impossible; only single instances of unpunctuality are possible.

Our initial definition, if it is to be free of contradiction, must therefore be amended to read: 'Unpunctuality is a singular and very rarely occurring instance of a particular person's failing to fulfil people's expectations regarding' etc. Simple logic compels us to the conclusion that unpunctuality cannot be anything other than an extremely rare and exceptional occurrence (for a connection between facts which cannot be deduced theoretically must present itself with notorious regularity if we are to consider it a stable and established connection and accept it as grounds for predictions about the future.)

Once this is accepted as a basic premise, the argument in praise of unpunctuality is simple to construct. The benefits of unpunctuality are manifold, both for individuals and for society as a whole. It is undeniable that if unpunctuality were a general and persistently recurring phenomenon, life would become extremely trying; but we have shown this to be logically impossible. Unpunctuality as a rare and sporadic phenomenon, on the other hand – which, as we have seen, is the only possible kind of unpunctuality – can be a very useful thing, and this for a number of reasons, of which we will here mention the two most important.

First, unpunctuality does much to inculcate the habit of logical thought. For if our expectations regarding people's future behaviour, expectations based on repeated empirical evidence of connections between their behaviour and their promises regarding it, were fulfilled in every case without exception, our illusory faith in the infallibility of ordinary numerical induction would be strengthened, and our ability to guard against the disappointment to which expectations based on induction of this kind might give rise correspondingly weakened. By the same token we would succumb to intellectual sloth, which could cost us dearly in our everyday lives, not to speak of the cost to our intellectual faculties themselves. If the conviction of the fallibility of reasoning based on purely numerical induction is to take firm root in our minds, our experience must provide the phenomenon of unpunctuality in the above sense.

Second, unpunctuality confers benefits of a moral nature. If our faith in the stability of the connections between people's states of consciousness (expressed in their declarations) and their behaviour were confirmed in every case without exception, our faith in free will would be destroyed, and we would be forced to conclude that people's actions are entirely predictable. By the same token we would stop treating other people as genuine moral agents. For if there is no logical connection between the two, there is a compelling psychological one: believing that human behaviour is utterly predictable entails failing to believe that people are responsible for their actions. Lacking any grounds for believing in the responsibility of other people, compelled by logic to treat them like machines with no will of their own, we would have no reason to hold their unpunctuality against them and berate them for it. Moreover, if everyone without exception was always punctual, unpunctuality could not be condemned as a bad habit. And since the condemnation of people who are unpunctual curbs or at least in large measure reduces their unpunctuality, the lack of this restraining influence would lead to a dangerous increase in the habit of unpunctuality among the population. Unpunctuality would thus turn against itself.

Thus unpunctuality is essential if punctuality is to exist. In other words, unpunctuality is a necessary condition for combating unpunctuality – not because there would be nothing to combat if it did not exist, but because if it did not exist, it would assume dimensions which would make it impossible to defeat; its spread would be uncontrollable.

A pedant might question the validity of this argument by pointing out that it concerns only relations between people who are assumed to be rational agents. For only rational agents would refrain from expecting punctuality until they had repeated evidence, over a long period of time, of connections between other people's promises and their later behaviour. But what if there are people who expect punctuality without legitimate grounds, thoughtlessly, for no good reason whatsoever? Then the whole argument will be undermined. This objection can be answered as follows: if there are such people, then unpunctuality becomes even more beneficial, indeed virtuous, for it will be just punishment for their intellectual sluggishness, lack of logic and groundless expectations. It would be our duty to flaunt our unpunctuality before such people as often as possible, on a grand scale, enthusiastically and without restraint.

Thus among rational agents unpunctuality is highly beneficial. Among non-rational agents it is equally beneficial, though for different reasons. Ergo…

1961

In Praise of Snobbery

I encounter the word at least ten times a week, in weeklies and dailies, in journals and magazines. Needless to say, it always comes shrouded in dark tones of condemnation: snobbery is absurd, contemptible, universally reviled, absolutely indefensible. I reach for my dictionary: what could it be, this snobbery business, to provoke such horror and outrage? I look it up in more dictionaries; I pore over lexicons. And what do I find? One dictionary says that a snob is someone who looks up to other people because of their high rank, social position or wealth. Another says that a snob is someone who imitates people of high social position, grovels before those of high rank and harbours particular respect – a pathetic and contemptible respect – for wealth. A third supplements this with a definition of snobbery as a mindless and contrived sort of admiration for things that are fashionable.

I read these explanations and I think: is that really what those who inveigh against snobbery mean? Do they believe, for instance, that following fashion is always to be condemned as snobbery? And if they do, would they, for example, want their wives and girlfriends to go about dressed in the fashions of fifty years ago, given that all changes in dress since then have come about through the influence of fashion? Do they themselves, in order to demonstrate their immunity to the fluctuations of fashion, go around in frock-coats, or perhaps togas, or chitons, or wolf skins? One occasionally sees the inveighers against snobbery in the street, but their dress does not seem to display any particularly ostentatious contempt for fashion.

So perhaps it is not fashion they mean, but something else? I go back to the dictionaries. They explain that snobbery is showing particular deference towards people of high rank and wealth. But as we know, it has been several centuries since wealth and high rank correlated perfectly. Certainly in Poland people of high rank are not immensely rich. I myself do not know any immensely rich people at all in this country; I only read about them in the paper, in the section where they report court proceedings. But when the inveighers against snobbery condemn a book or a play as snobbish, they surely do not mean that the work in question reflects particular deference on the part of the author towards clever currency traders or embezzlers on a grand scale. So maybe what they mean is high rank rather than wealth? Perhaps they think the author displays particular deference towards people who hold high positions in government. Can this be what they object to? It seems unlikely.

Let us try, then, to define snobbery in accordance with what we suppose to be the real motives of the inveighers against it. Let us give the name of snobbery to cases of behaviour adopted because that kind of behaviour is characteristic of people whom one regards as one's betters, either in general or in the domain to which that behaviour belongs.

On this definition, snobbery is a form of imitation undertaken not in order to get better at some activity whose goal we independently consider worth attaining, but with a view to self-improvement. We act snobbishly when we want to resemble people whom we admire – or perhaps not so much admire as envy – or whom we know to be generally admired; and achieving this resemblance is our only aim in behaving in this way.

But here is a question for the inveighers against snobbery to consider: what would civilization be like without snobbery? What other socially effective – and I stress, socially effective – motives of human behaviour are there that would have a chance of promoting general progress in human culture, both intellectual and material? If we exert ourselves to improve our behaviour, our work or our knowledge, it is for one of two reasons: either from a pure and disinterested desire for perfection for its own sake – that is, from a desire to become accomplished in some domain – or from a desire to be considered accomplished. Would you have me believe that if this second motive were not at work, the first would have the slightest chance of achieving anything in society on any remotely visible scale? Who was it, O inveighers against snobbery, who instilled in you this romantic, pathetic belief in an innate human desire for self-improvement, in a noble disinterestedness proper to the human race? Where did you pick up the absurd superstition that mankind, in every one of its individual specimens, is endowed with a natural desire for perfection, and yearns to be perfect for the sake of being perfect? And why on earth, why, I ask you, on the bones of Saint Isidore, should it make such a huge difference whether we try to be better because we just want to be better, regardless of any other motives we might have, and are drawn upwards by some pure ideal of virtue, or because we like being well thought of? To turn up one's nose at snobbery is to cut off the most viable (psychologically speaking) sources of progress.

Of course, you will say that such imitation is not always a striving for self-improvement; you will say that often it is quite the reverse. And you will be right. It is from snobbery that we take up smoking cigarettes at a young age, and then go on, without any snobbery, poisoning ourselves with them for the remainder of our days. The examples are legion, and there is no need to cite any more. But what of it? It shows only that snobbery makes us assimilate all the prevailing customs and values of a given social milieu, good and bad, worthy and unworthy, beneficial and useless.

Doubtless you will say that we should assimilate only the good ones and reject the bad. This is excellent advice. It was also the course advocated, for a considerable time, by the Church Fathers, without spectacular effect. Let us agree that we assimilate contemporary culture together with its less laudable aspects.

Snobbery is not, of course, a source of cultural creativity. But it is the most powerful instrument we have for disseminating all aspects and elements of culture. We can, if we like, deplore the wretchedness of human nature, which drives us to seek perfection through snobbery rather than for its own sake. But deploring human nature belongs to a different discipline. One thing, in any case, is certain: there are no greater snobs than children. It is only through snobbery that children in time become adults: they do it by imitating adults, and they do it not through some innate drive to perfection but because they are aping those whom they consider to be their betters. If the inveighers against snobbery know of any educational methods which dispense with this source of motivation, let them, by all means, present them to us.

1960

Crime and Punishment

I recognize that the title of this essay is not strikingly original; nor is the topic. I should say at the outset, therefore, that this is not an essay about Dostoyevsky, or even about legal theory – an area about which I am largely ignorant. It is rather about the traditional question of whether punishment can be justified, if at all, on other than practical grounds – and whether the practical, or instrumental, justification suffices.

Familiar justifications for punishment include the idea that the punishment is a deterrent for others; that it is a *preventive means* that makes the criminal physically incapable, temporarily or permanently, of committing further crimes; that it is an instrument of re-education; and that it is an act of retribution. One also finds some combination of the above. In the first three cases, the justification for punishment is practical; only in the case of retribution is it moral.

None of the practical reasons offered for punishment seem to require the notion of responsibility, at least if this notion implies freedom of choice. One may always argue, like Spinoza, that such a notion is irrelevant: do we not kill poisonous snakes without asking whether they enjoy *liberum arbitrium*, or even if we are certain that they do not? Do we not remove a stone from the road when it impairs our movement? On this view, punishing criminals does not differ from these sorts of practical measures.

The obvious trouble with this simple explanation is that we normally believe that people *do* differ significantly from snakes and stones. We believe that people are able to make choices, that there is a distinction between instinctive reflexes or mechanical movements and specifically human behaviour mediated by reflection, and that our thinking about crime and punishment naturally involves the ideas of justice, responsibility, and duty.

Of course, a consistent behaviourist can easily dismiss such doubts. Maintaining that the concepts of justice, responsibility, and duty are no more than philosophical fancies or remnants of religious superstitions, the behaviourist holds that we would be much better off scrapping such concepts altogether (though it is not clear how he knows that we would be better off). According to him, our behaviour – whether or not it is mediated by reflection – consists of events determined entirely by prior conditions (again, it is not clear how the behaviourist knows this). Consequently, he regards punishment merely as a technique for modifying human conduct: for him, punishment needs no other support. Whether it does or doesn't need additional support is the question I wish to address.

That no human society could survive without deterring its members from what it considers anti-social behaviour is obvious. At least in our time, whenever legal restrictions become for any reason unenforceable, the result almost invariably is mass looting and vandalism. And this is true not only in Somalia or Liberia but in New York as well, as we saw after the sudden blackout there a few years ago. Not everyone goes wild on such occasions, to be sure, but an anarchic minority suffices to break society apart and make life impossible. If my heart is rather on the side of anarchy, my reason is not, and I have to admit that anarchy is (alas) a childish dream. No doubt there are encouraging counter-examples. Alexander Solzhenitsyn tells a story about a Soviet concentration camp in which the inmates overpowered the guards and seized control for about three days. On that occasion, miraculously, the camp remained in order: there was no violence and no rape, even though the population consisted mainly of hardened criminals. The suddenly regained feeling of freedom created a kind of fraternity. But such examples cannot, unfortunately, be extrapolated into a general principle. We have to admit that no human community, unless it wants to disintegrate, can dispense with the institutions that deter would-be criminals with the prospect of suffering.

But the idea of deterrence is not above criticism. It has often been observed that there is something wrong with inflicting suffering on some people in order to terrify others. Doesn't it run counter to the Kantian principle which demands that we treat every human being as an end in himself, never as a means? What right do we have to employ people as instruments of deterrence? Moreover, the very idea of deterrence suggests that its validity is to be measured by its effectiveness. The simplest example: in all debates about capital punishment, its opponents argue that it is useless because it does not deter terrorists or murderers; it is said that statistics do not reveal any clear correlation between the abolition or reimposition of the death penalty and increase or decline in the number of relevant crimes. Perhaps. But surely the death penalty would work as a deterrent if it were applied swiftly and infallibly – preferably amid horrid tortures in a public square – to people who ride city buses without a ticket or fail to fasten their seat belts when driving a car.

A silly joke? Not necessarily, if we wish to measure the validity of punishment solely by its efficacy as a deterrent. Everybody would say, of course, that my suggestion involves a glaring disproportion between the offence and the punishment. But how do we know what is or is not proportionate in such matters? In various historical periods, people were hanged for stealing a few shillings, buried alive for adultery, and burned for not believing in the Holy Trinity. The present penal system in Western civilization is of relatively recent origin and has by no means acquired universal recognition or approval. What penalty is proper for what wrongdoing is a matter of changing conventions, feelings and sensitivities – as is, for that matter, the scope of acts that are penalized. In countries without a strict penal code, we still observe wild discrepancies between penalties meted out for the same crime, depending on the judge. There is no *a priori* and no empirical foundation, no transcendental wisdom and no religious tradition, on which we could rely in establishing the right proportions between criminal acts and the ways in which they are punished. In those matters, justice is always arbitrary and there is usually no way of reducing crime and penalty to the same currency.

The idea of punishment as a preventive is not liable to the objection that it views individuals merely as a means to instil dread into other people. It seems to justify the ultimate prevention – the death penalty – even better. And in cases in which there is practically no probability that the criminal might commit the same crime again – and such cases are frequent – it suggests that there is no need for punishment at all. As to the question of proportion between punishable acts and the punishment, the idea of prevention does not seem to provide any better clues than does the idea of punishment as deterrence: here, too, the matter is bound to be decided by historically relative consensus.

The concept of re-education as a theoretical foundation of the penal system provokes other doubts. Whether and how punishment educates criminals is a matter of empirical inquiry, and I am not competent to venture into this area; it is enough to say that, according to the considered opinion of many knowledgeable people, prisons are more likely to provide an education for crime than for decency; and if this is the case, the idea of re-education as a justification for punishment is simply pointless. Setting this empirical question aside, however, we should ask what is meant by re-education. If it consists in instilling fear, in altering a person's conditional reflexes so as to dispose him to change his conduct in the future, it does not seem to differ fundamentally from prevention, in that it acts on the criminal himself, rather than on other people. And if moral education in the proper sense is meant, then punishment seems altogether dispensable if other means – for instance, ordering people to attend classes in moral philosophy instead of sending them to prison – prove more efficient (unless, of course, attending such classes is in itself a penalty heavy enough).

But even if we grant the uncontestable assumption that it is impossible to dispense with the instruments of deterrence lest the whole fabric of society fall apart, there is still another question: can the idea of deterrence and, in general, practical justifications of punishment, suffice to ensure a level of community without which life becomes intolerable? In other words, do we need the idea of retribution?

The concept of retribution seems close enough to that of revenge to provoke understandable suspicion. But the two concepts can be separated. Revenge is neither punishment in the legal sense nor retribution in the sense of natural law. It is an emotionally motivated act with the exclusive aim of doing harm to people who, in our opinion, did harm to us directly or indirectly; the intensity of the thirst for revenge has little to do with the extent of the harm caused by the person involved, as we can see from many cases of people killing each other for ridiculously slight reasons. The desire for revenge is perhaps natural and unavoidable, but a widespread moral intuition recommends that we forbear from actually taking revenge, even in cases of obvious and serious wrongdoing, since taking revenge would make us at the same time plaintiff, judge, prosecutor and executioner in the conflict – a state of affairs that runs counter to the very concept of law. It is true that vengeful feelings often make up the background of public pressure exerted on penal legislation. Indeed, we all know of crimes so hideous, so abominable, that the demand for the death penalty is understandable. In countries where the death penalty has been abolished, this generally came about through a legislative decision against the opinion of the majority of the population. The same can be said of the abolition of witch-hunting.

While we can, and probably should, dismiss the idea that vengeance is a compelling justification of any penal system, we may still wish to retain the idea of retribution and argue that it is important to keep it. Retribution is not revenge, nor is it necessary as a concept of positive law. It is not revenge because it does not imply an emotional urge to hurt the wrongdoer; it is not part of positive law because cannot be properly defined in legal terms. The idea of retribution could retain its validity even if it were proved – and this is an empirical issue – that punishment is inefficient as a deterrent, as a preventive measure, or as an educational device. It is a moral – as opposed to practical – justification of punishment. To be sure, it cannot, any more than can practical justifications, define the proportion between the nature of a crime and the extent of the penalty. One may say nonetheless that, without it, human communal life would be devoid of substance and would probably collapse.

The idea of retribution has, I believe, mythological origins. We cannot *prove* its validity empirically or give it *a priori* grounds. Yet there seems to be a widespread mythological belief – perhaps more often implied than explicitly stated – that there is a kind of moral mechanism of equilibrium at work in the arrangement of the cosmos whereby evil must be repaid, or cancelled, by suffering; and that therefore suffering has redemptive power, and restores the order of Being which is continually disturbed by our evil acts. Suffering thus has a meaning that cannot be reduced to its hypothetical functions in legal machinery: it has a place in our lives, since we are participants in the cosmic order of things, and it has a place in mankind's moral order – an order that was not arbitrarily invented by us but was found ready-made, sacred, compellingly imposed on human communities.

In the legal order, crime is what is defined as such by penal law. The scope of what is considered criminal may change one way or the other; some items are decriminalized, others are added to the list of punishable actions. Legal punishment is for transgressions of the law, but retribution is for sin, and sin is part of the moral order of the universe. The ideas of sin, of evil, of guilt, of repentance, are beyond the scope of the legal system; the law can function well without them. But can we? In terms of secular constitutions, our only duty is not to violate the laws set by the state. Duty in the moral sense has little to do with positive legislation. We have duties that no positive law can prescribe; we may even, on some occasions, have a duty to defy or violate the existing laws.

In secular states within a nominally Christian civilization, the areas of sin as defined by church doctrine and of crime as defined by the law overlap. Some criminal acts, such as murder, rape and stealing, are sinful in a religious sense, while others may be considered *adiaphora*, or indifferent, by religious rules. Conversely, some sins are not crimes according to the law. Lying, for instance, is a crime only in special circumstances, as in the case of perjury; but Christian doctrine teaches that all lies are sinful. Certainly, any Christian Church is in an ambiguous position: it is supposed to convey to the faithful the divine Commandments, but it is a legally ordered institution as well, and it would be impossible to claim that everything in canon law or in the Commandments of the Catholic Church is *de iure divino*. Therefore the area of what is defined as sinful is not immutable. One no longer needs to confess to a priest the sin of eating meat on Friday, and even though a married priest is still a sinner, exceptions are permissible and nobody maintains that the celibacy of priests is *de iure divino*. The use of contraceptives is in principle still a sin but probably so few Catholics bother about it nowadays that it is practically, albeit grudgingly, tolerated, like premarital sex.

But although sin cannot be defined in formal terms, i.e., in terms of currently binding ecclesiastical rules, and the Church as a legal order – as distinct from the Church as *corpus mysticum* – cannot be considered infallible on the question of what sin is, we may still believe that evil is real. That is, we may still believe that evil is a real characteristic of life and that we carry in us a kind of moral intuition that enables us to recognize it as such. We intuitively know, or at least we are capable of knowing, when we do evil and when our fellow men do it, whether or not this evil is defined as a crime in penal legislation.

The question of the *desirable* relationship between sin and crime has been the crucial area of conflict between theocracy and liberalism in modern civilization. The theocratic tendency in its strongest form – which is hardly noticeable in the history of the Christian West – consists in the demand for direct rule of the state by the Church and the clergy. A weaker version, while accepting the distinction between secular and spiritual powers, wants everything that is sinful according to the Church's moral doctrine to be punishable by secular law – as was often the case in medieval civilization and later – apart from sins for which the punishment would, for technical reasons, simply be unenforceable (for instance, mental sins). If this tendency prevailed, such sins as adultery and homosexuality would be illegal, not to speak of atheism and heresy. It took a very long time before such sins were decriminalized; homosexuality was punished in Britain until quite recently, and it is still illegal in some American states, regardless of the extent to which such laws are enforced (and this in Western civilization; in Islamic states the theocratic tendency has always been much stronger). Orthodox Jews would like to impose Old Testament law on the state of Israel, including the interdiction of the sale of forbidden food, the interdiction of travel on the Sabbath, etc.

The liberal tendency refuses to abide by religious doctrine in defining the limits of the forbidden and the permissible, and defends the principle of the separation of church and state. But it must still answer the question: what are the sources of law in such matters, once the validity of religious tradition has been done away with? To say that it is the voice of the people, or public opinion, is not always convenient, because public opinion often opposes liberal legislators; as I have mentioned, a number of important decisions have been made by legislative bodies against the views of the majority. Whatever the mechanisms of making law, liberal doctrines cannot accept that their spokesmen in legislative bodies should merely follow the current voice of the majority without correction. Liberal ideology *is* an ideology, and it is bound to fight for its principles, whatever the majority might think. Liberal doctrine on this point can perhaps be summed up in the principle that only those acts may be declared illegal which, if permitted, would make life in this society intolerable and cause the peaceful order to collapse or to deteriorate significantly. Murder, obviously, belongs to this category, but homosexuality, for example, does not. Some cases are debatable – the use of drugs, for instance – but it is supposed that arguments for or against a given activity can be based on empirical evidence.

This principle seems to be reasonable and to conform to current perceptions about the law. Liberal legislation has been gaining ground since the sixteenth century in Western civilization, and the vestiges of the theocratic tradition, though still discernible, are now of little significance. Islamic countries will probably move in the same direction, although we cannot know how long it will take. But accepting this principle, with all the problems and ambiguities it must create, does not help us answer the question with which I am concerned. If all we have at our disposal is penal law, more liberal or less, based on practical considerations alone, and no living moral beliefs that give validity to the ideas of evil, guilt, sin, freedom of action, and retribution, can human communities survive at all? Penal law, supported solely by practical considerations, acts by fear of punishment alone. Can fear suffice? Fear may restrain the natural human impulses of greed, aggressiveness and lust for power. But can we assume that such a morally emptied Hobbesian society, in which fear is the only binding force, would be viable?

Or, to put it differently: can we live without feeling that the law is to be respected, not only feared?

This distinction between respect for and fear of the law is, of course, crucial in Kantian moral philosophy. Respect, in Kant's view, is not supposed to be an emotion (emotional motivations are morally worthless) but a phenomenon *sui generis*, neither fear nor love. But can we respect positive law for no better reason than that it is law? And why should we? Most of us know only a tiny part of the immense body of legal regulations that proliferate endlessly, from one month to another. And these regulations are frequently changed, for good or bad reasons. What could produce in me a quasi-religious feeling of awe in the face of this *mysterium numinosum valde ridiculum*, this ridiculous deity, that consists of paper mountains which I would never be able to wade through? And I leave aside cases of oppressive codes in totalitarian or tyrannical regimes, where obeying some of the laws would be morally repugnant and defying them is strongly recommended.

No, we can neither expect nor demand respect for the law just because it has been promulgated, regardless of its content. What matters is not respect for this or that (often accidental) decision of the majority in a parliament or of a judge. Rather, what matters is respect for the moral law, which may or may not coincide with the positive law and which involves the legally irrelevant distinction between good and evil.

Kant, when he talked about respect for law, had in mind moral law as he understood it; but I do not think that this part of his doctrine is entirely acceptable. To be sure, the Kantian distinction between obeying a law for prudential reasons and obeying it for moral reasons is obvious and valid. We may not normally steal packets of butter at the grocery store, but this does not mean that we are honest people; we do not do it simply because it would be silly to do so, as the gain is minimal and to be caught would have unpleasant consequences. This is admittedly a very simple example. But even when we do something apparently honest, without calculation and without any risk of punishment if we fail to do it, this by no means proves that we are up to Kantian standards. When I do something apparently good – help other people, save them, even sacrifice myself – if I do so out of compassion, that is, if I am moved by an emotion, my act is morally worthless in Kantian terms, since only those acts are moral which are motivated by the pure will to fulfil the moral law and nothing else. Kant admits, first, that such acts are rather unusual and rare. He admits, second, that when such an act does occur it is impossible to be certain that it really has occurred, since we have no means of establishing the real content of other peoples' minds. He admits, third, that the agent himself is, practically speaking, incapable of stating firmly that his action is as pure and as devoid of emotional admixture as the moral imperatives demand. Self-deception is easy, and we often attribute to ourselves nobler motivations than we actually possess.

Moreover, it is plausible to argue that when Kant speaks of acts that externally conform to moral law but are performed for the wrong reasons, he uses a concept that is invalid on his own premises. For in order to conform to moral law, our actions should be precisely what the formal imperatives say they should be: that is, they should be motivated by a 'maxim' that the agent is prepared to make universal. It seems, therefore, that there is simply no such thing as 'external' compliance with the moral law: compliance must involve the proper motivation. And, since evil is defined as disobedience to the law, we may even suspect that in Kant's terms – although he does not say this in so many words – when I do something out of compassion and love, my act is not just morally worthless but positively evil, which sounds outrageous to our normal moral intuition.

Kant's moral doctrine seems very poorly designed as an educational device, more poorly even than the Augustinian-Calvinist theology of Grace that it partially resembles. It suggests that as long as I am not perfect and holy I am simply evil in whatever I do, and to suggest this is the best recipe for nihilistic indifference – for we know, and Kant knew, that nobody is perfect. In other words, in practice we do not need to bother much about our conduct, since we are certain in advance that holiness is beyond our reach.

But however impracticable Kantian philosophy may be as a tool of moral education in the real world, it was the boldest attempt the Enlightenment ever made to establish moral principles as a separate realm of reason, logically independent from the legacy of a revealed religion and irreducible to empirical grounds or to hedonistic justifications. The idea that no empirical evidence can be miraculously transmuted into moral rules was one that Kant shared with Hume, but he did not conclude that therefore no such rules can be rationally constructed.

I am not here concerned with the validity or soundness of Kantian ethics as a whole. But Kant was right, I believe, when he said that if we deny the validity of the distinction between right and wrong, good and evil, we are denying the very possibility of morality in the normal sense of the word; and if we deny this, there is no longer any way that respect for the moral law can be distinguished from fear of legal punishment. To accept this does not entail that one is logically compelled to embrace Kantian formalism, with its subsequent elimination of compassion and love from the catalogue of worthy motivations for morally good acts. Yet if the distinction between respect and fear is real, it seems to imply the validity of the concepts of sin, guilt, responsibility and retribution. It implies, consequently, the idea of freedom of choice as well. And if freedom is empirically unprovable, this may be for reasons other than those adduced by Kant. Indeed, it might be precisely because freedom is a perfectly simple and very elementary experience which, being so simple and so elementary, is not analysable any further – like the idea of the self. It is one of the building blocks of our world of experience, but is not itself validly deducible from any empirical evidence that would be admissible in scientific procedures.

The same may be said about the distinction between good and evil, between moral duty and legal duty, between legal punishment and retribution. To believe that those distinctions are valid is to believe that there is a kind of natural law that binds us, that does not depend on arbitrary conventions or decrees, and that is accessible to us through moral intuition. Throughout history many people have believed, and indeed still believe, in such an order of things, no matter how this insight is phrased and how it is connected with – or disconnected from – its religious background. Are we still capable of sharing this belief? Certainly not if we surrender to the dogmas either of empiricism or of historicism. But why should we surrender? That there is anything compelling in these dogmas has not been persuasively demonstrated.

In addition to making philosophical arguments for or against natural law, we may reflect on the likely outcome of a process whereby the notions of good and evil, of sin and retribution, would simply disappear from human minds. They have not disappeared yet, but they have been severely eroded in our civilization. Many people still believe that they ought to do something simply because it is right, or refrain from doing it simply because it is wrong, not because they are terrified by the spectre of the police, judges, prison or execution. My naive question is: could mankind survive without such people? And my answer is no. Mankind as we know it would not survive if the only means of preventing us from following our desires and indulging our passions was the fear of legally inflicted suffering. This seems to me to be common sense, based on the distinction between the human race and rats. It is also based on a strong disbelief in the doctrine according to which human behavior is entirely reducible to a system of inherited instincts and conditional reflexes.

Because there is evil in us, we do, of course, need penal machinery: laws, threats and fear. But if there were nothing but evil in us, the very concepts of good and evil – as distinct from the concepts of pleasure and pain, profit and harm – would be so redundant, so utterly useless, that it would be hard to see why mankind should have concocted them at all. And the same may be said about the pair sin/retribution, as distinct from crime/punishment. Because we are not entirely and irredeemably evil, it is good for us occasionally to think that we deserve retribution or that retribution may restore the order of the world we have disturbed by our sins. To dismiss this belief as a myth is easy, but it leaves unanswered these questions: Why has mankind, throughout its history, required a mythological order of the universe in addition to a technical one? And what might happen should this order evaporate altogether?

1991

On Natural Law

My topic is not constitutional. It is, to put it somewhat pretentiously, the metaphysical, perhaps even theological riddle that may emerge from reflecting on constitutions as such, that is to say, reflecting on natural law.

Natural law is supposed to be law that is not invented by us, but found ready-made, independently of our conventions, customs and regulations. It provides us with supreme normative rules; and it is to those rules that our constitutions and codes have to conform if they deserve to be called *just*.

The concept of natural law has been criticized for centuries, in a variety of theoretical idioms, and it is much easier to repeat these criticisms than to articulate the principles of natural law. The critic asks: where is this supposed natural law to be found? One cannot infer it – as Locke suggested that we could – from what is common to all legislative systems, or even from any tacitly assumed principles underlying their foundation. There is no universal core for all legal codes; not even rules that might seem to us intuitively self-evident – such as the principle that only people who have committed a crime should be punished, and not others – are universally accepted. (According to an old Polish anecdote, a locksmith once committed a crime for which the penalty was capital punishment; but there was only one locksmith in the village whereas there were several blacksmiths, and so it was decided that a blacksmith should be hanged instead.) Under the Hammurabi Code it was legitimate in some cases to kill people who had not contributed at all to the crime: if John had killed Martin's son, Martin had the right to kill John's son, who was not guilty of any crime. In Stalin's criminal code, there were some political crimes that demanded punishment not only for the criminal, and not only for all those who had known about the crime and failed to inform the authorities, but also for members of the criminal's family or even of his household – people who knew nothing about the case. (Thus innumerable thousands of women, known by the acronym 'Zhir' – wives of traitors to the Fatherland – lived out their lives and died in Soviet concentration camps. This was according to the letter of the law, but the practice was far worse.) Nor is there any universal acceptance of the (no less intuitively self-evident) rule that it is our duty to keep our promises (a principle that may perhaps be considered the supreme principle of civil law); or of the rule that law cannot be valid retrospectively. And there is no need to point out that equality before the law, religious freedom, freedom of speech and so on, are relatively new, and were absent even from many modern constitutions.

A more sceptical critic could go further: even if we discovered norms common to all known constitutions and codes, past and present, such a discovery would be just an empirical fact. We could not infer from it that such norms are inherently just, right or true. Universal agreement, a *consensus omnium*, is not a criterion of scientific truth, so why should it be the criterion of the validity of a norm? When philosophers asked about the content and the grounds of natural law, what they wanted to know was not when and where particular legal norms have been accepted, or even whether there are any moral or legal norms that are accepted always and everywhere, but which norms are really legitimate and how we might go about establishing their validity.

Let us suppose that one day a sensational archeological discovery is made: archaeologists find the Ark of the Covenant and in it the stone tablets on which Moses carved out the Ten Commandments. We would still be unable to prove that this was really a text dictated by God and thus absolutely valid.

Should we then, in the face of this criticism, reconcile ourselves to the view – expressed countless times by so many: by some of the Sophists in Plato's dialogues, by Hobbes and by many more recent authors – that what is just is what has been laid down as law by the legislator, and that there is no other valid law apart from this? This view can of course be expressed with varying degrees of consistency. The radical version says that whatever a sovereign or ruling power has established is indeed just: Hitler's Nürnberg laws, and Stalin's codes, and the American Constitution – all are equally just. But this compels us to accept the inconvenient conclusion that norms which contradict each other may be equally legitimate and equally just. Advocates of this view, therefore, usually try to circumvent the problem by arguing that the value-laden concept of justice has no discernible meaning if it is taken to suggest a supreme paradigm according to which we can measure and assess existing legislation; if, on the other hand, 'justice' means nothing except positive law, i.e., what is established in existing legislation, it is a misleading and useless concept.

A critic who scorns the idea of natural law as a myth, a fabrication with no basis in reality, can still try to rebut the objection that in his view both the Nürnberg laws and the American Constitution must be equally good – not in the sense of 'just,' but in the sense of 'valid,' because they were established as the law of the land. He might protest that nothing imposes this conclusion on him; he might say, 'Of course I don't believe that it is all right for me to express opinions that contradict each other. Accepting such a conclusion would be evidence of my intellectual feebleness. No,' he will say; 'these opinions would be contradictory only on the assumption that the quality of being 'good' or 'just' applied *in fact*, independently of my or anyone's judgments. But there is no contradiction if what we mean when we say that some laws are good and others not is that we approve of them; we are simply expressing our moral feelings, feelings that we share, to be sure, with many other people.' Thus the critic will maintain that when he says, for example, that the Nürnberg laws are evil and the American Constitution is good (or vice versa), he is not making a statement about those laws or this constitution, but about himself, and about those who share the same opinion.

Does this conclusion, which must seem difficult to stomach for many people, actually follow from the rejection of the idea of natural law? It seems to. Critics of such a conclusion might argue, for instance, that the American Constitution, which says in the Preamble that it serves justice, peace, human welfare and freedom, and goes on, in the text proper, to set down the details of the representative system and, in the Amendments, to establish religious freedom, freedom of speech and the illegality of slavery – one might argue that it is a good thing, because it is impossible to deny that peace is better than war, freedom better than slavery, etc. But the critic would reply, 'Not at all. For centuries slavery was considered part of the natural order of things, also by the United States, under this very Constitution, up to Amendment 13 of 1865. War, too, has been exalted, and for centuries seen as part of the natural order of things. And religious freedom in the Christian world is a very recent phenomenon, a novelty by no means everywhere accepted, even today. All such things are conventions; they are accepted in some historical eras but not in others. And there is no proof that these conventions – which we may accept if we wish – reflect any normative order of the universe, any order that is embedded in the nature of things and which we can discover ready-made.'

Thus, according to this critic, if someone refuses to recognize that freedom is better than slavery or peace better than war, or that torturing people is evil, or that people are equal in a fundamental sense (i.e., in their dignity), there is no way of convincing him otherwise. One cannot, for instance, reproach the rulers of Communist China because they repudiate the idea of human rights as a bourgeois or specifically European doctrine. According to this view, to say that certain norms are valid is meaningless without explaining, 'valid for whom?' They may be valid for a specific historical period, for a civilization, for a well-defined social milieu; to say this is to say that they are accepted in that period, or in that civilization, or in that milieu, and that, of course, is just an empirical statement, without any normative content. But to say that a norm is valid in itself is a fantasy, born of myth.

Those who believe in natural law have frequently been accused (for example, by John Stuart Mill) of committing what analytical philosophers call the naturalistic fallacy: that is, of attempting to deduce normative propositions from empirical ones (an impossible feat), or confusing the two. According to this criticism, believing in natural law amounts to failing to distinguish between law as a regularity in nature, such as Newton's laws, for instance, and law in the sense of a norm established within a legal order. This charge can be justified in some cases of natural-law theory, but not in others. Aquinas believed that all things in the world participate in the eternal, God-created order, but human creatures, being endowed with reason, participate in it by conscious obedience: the rules of natural law, including the distinction between good and evil, were inscribed by God in our minds, and so everyone, including pagans, participates in this knowledge.

Clearly, however, 'participation' in the physical and moral order is not the same. All things in the world, including human beings, are subject to the law of gravity, which no one can invalidate or violate. If, however, we 'participate' in the Ten Commandments, it is in the sense that those commandments bind us. In this sense of participation, we also cannot invalidate the laws in which we participate, but we *can* violate them. The failure to distinguish between these two kinds of 'participation' may justify the accusation of naturalistic fallacy.

But the accusation need not apply to the theory according to which the divinely established distinction between good and evil is legitimate, i.e., that when we say that something is good or evil we are saying that this is *really* the case (even though, being endowed with free will, we may act in a way that ignores this distinction). On this view the laws concerning good and evil are as valid as the laws of chemistry, because they are founded on divine decree; and for God, who is absolute unity, there is no distinction between a truth that describes a natural regularity and one that expresses what God has decreed about good and evil. Both kinds of laws are true and of equal status, despite the different ways in which we 'participate' in the laws of nature on the one hand and moral laws on the other. And both are of divine origin. But they do not result from an arbitrary decree which would have been as valid had it been different: they are rooted in God's infinite wisdom. Thus it is wrong to say that the content of the divine commandments is the result of the Creator's whim, and equally wrong to say that the Creator is subject to external laws, ready-made rules that exist independently of Him which it is not in His power to invalidate. The first would question God's infinite wisdom, the second His omnipotence – His position as the unique and ultimate source of all creative energy. From the Thomist standpoint it is utterly wrong to say (as did some later nominalists and some modern thinkers, including Descartes) that all truths – both mathematical and moral – are freely decreed by God and could have been different, so that, if God had so wished, He could have decided, for instance, that two and two is seven, or that two propositions which directly contradict each other can both be true, or that it is a virtuous deed to murder one's parents. Those who held this view claimed that to doubt this would be to question God's omnipotence. This is wrong in Thomist terms because in God there is no distinction between intellect and will; one may not attribute to Him the distinctions that appear in human beings. And although we cannot truly inderstand the divine mode of existence, we can know *a priori* what must be true of God – or, rather, what cannot be true of Him.

For the Thomist it is obvious that natural law presupposes the existence of God. But is this a necessary, logical implication? Is it not logically possible to believe in natural law without believing in God? Modern theorists of natural law, such as Grotius and Pufendorf, say that it is, and affirm the logical independence of the two. Grotius allows that some of God's commandments would be unknowable without Revelation; we could not discover them with our own reason. Divine legislation *makes* some acts virtuous or forbidden. But apart from these laws there are the commandments of Reason, whereby we can discern good and evil in all human actions according to their conformity, or lack of it, with human nature. Such laws, says Grotius, do not depend on divine decrees, and God Himself could not alter them any more than He could invalidate the rules of arithmetic. Natural law operates in human life only; the concept of justice does not apply to animals. But it is not a man-made convention. Nor is it a decree freely made by the Creator. It is a set of rules which are, as it were, embedded (Grotius does not use this exact expression) in the ontic condition of humanity – in human dignity; without knowledge of these rules, we would not be human.

According to this view, then, natural law is present in the world, but it does not logically presuppose a legislating personal God. It does, however, imply a certain metaphysical faith: the faith (which goes back to the Stoics) that there is a Reason which rules the universe, a Reason whose nature we can recognize and which enables us to distinguish truth from falsity as well as good from evil. It was a widespread (though not universal) view in the Christian Middle Ages that knowledge of natural law is accessible to us apart from Revelation because the Creator endowed us with the intellectual faculties necessary and sufficient for this purpose. In this respect our natural knowledge of the world does not differ from the natural recognition of moral principles. Cicero observed, in a number of his writings, that the rules which command that we help each other, do no harm, display gratitude for other people's kindness, and so forth, were created not by man but by nature, and that they are eternal; despite the evil things we do and despite our corruption, which often stamps out in us the power of Reason, we do know what is good or evil.

Belief in natural law was popular among the writers of the Enlightenment, too, although it was variously expressed (as becomes apparent if we compare, for example, Montesquieu and Kant). Kant argued that our duty is to do good because it is good and not because God orders it; if we do something because it is a commandment, we are not truly free and rational agents. He also thought that we are capable of discovering which fundamental moral rules are obligatory, because we participate in a universal Reason that was not created by divine decree but is simply there, indestructible and eternal.

Many thinkers, Christian and otherwise, have believed that natural law provides us with a paradigm according to which we can judge positive law. Many of them thought that we have no obligation to obey laws that are incompatible with natural law; we may, even should, reject and violate such laws.

Here, then, is my main question: mindful of the sceptical

challenges I have reviewed above, can we still believe in natural law? My reply is yes. Not only may we believe in natural law, but by denying it we deny our humanity. We may believe that good and evil, instead of being projections of our likes and dislikes, emotions, or decisions, are *real qualities* of human life – of our actions, thoughts, desires, our conflicts and our friendships. And if someone were to say, 'We can determine the speed of light and the chemical composition of ethyl alcohol, and we can prove that heat causes gases to expand, but we cannot prove, in the same sense, that torturing people is evil and helping the homeless is good,' we may reply, 'No, such moral judgments cannot be *proved* in the same sense as the laws of chemistry and physics, but need we accept the kind of proofs required in experimental science as the only model for all our truth-judgments?' Nothing compels us to embrace the view of proponents of logical empiricism that only propositions which are empirically verifiable (or perhaps falsifiable), in the same way as propositions in the sciences, are meaningful. The principles of empiricism, as many have pointed out, are not themselves empirical propositions. They are norms, commandments, and we may ask about their justification; they are by no means self-evident. Empiricism is not an empirical theory. Similarly, large areas of our knowledge have their indispensable foundation in intuition, the intuition of experience, and we do not for this reason dismiss them as figments of the imagination. Why, then, should we dismiss our intuition about moral experience? There is a moral intuition by which moral truths can be recognized, just as there is the intuition of sense experience and that of mathematical and logical truths. These three kinds of intuition are not reducible to each other; they work separately. Moral intuition is also a kind of experience, different from sense perception – and neither of them is infallible.

Our belief in natural law is not impaired by the fact that the results of this intuition are not necessarily identical in everyone's mind, always and everywhere, nor by the fact that centuries were needed before people recognized the good and evil of their various actions and institutions – before they admitted, for example, that torture is evil and equality before the law good. This has also been the case with many discoveries in empirical science: it took centuries before people realized that their ordinary intuitions were wrong: that the sun does not revolve around the earth, or that a force is not necessary to cause movement, or that events are never absolutely simultaneous. All these erroneous beliefs were natural and understandable. So why should we not accept that the principles and norms of natural law reveal themselves to us gradually: that we must go through a process of growth before we understand certain moral truths and laws and recognize them as such? (Although it should be said that since antiquity there have been people who preached those principles and norms with full conviction – without, however, gaining universal approval.)

There is no reason to accept the nihilistic doctrine that because various contradictory norms have been accepted and applied at various times and in various places, they are all, in terms of Reason, equally justified, which is to say equally groundless. While belief in natural law does not – I repeat – require belief in the existence of God as a necessary premise, it *does* require the belief in something that one might call the moral (in addition to the physical) constitution of Being – a constitution that converges with the rule of Reason in the universe. All the evils of the human world, its endless stupidity and suffering, cannot impair our belief in natural law in this sense. Two other realms of intuition – perception and mathematics – also require suppositions that cannot be proved but are indispensable for the knowledge we acquire by those intuitions. Our life as rational creatures occurs in a realm that is constructed with the aid of various non-empirical but fundamental courts of appeal, among them truth and goodness. Nor need our belief in natural law be impaired by the fact that it is not universally observed. This fact was well known to Seneca and Cicero, to Gratian and Suárez, to Grotius and Kant, but it did not weaken their conviction that the rules of natural law are valid, no matter how often they are violated.

Natural law does not, of course, allow us to infer from it the details of any constitution or civil or penal code. It does not allow us to infer, for instance, whether or not capital punishment or voluntary euthanasia is permissible, whether a proportional or a majority voting system is better, whether or not monarchy can be a good thing, whether property rights should have priority over other rights in case of conflict, whether censorship can be recommended on moral grounds, and so on. Nevertheless, natural law erects barriers that limit positive legislation and do not allow it to legalize attempts to infringe the indestructible dignity that is proper to every human being. Natural law is built around human dignity. Thus it invalidates legislation that, for instance, admits slavery, torture, political censorship, inequality before the law, compulsory religious worship or the prohibition of worship, or the duty to inform the authorities about the non-conformity of people's political views. Within these limits various constitutions and various codes are possible; natural law does not dictate their details.

The barriers mentioned above are usually accepted today in the legislation of civilized countries, but we must keep in mind that they are relatively recent; that they are not recognized everywhere; and that in many places where they are present in constitutions they remain mere words on paper. Natural law should be like an uncompromising demon breathing down the neck of all the legislators of the world.

2001

On Collective Identity

It is not collective identity in the Leibnizian sense that will concern us here. For Leibniz the concept of identity was mainly a logical device, and was applicable only to entities such that every proposition which is true of them at one point in time is true of them at all times; it was not applicable to single entities (material or not) with a continuous existence in real time. It did have a metaphysical sense, insofar as it entailed two assumptions important for Leibniz's metaphysics – a system where all relations that obtain between monads must have their equivalents in each monad's immanent properties. It entailed a universal (but only phenomenal) interdependence between all the elements of the universe; and it entailed the identity of indiscernibles: that there cannot be two objects (monads) which differ from each other only numerically. Leibniz thought that if two objects are identical in all respects (indiscernible), they must also be numerically identical – i.e., they must be one and the same object. But Leibniz's metaphysics is irrelevant to our present purposes. The question I want to consider here is how a monad or a set of monads can retain its identity over time, regardless of the changes it undergoes.

When we consider the question of the identity of human collective bodies (keeping in mind the obvious caveat that all definitions of non-mathematical objects will inevitably be shaky and imprecise), we observe that it is analogous to the time-hallowed problem of personal identity discussed by Locke, Hume and many contemporary philosophers. Conversely, certain aspects of personal identity have their equivalents in collective identity. In short, it is impossible to talk of one without considering the other.

Of the aspects common to both personal and collective identity, the first is substance, or soul – the non-material aspect of personality – and the problem of its connection with the body. This connection has been defined in a variety of ways, depending on the metaphysical doctrine one chose to adopt – Platonic, Thomist, Augustinian or Cartesian. For as long as the concept of substance (whether considered to be a separate entity or, as in Aquinas, a composite of body and its form, i.e., the soul) retained its unquestioned legitimacy in philosophical discourse and was accepted as the immutable seat of mental life, the thing that preserves its *ipseitas* through all changes, personal identity was easily defined by reference to it. But once empiricist critique had undermined and dethroned it, pointing out that its presence could not be established, either directly or indirectly, substance was demoted from the status of empirical fact to that of metaphysical presupposition. Of course, the dogmas of empiricism are themselves far from immune from criticism, in particular from the (frequently made) charge of being arbitrary. However, even if we abandon the idea of substance, we are still left with the problem of how to define the experience of self – the 'I' at the root of personal identity.

The followers of Hume and Mach insisted that the word 'I' had no referent, and claimed that the idea of the ego was no more than an artificial construct; but such a claim is even shakier than the arguments for rejecting the idea of substance. For one might reasonably argue that 'I' am the object of my own experience, and hence that the issue is an empirical one after all. To this critics might object that the word 'I' is used here as if it corresponded to some reality: that it presupposes a referent, and that it is, in fact, exactly the same thing as 'substance,' and therefore liable to the same charge. But such an objection would be groundless; there seems to be no compelling reason to extend the scope of this charge. To be sure, the content of whatever the word 'I' refers to is accessible only to me, but then it is equally true that in general my perceptions are uniquely my own and no one else's. I am the referent of the word 'I.' There is always something awkward about using this pronoun as if it were an ordinary noun (or replacing it by other artificial constructs such as 'the self' or 'the ego'), but this philosophical parlance cannot be avoided, even if it makes our speech sound odd. When I say, 'I had dinner last night,' I assume (and so does everyone else) that I am the same person I was last night, and I assume this without appealing to any metaphysical idea of substance. Indeed, it is hard to say what exactly is wrong with this ordinary way of speaking – particularly since dismissing the continuity of the 'I' entails, among other things, abandoning the idea of personal responsibility, without which life in a human community would be impossible. The referent of the word 'I' is established in experience, and no one, with the exception of a few Buddhists at a very advanced stage on their path to enlightenment and an even smaller number of philosophers, can cast any real doubt on the validity of this experience.

However, the experience of the continuous 'I' also presupposes memory. *Memory* is the second element inherent in the idea of personal identity, and it is an essential one. There would be no continuity of identity if the entire memory of a person were erased; there can be no personal identity without the memory which makes it conscious, without, in other words, the consciousness of one's history. Christian theologians maintain that God is both a person and a timeless being. Such a statement may be meaningfully uttered, but we lack both the conceptual and the empirical tools to understand such a being or gain any insight into its existence.

In discussing the question of personality, Freud introduced a distinction between two kinds of growth: between things which change like cities, with new buildings and streets growing up around the old centre but leaving it untouched, and others which do not grow by accretion but change like living organisms, their structure remaining unaltered as they grow. Freud thought that the growth of personality is more like the former, preserving what was there at the beginning: he thought that the minds we had as children are still there in us, are a part of what makes up our adult identity, as if our entire stock of memory, whether conscious or unconscious, were indestructible. Whichever of these metaphors is the more accurate, there is no doubt that memory is an essential part of identity.

Personal identity requires not only the consciousness of one's past but also, and in equal measure, an attitude with regard to the future: a conscious anticipation, usually tinged with a variety of emotions like hope, fear, uncertainty, joy or despair. *Anticipation* is a feature of human existence which a variety of philosophers, usually those of an 'existentialist' bent, have attempted to describe, and it is the third element of identity.

The fourth element is *body*. The body is an essential part of the very idea of personality, but this claim does not settle the question of whether disembodied human life is possible, and is logically independent from it. We have no reliable empirical access to disembodied persons.

Bodily identity has been a subject of controversy at least since the paradox of Theseus's ship: if we gradually replace every part of a ship by a new one until all its parts have been replaced, is it still (given that neither its structure nor its appearance has changed) the same ship? The problem with the human body seems similar, but there are important differences. First, the human body is a conscious thing, and we cannot consider its identity over time without considering the contribution of memory to that identity. I remember my body as being my own: it is always the same body, *my* body, no matter how much it has changed since I was born and regardless of the constant changes taking place in its constituent parts. Second, we each of us have, as we now know, a unique and constant genetic make-up which defines the identity of our body, not only during our lifetime but even after death. The fact that we are conscious of only a fraction of the processes which take place in our bodies does not alter the status of the (conscious) body as an essential part of identity: however large or small that fraction might be, we still experience the continuity of the organism to which we belong (or which belongs to us, if it seems more appropriate to put it that way – either way will do). The fact that personal identity is only partly remembered in no way affects the continuity of personal identity through memory.

The fifth element in personal identity is the consciousness of an *identifiable beginning*. We do not, and perhaps cannot, remember the first event of our lives – our own birth – but we know that it took place. This knowledge is so basic and so patently indisputable that it might seem unnecessary to mention it at all, but it is indispensable, for it is what allows me to utter with conviction the apparent tautology 'I am I.' If at some point I simply discovered myself as a conscious and thinking being and had a Cartesian uncertainty about where I came from, the feeling that 'I am I' would probably be impossible. I imagine that people who are uncertain about their origins in the weak, not the Cartesian, sense – i.e., people who, although they know they must have been born somewhere, some time, do not know who their parents were or where and when they were born – must have a seriously damaged sense of identity.

Substance, memory, anticipation, body and an identifiable beginning – these are the five elements (four if we set aside the first as empirically inaccessible) which together make up personal identity.

But personality is of course a cultural as well as an 'existential' phenomenon. My belonging to various collective entities is also part of what makes me a person (although this does not entail that I am no more than a part of these collective entities, nor that I am literally nothing if I do not belong to them). And human collectivities have identities of their own, which can be described in similar terms and categories.

Collective identity is, even more than personal identity, a matter of degree. This is evident as soon as we begin to think about it, from the fact that we need a number of independent criteria to describe it. The concept of collective identity is a legitimate one; its legitimacy is not undermined by the fact that both personal and collective beings are only 'more or less' self-identical. Their identity is no more suspect in this regard than that of physical objects. This becomes clear when we look at examples of collective entities such as ethnic communities and nations.

It is an obvious truth that no nation can survive without a national consciousness. How strong that consciousness is depends on a variety of historical circumstances. When we speak of nations, we usually have in mind historically well-established ethnic communities, most often European ones, and we are reluctant to use the term more widely: to apply it, for example, to African or Asian tribes or even to remote outposts of European civilization in North or South America or in Australia. States which lack ethnic homogeneity naturally have their own interests, and some of them may one day establish themselves as nations on the basis of the common aspirations of their people, if these prove stronger than ethnic divisions. But when we consider peoples whose status as nations is not in doubt, as in the case of nearly all European states, we see that their collective identity is made up of the same five elements discussed above.

The closest thing in collective identity to the metaphysical idea of substance is the vague idea of 'national spirit' or '*Volksgeist*,' which finds its expression in cultural life and collective behaviour, especially at times of crisis. The *Volksgeist* is supposed to be something that underlies cultural phenomena but is not identical with them; unlike them, it is not an object of historical experience or a collection of facts, but a metaphysical entity (discovered by Hegel and the Romantics) with explanatory powers similar to those of a *res cogitans*. Like the *res cogitans*, it is a substance which is not reducible to the sum of its thought-acts, but is an essential condition of their occurrence.

While the idea of the *Volksgeist*, like the idea of substance, is not empirical, and easily disposed of by empiricist philosophers, the other elements of collective identity are less problematic.

No long proofs are needed to establish the obvious fact that national identity requires *historical memory*. It does not matter, for this purpose, how much of the content of that memory is true and how much half-true or altogether legendary. What matters is the consciousness of a past: no nation can survive without the awareness that its present existence is the continuation of a past one – and the further awareness that the older those (real or imaginary) memories, the deeper they reach back into the past, the more firmly its national identity is established. The past is preserved not only in historical knowledge but also in such things as symbols, idioms and other particularities of the language, old buildings, temples, tombs and so on.

These observations are all platitudes, so obvious that they hardly need saying. It is worth adding that what decides whether a nation is the same nation now as it was at any point in its past is that nation's present collective consciousness. If contemporary Greeks, Italians, Indians, Copts or Chinese genuinely 'feel' that they belong to the same, continuous ethnic community as their ancient forebears, then one cannot convince them otherwise or argue that they are mistaken. Some emerging nations – a number of cases come to mind – have simply invented a past for themselves, *ad hoc* and without any genuine or verifiable historical continuity. Such inventions are tolerated because they are necessary.

National cultures change imperceptibly; we cannot pinpoint the moment of their metamorphosis. They evolve like languages and, like languages, at some point they do evolve into what is clearly a different entity. We have no doubt, for instance, that the language of Montaigne is the same language as modern French, despite all the changes which have occurred in the meantime, and we also know that Latin is not: it is a different language. But a nation can lose its language without losing the consciousness of its identity (Ireland might be an example of this sad fate).

Anticipation is as essential to national as to personal identity. A nation, like an individual, looks to the future and thinks in terms of its future interests; it worries about what might happen, tries to assure its survival and takes measures to protect itself against possible adversity. There is, however, one important difference: a nation, unlike an individual, does not usually anticipate its own demise.

The fourth aspect of the collective national 'personality' is body: the nation's territory, the natural particularities of its landscape and the physical artifacts which have reshaped it. A counter-example which immediately springs to mind is the case of the Jews, who survived for so long without a land of their own. But they had their substitute for body: their religious identity. This was what ensured their distinctness throughout all the centuries of life in the diaspora. In the past, the Jewish religious and ethnic identities were virtually indistinguishable, and the Jews would surely not have survived as a distinct ethnic community without their religious identity, their laws and their rituals, to support and distinguish them.

The fifth element essential to national identity is a nation's awareness of its origins – of an *identifiable beginning* at some point in time.

Every nation has myths which testify to this: legends about founding events or ancestral figures to which the origins of the nation can be traced. Sometimes these events and figures cannot be precisely located in time, but this does not matter: it is enough that they represent an *exordium temporis* – a beginning of the nation's historical time.

These five elements, through which the collective 'person' can identify itself as a distinct entity with a continuous identity in time, are also clearly visible in the way in which religious bodies define themselves.

In no religious body is continuous identity so firmly established as in the Catholic Church; and the same five elements which make up its identity are also present in its constitution. This is partly because of its high degree of institutionalization, unequalled by any other religious community.

In the case of the Catholic Church, the idea which most closely corresponds to that of *substance* is the idea of the Church as a *corpus mysticum* – as the bride of Christ. Just as the idea of substance is not an empirical one, so this, too, is unverifiable: it is a question of faith. But it is essential to the preservation of the idea of the Church, the *Ecclesia*, as a charismatic body established by God and deriving its legitimacy directly from divine intervention in human history – an intervention more momentous than any except the act of Creation itself. And the Church as a mystical body owes its unblemished purity and sanctity not to the impeccable moral conduct of its members, but to its divine origin and mission. This is why, for example, St Augustine's battle against the Donatist heresy was so important: if the validity of the sacraments depended on the moral qualities of priests, or the perfection of the Church on the perfection of the faithful (as the Pelagians thought), the identity of the Church body would soon have been destroyed. The Church's substance, the *corpus mysticum*, cannot be damaged or polluted by human sins or offences.

The collective *memory* of the Church is preserved not only in its sacred books, in historical records of its vicissitudes, in the lives of the saints and in material monuments of faith such as temples and works of art; it is also embodied in the long tradition of Church dogmas, considered (along with Scripture) as a source of doctrinal truth, and not merely as the product of the exegetical labours of theologians, popes, Council Fathers or the Holy Office. This tradition (when articulated in the official pronouncements of authorized bodies) is considered to be the true interpretation of Scripture, not the product of human thought: it is divine truth, not human opinion. It extends our understanding of the meaning of Revelation, but that meaning, although hidden, must already have been there if the dogmas are to be valid: it is discovered, not created.

Here we touch upon the delicate question of the 'evolution of dogmas' – an idea developed in the modernist heresy, condemned by the Church and revived by Bultmannist theologians. How far the matter really affects the Church's sense of identity depends on how one interprets this 'evolution.' It is obviously important for the continuous identity of the Church body that the basic tenets of faith be preserved forever as they are, untouchable, like the Apostolic symbols; it is equally obvious, however, that there is hardly a word in them that has not been the subject of theological and philosophical examination, questioning, argument and dispute – beginning with the adjective 'omnipotent' (apparently stronger and implying more than the Greek '*pantokrator*'). Both the scholastics and modern philosophers like Descartes and Leibniz have struggled with the perplexing questions to which this word gave rise: Can God reverse time and change the past? Do the truths of logic and mathematics depend on His will? And so on. The Church, understandably, has always insisted on the absolute validity of the *credo*, regardless of all the hermeneutics and debates, and this insistence is one of the forms in which it asserts its doctrinal identity. Whether the (tacit or explicit) consensus of the community of the faithful as to the meaning of this and countless other words has changed over the centuries is a matter for historians to investigate; but it seems reasonable to suppose that there is a core of basic beliefs (and thus a basic collective memory) which has withstood the efforts of theologians and philosophers to erode it. On some points of detail we may doubt the perfect consistency of the proclamations issued by the Holy Office at various times over the centuries, but the majority of the faithful is not much concerned with subtle theological distinctions, and the basic foundations are strong enough to allay the suspicion that they are 'evolving' (in the sense in which this verb is used in the modernist heresy). Interpretations may change, and do, as do the liturgy and canon law, and forms of organization, and Church policy on various matters; but dogma, strictly speaking, does not, and nor do the basic divine moral commandments. For a truth cannot cease to be a truth – a statement to which not only Catholics, but also many rationalists, would assent.

The third element of the Church's identity, corresponding to *anticipation*, is its *orientation toward the future*. This, of course, remains as it has always been: the Church is the guide which will lead humanity to the harbour of salvation. But in the case of the Church there is an additional sense to this element which is absent from, or at least not always present in, other kinds of collective identity: it is not just anticipation of the future and future interests, but the consciousness of having an active mission. The idea of a mission can – but need not – be part of both a nation's and an individual's perception of themselves: nations, and their ideologues, can, in addition to proclaiming the superiority of their culture, believe that they have a duty to propagate it, or that they have a special role to fulfil in world history; individuals can believe that God's will or destiny has entrusted them with a special mission, or they may believe that their calling in life is to serve others. But for the Church its mission is an essential part, indeed the basic core, of its meaning; it is built into its very constitution.

The fourth component of the Church's continuous identity, corresponding to *body*, is the *Apostolic Succession*: the perfectly traceable and uninterrupted continuity in the handing down, over the centuries, from one generation of priests to another, of the gifts originally bestowed upon the Apostles. Individuals are born and die, but the body of the Church, in the form of this succession, retains its identity as the treasury of redemption. It is the Apostolic Succession that lends the Church a bodily identity which is stronger and clearer in its continuity than that of other collective organisms, such as states, political parties, corporations or universities. These may claim continuity over generations, as new members take over from those who have left or died, but there will always be an element of doubt (similar to the doubts about Theseus's ship), whereas the Apostolic Succession provides the Church with clear criteria for the legitimacy of each new generation: it is always clear who may take his place in the collective body as the rightful successor of the Apostles, on what conditions and on what grounds. In this very particular sense it is not a collection of physical persons that makes up the body of the Church but the 'spiritual body' which these persons together represent.

The fifth and last element of the Church's identity is its *identifiable beginning*. This, of course, is the birth and baptism of Christ, as well as the miracles he performed, his teaching, his transfiguration, his passion and his resurrection. In this context it need not be established when precisely, in historical terms, the ultimate separation of the Christian community from the Jewish temple took place; the question is irrelevant here, and it is not one I am competent to discuss. What matters is the beginning as perceived and accepted by the Church for centuries.

For all these reasons the Catholic Church retains, in spite of all the changes it has undergone, a clearer, stronger and better-attested continuous identity than any other collective body. The fact that all the elements of its identity are strengthened by or dependent upon the power of faith is immaterial; self-perception is an essential element of continuous identity, just as in the case of personal identity. I will not go into the question of how and to what extent these criteria apply to other religious bodies, Christian and non-Christian; none has such a well-grounded identity. The position of Christian communities which broke away from the Church of Rome in the sixteenth century or later is shakier with regard to their apostolic legitimacy. Although their history from the moment of the split is well known, they have often been accused of breaking the continuity which is essential to the Catholic Church, for they abolished the sacrament of the priesthood and denied the validity of tradition as a separate source of doctrinal authority. The Jewish religious identity does not meet all five of the criteria discussed above, but this is compensated for by an insistence on the immutability of divine law, which in Jewish religious communities is handed down uninterruptedly from generation to generation. The great Oriental religions have their sacred books, of course, but none of them has a well-defined body of scripture endowed with the status of divine revelation, as in the case of Christianity, Judaism and Islam. Here, too, identity is a matter of degree.

It is worth noting that the Church's recent expansion of ecumenical spirit and increasing openness toward other traditions is perceived by many as an erosion of its identity. And it is true that this trend to openness (of which the Church's decision to stop condemning heresies is also part), however laudable, might blur the borderline which makes the Catholic Church distinct from other churches. But acceptance of tolerance and religious freedom can coexist with the Church's persistent will to assert its distinctness and its unique place in the world.

Since the Devil, as theologians used to teach, is the ape of God, there is nothing astonishing in the fact that some more recent, secular ideological bodies appeal to similar criteria of identity. The communist movement had an analogous attitude to its sacred texts (*memory*), which could be reinterpreted and applied in new conditions without in any way undermining the eternal validity of the originals. The movement was supposed to be embedded in the great plan of History, and its aim was to further the realization of this plan; thus it acquired both its universal meaning (*substance*) and its mission (future-directedness, i.e., *anticipation*). It had a hierarchy and a supreme authority, whose members were empowered to pass judgment on the validity of its particular elements (*body*). It considered itself appointed by History as the carrier of truth and the leader of mankind on its march to ultimate salvation, but it could also point to a well-defined origin in time (*an identifiable beginning*), namely the birth of the collective messiah. Similarly with the orthodox Freudian movement, where we can observe a fairly exact parallel with the Apostolic Succession: the healing art may be practised only by those who have been anointed by another who has been similarly anointed, and so on down to the initial, self-anointed Founder (the only one who could, and did, apply the liberating therapy of psycho-analysis to himself; no one after him was able to repeat this feat).

Both ideological movements and religious bodies consider themselves to be the bearers of truth; the *claim to truth* is inscribed into the very meaning of their existence. Such a claim is not among the criteria of identity which can be applied to other continuous entities, nations or individuals; but such entities do make a claim which may be considered roughly analogous, namely a claim to *legitimacy*. Both persons and nations claim legitimacy by the very fact of their existence: they are there, so they are there legitimately, just because they are there. Moreover, they are there necessarily, not contingently: both persons and nations, in their act of self-assertion, assert the *necessity* of their existence, for they cannot conceive of a world from which they are absent. Their being there not only entails that they are entitled to be there but belongs, as it were, to the very constitution of the world. This claim of legitimacy and necessity is similar to the truth claims of religious and ideological bodies.

There is one more thing that should be mentioned. The assertion of self-identity, whether by an individual, an ethnic group or a religious body, always involves a danger: the danger of aggression or of a desire to dominate others. In defending his legitimacy, an individual may easily come to feel that he must affirm it by expanding his power; a nation will protect its identity by hostility to other nations, by conquest and domination; a religious body, as the bearer of truth *par excellence*, is easily tempted to believe that it is its right and its duty to destroy the enemies of truth, i.e., other religious communities and forms of faith. Even if we admit that the desire to assert one's identity by hostile expansion is by no means always and everywhere inevitable, the truth remains (however Nietzschean it may sound) that it is ultimately the stuff of which most of the world's history is made.

1994

The Demise of Historical Man

Homo historicus in the sense I have in mind here is a modern invention. More specifically, he is an internal reaction against the modern world.

It has often been claimed that to be human is to be historical; that mankind robbed of historical consciousness is a monstrosity, even a contradiction in terms; and that collective memory, crystallized in historical knowledge, is not only a necessary condition but the very foundation of our self-identification as beings that live in a community – that is, as humans. This commonplace is hardly controversial. But the fact of our being historically oriented in this obvious way does not make us historical beings in the modern sense. Of course people have always been interested in their collective past; of course they have always needed – as a tribe, as a nation, or as a religious community – a mythological foundation for their existence that told them about the origins of their world and allowed them to grasp its sense.

History as knowledge of origins played the role of myth, irrespective of the varying proportions in which it combined truth and poetry. Its function was to provide a self-grounding: to give the community a sense of the legitimacy of its existence, to ground it in its ancient origins. History-as-myth provided more than just interesting information about a community's genealogy; it also provided a principle of legitimacy, and thus gave meaning to the community's continuing existence – a meaning defined and situated, so to speak, at the source of being. A 'grounding' fact was more than just a fact, a chance event that could just as well not have happened; it contained within it its own necessity, and in this sense it seemed timeless, outside the temporality of facts.

This awareness of origins and grounding in history, the sense of an existence rooted in an absolute beginning which, petrified in a timeless moment of the ancient past, endowed it with meaning and legitimacy, was indispensable for societies whose distinctive feature was what Edward Shils calls 'primordiality': the bond created by a common ancestry, the self-definition of a tribe by 'blood,' its rootedness in a common, more or less legendary, past in which all individual genealogies converge. A similar, although not identical, phenomenon can be observed in religious communities, which also define themselves through participation in a common past. This is also true of the so-called universal religions, where ethnic bonds play no role; belonging to a religious community is defined by spiritual, not biological, kinship. And spiritual kinship is defined historically: through participation in the same holy history which goes back to the beginning of things, when God – or gods or a messenger of God – called this spiritual tribe to life, endowed it with certain privileges and imposed certain duties, giving it access to the truth which brings salvation and entrusting it with a mission.

In both cases of kinship – spiritual kinship and kinship defined by blood ties – history is the binding force whereby a tribe identifies itself by opposition to the rest of the world. People are historical beings in the sense that they are sole owners of the past in which their world, their tribe, or their religion were grounded and shaped; and they naturally need this past in order to give meaning to their lives and to the universe as a whole.

This 'historicity' which binds all communities has not been utterly extinguished; it still exists both in national consciousness and in religious bonds. But it is a vestigial existence. The victorious march of Enlightenment rationalism, and the transition from tribal life to civil society, have radically enfeebled it, and driven it out almost entirely.

The connection has often been remarked between the rationalist view of the world, which evolved upon the ruins of religious tradition, and civil society (in the Rousseauian, not the Hegelian, sense), which replaced tribal kinship. In civil society the individual acquires his belonging to the social 'whole' not through blood ties or the bonds of a common genealogy, but through his participation in an abstract legal order; historical considerations are not needed to determine or establish this belonging. What makes us a society is the power of the law: a law which extends over a certain limited area and before which all individuals are equal. (It took a long time, of course, for the belief in equality before the law to become entrenched; as long as legally defined estates and aristocratic privileges were upheld, historical criteria continued to function, albeit more and more feebly.) In short, history is no longer needed to establish the legitimacy of a social order and the place of the individual in it.

Rationalism in the modern sense of the term – that is, the rationalism we associate chiefly with the Cartesian heritage – emerged as, roughly speaking, the belief that the criteria of validity in the intellectual realm are the same as those applied in scientific procedures. Rationalism and civil society (regardless of which came first or was prior in the order of causality) converge in their common indifference to history. They share the belief that *history cannot confer validity*; it cannot establish, justify or explain the validity of anything. It is naive superstition to imagine that the truth of a proposition can be established by the fact that it has been believed for a long time, that our ancestors believed it, that it was revealed as God's word by some prophet, etc. In order to establish the truth of any opinion, we must apply the clear and absolutely binding mathematical and empirical criteria elaborated by science. Religious truths, too, are valid only to the extent that they can be rationally – i.e., 'geometrically' or empirically – verified. Nor is the history of science relevant to the understanding of science: we want to know the truth, so what use is there in studying a series of absurd blunders? Similarly with issues concerning laws and government; these must be decided by considering what form of government would best preserve the peace, ensure social order and serve people's interests, not by appealing to tradition. In such matters the theory of social contract and enlightened egoism provides sufficient guidance: everyone attends to his own affairs, and from these countless egoisms the 'invisible hand' of the market forges a functioning whole. Scientistic rationalism, the development of civil society based on equality before the law, the theory of enlightened egoism and social contract, the spread of the market, economic theory – these things together are a tightly woven whole, and all its components give rise to indifference or disdain for history, which is rejected as a source of legitimacy both in the intellectual realm and in social affairs.

The view of the world I have sketched here, in a rough and simplified form, determined the ideological framework of modernity, and exerted a tremendous influence on eighteenth- and nineteenth-century European thought. Not, of course, without encountering a good deal of resistance: the strength of ethnic bonds and the vitality of religious tradition were still such that rationalist attacks could not defeat them entirely. The doctrine according to which the interplay of colliding egoisms in a society based on greed ultimately brings universal happiness proved highly dubious in light of the effects of the Industrial Revolution – a fact to which representatives of early socialist thought did not fail to draw the attention of the European public. And once rationalist and skeptical attacks had deposed first divine authority, and then also natural law (which had been treated as a sort of watered-down form of divinity, or a more modest substitute for God), the simple question of how good could be distinguished from evil seemed unanswerable. The reply that the question was meaningless or wrongly put could not really make people happy.

To be sure, Kant tried to prove that the question could be answered within the framework of a rationalist worldview, without appealing to history; he argued that the foundations of moral judgment could be established by transcendental rationality, in which we all participate. However, very few Enlightenment sceptics were convinced by this.

The Romantic movement seemed to be an attempt to return to the old historicity: to the belief in the legitimizing power of the national bonds established in an ever-present past. The Catholic temptation in this movement is entirely understandable, for the Church of Rome could boast of the uninterrupted continuity of its existence and lay claim to being the guardian of the original treasure of Christianity.

Both liberals and socialists have ignored the reality of nations; most of them saw nations as the remnant of a past era, doomed to extinction by the all-unifying force of modernity and the development of communication and of the global economy. Their predictions were based on sound arguments; they would surely be astonished if they could witness the rebirth of nationalism in our time. And yet the socialist movement was nourished and given its impetus by the same instinct that nourished Romanticism: not in the sense that the socialists extolled the values of national tradition (although in fact some did) or the beauty of an idealized medieval spiritual unity, but in the sense that they deplored the domination of egoisms and the loss, in the market economy, of natural human solidarity; they dreamed of a society in which every individual would spontaneously and disinterestedly identify with humanity, thus ensuring everlasting harmony. But if remnants of the old historicity – the belief in the happiness of primitive, classless tribes – have survived here and there in socialist ideologies, it is no longer as a validating principle of present society, but rather as an abstract, ahistorical image of a Golden Age; a model, not a source of energy as in the past. Thus this belief was not properly an instance of the old historicity. And the most powerful theoretical expression of the socialist idea, the Marxist doctrine, evolved from an entirely different kind of historicism, associated, of course, with the name of Hegel.

The issue here is not to interpret the Hegelian idea or to ask whether and how this idea – a reaction to the antihistoricism of the Enlightenment – was itself unambiguous and coherent. The point is that two mutually incompatible varieties of a new historicity seem to have grown – whether legitimately or not does not matter here – out of the Hegelian legacy; and the *homo historicus* I have in mind here was shaped by one or both of them.

It was also Hegel who taught us – directly or indirectly – that we live in history and contribute to its shape; that history includes what occurs here and now. The widespread feeling that we shape history is probably Hegelian in origin (though it was anticipated by Vico). It irrupted into our language and ensconced itself in it so comfortably, with its aura of pathos, that we do not think to question it. History used to be either simply a chronicle of past events or – on the Augustinian approach – a succession of divine interventions in human affairs. But today it is no longer either of these things. I eat breakfast, lecture at the university, talk with friends, go to an art exhibition, and doing all these things I am not only surrounded by 'history' as a kind of invisible natural environment, but contributing to its progress. We either internalize history as our way of life or we interact with it in an intimate, quasi-erotic way, as if history were a lady one could seduce. In doing something, I am not simply doing this or that, eating breakfast or visiting an exhibition; in everything I do, I am making history.

What use do people have, or what use did they have, for this curious and unnatural feeling invented by philosophers? The Enlightenment, having pronounced the death sentence on divine providence and then on God himself, rejecting Him as the source of meaning and as the tribunal that could be entrusted with matters of good and evil, soon went on to kill Nature – a substitute for God that provided both moral rules and principles of rationality. History became a substitute for the substitute – a newly discovered infallible foundation on which meaning could be built, and the binding power that could reconstruct a meaningful whole from disconnected pieces and define our place in it.

Historical man need have no historical knowledge or interest in real history; he knows history simply as a reliable and trustworthy legislator. And he believes that history is *real*: not simply something that once was, but a living being. History 'marches on,' like an army; it will 'decide if we were right,' like a judge; it will 'be the judge of events,' like a scholar. And so on.

This, then, was an attempt to make history the carrier and guardian of all human values, the divine authority that could issue verdicts about good and evil and provide access to the sources of higher reason and meaning. But – as the later career of this idea shows – it was doomed from the outset by a fatal ambiguity, as a result of which the authority of history not only broke apart into two irreconcilable tendencies but was also brought, ineluctably, to its own destruction, dashing all hopes of rebuilding meaning.

Both God and Nature were immutable; and their judgments about human duties and human dignity, the meaning of life, justice and injustice, truth and falsity, were supposed to be immutably valid. History is by definition incapable of issuing such judgments, for it is mutability itself; change, and nothing other, is precisely what history consists of. How, then, can we trust it and profit from its wisdom?

One of the Hegelian answers is that the actual historical process is the only authority that can produce reason and truth; only it can confer absolute validity. Abstract moral judgments about the historical process are empty and fruitless. From this assumption some Hegelians concluded that this process *in toto*, with all its cruelties and atrocities, must simply be accepted as rational and therefore good. But history so conceived can no longer be a source of wisdom or rules of behaviour; it cannot be our teacher and guide in life. Like a tyrant, it demands to be worshipped as it is, for what it is. At best, all we can say is that what is good and rational today was absurd and wrong yesterday, and may also be wrong tomorrow. This relativist and ultimately nihilist interpretation of Hegel was certainly a great simplification, but it was not entirely wrong; and 'historicism' in this sense could recognize some of its ideas in the Hegelian construction. But this form of historical relativism was, of course, much older than Hegel; it had been present in European thought since Montaigne: 'Diabolical today, holy yesterday,' 'Just on one side of the Pyrenees, unjust on the other,' etc. This simple scepticism cannot be attributed to Hegel without restrictions, but then – as Hegel himself pointed out – we do not read philosophers the way they would like to be read, but the way our era dictates that we should read them. And on this reading, history is self-sufficient and self-supporting; it has no ontological background except itself; and everything – every truth, every validity, every kind of Reason – is immanent in it.

So conceived, the so-called historicism inevitably turned against itself. For to say that truth is historically relative, that something is true only 'for a certain era,' is tantamount to saying that there is no truth in the normal sense. Thus we no longer need history or historicist philosophy; the question of truth has simply been abolished. Nietzsche knew this; he also knew that he had drawn all the conclusions from God's death, and wanted to make us face the world as it is – without God, and thus without meaning, without good and evil, without truth. For the next hundred years the European spirit was to live in the shadow of his nihilism. Nihilism is still with us, and it does not need to express itself in so-called historicist categories; universal relativism and nihilism are plentiful enough.

But there was another side to the Hegelian heritage: belief in progress and in the fulfilment of history. The idea of progress, however defined, necessarily implies that we have at our disposal certain non-historical criteria, criteria that are not entirely dependent on the actual course of events, which allow us to say that truth – truth *tout court*, not truth for some historical era – increases, or evolves, or manifests itself increasingly, in history; or that the essence of humanity develops and matures in time. And the idea of fulfilment suggests that there will come a point in the historical process at which an absolute state will have been achieved – not just in the sense that history will tire of going on, or exhaust itself, and just decide not to progress any further, but also in the sense that it will attain its plenitude, its perfect form.

Hegel, despite his intransigent anti-utopianism, did believe in an ultimate stage of the evolution of mankind. His anti-utopianism was directed against all the arbitrarily constructed visions of the perfect society that people have thought they could deduce from moral principles alone, without taking into account the actual historical process; there was no conflict between this criticism and his belief in the fulfilment of history.

The tension between the belief that all truths and ideas are historically limited and the anticipation of mankind's ultimate fulfilment was inherited by the most successful form of historicism in our century – Marxist philosophy. According to Marxist doctrine, there are no eternal ideas; every product of culture is a disguised expression of the real interests of various social classes. According to this same doctrine, however, we also know what the essence of being human is and what is required for its actualization; only on this assumption can we use words like 'alienation,' 'liberation of mankind,' 'the end of alienation,' etc. Thus on the one hand everything is historically determined, but, on the other, the ultimate state of humanity, which may shortly be expected, will – though it is called the 'beginning' rather than the 'end' of genuine history – be the fulfilment of mankind. So it seems that not everything is historically determined after all.

But the Marxist utopia can hardly be described as historicism in the proper sense. It certainly included the belief in 'laws of history' that would unfailingly, and within a very short time, elevate us to the heights of perfection and bring about an ideal world. But the past was irrelevant; the anticipated future would consign it to oblivion. The meaning of the past can be grasped only from the vantage point of the expected ultimate fulfilment; it is the future – something that is not empirically given – that defines the meaning of both present and past. History in itself is unproductive; it can give us no guidance and no access to truth, or only in a perverse way, in that it acquires its meaning from the future – i.e., from something that does not exist.

And thus history, the last rampart from which the Enlightenment hoped to defend itself against nihilism – its own creation – and rediscover the source of meaning, collapsed under its own weight, unable to go on performing its task. 'Historical man' split into two figures, and for both history gradually became less and less significant.

For those who drew their utopian dreams from Marxist ideology, history was no more than a pretext for believing in a quasi-natural inevitability that would soon transform their fantasies into reality. Messianic hopes justified all means, all forms of violence, which might bring millenarian happiness closer. Nothing in the present, and thus all the more emphatically nothing in the past, was of any significance; only the future mattered. The reality that did not yet exist had much more importance – indeed, much more existence – than the real, palpable world. 'Historical man' abolished history.

The variety of historicism which saw history as an all-encompassing, all-exhaustive, self-grounding absolute was also forced, in the end, to deny history. The logic of this peculiar self-devastation seems simple enough. People were aware that different periods and different civilizations gave rise to different beliefs; historicism was the generalized theoretical expression of this ancient discovery. Consistent historicism entailed the belief that something could be valid only for a given era, for a given *Zeitgeist*, within the context of a given culture, etc. And this meant that nothing is valid in itself. To say that something is valid for a given historical epoch, a *Zeitgeist*, a culture or civilization is tantamount to saying that it was considered valid, or true, or obvious, or uncontroversial, in that era or for that culture; apart from this context the adjective 'valid' has no meaning. Thus universal relativism no longer has any need of history. And the path from historicism in this sense to simple, all-embracing and all-engulfing relativism was a straight one. The next stage – the structuralist ideology – was to proclaim that knowledge of history in the traditional sense (which included knowledge of conscious human intentions) is neither possible nor useful; following swiftly upon it was the further discovery that all meaning we imagined ourselves to have found in the past is our own meaning, imposed by us. For instance, no text has any meaning in itself (presumably with the exception of texts by those who make this very claim). A convenient theory, one may note in passing, in that it frees us from the need to read, since whatever we read, we are in fact reading nothing.

Thus 'historical man' committed suicide and was resurrected – as nihilistic man.

Where do we stand now, at the century's close, with our uncertainty about history, and at the same time our unease in it and our longing for it? Will relativism and nihilism (which Husserl warned us against at the start of the century), first historically grounded, then ahistorical, be definitively, irrevocably victorious?

The utopian mentality, after so many great disillusionments, seems to be in decline. Fewer and fewer people seem to believe that there is a technique that will lead us infallibly to a paradise where all human needs have been satisfied and all conflicts reconciled. There is no doubt, on the other hand, that more and more effort, toil and money will be needed to repair the damage we ourselves have wrought, to ward off ecological catastrophes and to solve demographic problems. It would be naive to hope that in some indefinite future we will all have more and more of everything. The utopian faith in the benevolent designs of history seems to be waning.

But relativism, freed from its 'historicist' origins, seems to be enjoying continuing good health. In its popular and most widespread form, it tells us that we have no absolute criteria whereby we might evaluate and compare different civilizations, belief systems or norms, and that all elements of all civilizations are therefore equally legitimate. In short, slavery is as good as freedom, or at any rate neither is 'better' in any real sense. A pragmatic variety of relativism, with a more developed theoretical framework, is based on the idea of consensus: it claims that everything will be fine, we won't have to worry about a thing, if only we can reach a consensus.

Since this relativism is associated particularly with the American mentality, it is perhaps not out of place here to remark on the difference between the American and the German approach. The American approach is to say, for instance, 'No one here defends slavery; it would be very hard to find someone who believed there was nothing wrong with slavery and expressed regret that it had been abolished. Thus we can say, without a shadow of a doubt, that there is a consensus about slavery, and nothing more is needed.' The German spirit, however, is not satisfied with this solution. The German approach is to say, rather, 'Consensus is never enough. I want to know whether slavery is in fact evil, not just what people think about it. Otherwise, if someone says that slavery is evil, he can be taken to mean only that most people in a given society consider it to be evil. But that is not what he means: such a reduction is contrary to people's real intentions; this is not the meaning people assign to their words when they make such a statement. When I say that slavery is evil, I mean that slavery is in fact evil – that it is evil in itself, not that other people, or even most people, believe it to be evil. Moreover, this reduction implies that while slavery might be evil today, it was not evil in the past, when it was considered quite normal. But those who fought against slavery did so because they believed that it was evil and contrary to human dignity, irrespective of any consensus in the matter. If they had not believed this, slavery would never have been abolished. And if the words "good" and "evil" have no meaning except in this sense, then, if slavery were re-established and again considered quite normal, it would become good *in fact.*' Thus the German spirit wants to know what is good or evil, real or unreal, true or false. It found its expression in the Kantian and Husserlian tradition; it even invaded the Frankfurt School, which never abandoned the hope that a *logos* free from all contingency might be discovered that would provide us with genuinely valid rules, both for thinking and for issuing value judgments.

Historical man may be in decline, he may even have died, but his offspring, the carrier of generalized relativism, lives on and flourishes. A number of features peculiar to our time may be put forward to explain his resilience. One of them is the all-pervading spirit of popular scientism, which rejects everything that cannot be assessed in terms of visible goods; on these criteria, the distinction between good and evil, and that between true and false in any but a pragmatic sense, is meaningless. Another reason is the aversion to ideological fanaticism, whether religious or secular, whose inhuman consequences we have had so much occasion to observe in our century. However, this admirable rejection of fanaticism often seems no more than a disguise for quite a different attitude. For relativism is convenient; it is convenient because it sanctions our *indifference.* And we would like to ennoble this indifference, to give it a good name – as if there were no difference between fanaticism and the search for truth, or between tolerance and indifference to truth; as if nihilism were a defence against fanaticism.

So we can find reasons why 'historical man' was born and why he died – though not without progeny. Faced with the progressive waning of religious belief, with the loss, too, of faith in the wisdom and immutability of nature, our culture set up history as the tribunal in which we can put our trust if we are not to be engulfed by the desert wastes of nihilism. But this contrivance proved weaker than the cultural forces against which it was meant to defend us. Historicism was transformed into relativist indifference, leaving us in the same spiritual wasteland, with the same void it had promised to fill.

This wasteland is comfortable, but also hard to bear. People need, and have always needed, to believe that the world can be not only dominated but also understood; this need is surely part of what it means to be human. This is why we have seen, in our brutal century, various attempts to find a way back to the meaning we have lost. It seems unlikely that traditional historicism will find this way for us: unlikely that we could ever again be persuaded to put our faith in history as it actually is. If anything, we seem, rather, to be witnessing a new longing for the old historicity. In defiance of all rational expectations, the need to establish one's identity through tribal membership, to define oneself through the values of a national culture, is not fading; it is getting stronger. (And we know the dangers to which this quite understandable need gives rise when it degenerates into militant chauvinism.) Above all, and again in defiance of rational expectations, there is a renewed longing for self-identification through religion. In all the chaos and uncertainty of our times, our religious heritage seems to provide a more reliable source of support than anything else.

Of course, it is hard to make predictions on such precarious ground. But it seems safe to say that we have seen the demise of secular history as the grounding for existence and the source of meaning, and that the third Christian millennium, which is almost upon us, will have to rediscover our old religious roots – so that we can survive.

1989

On Our Relative Relativism

According to Heraclitus, in the eyes of God everything is beautiful, good and just. It is not so in our eyes, of course. But Heraclitus's assertion does not imply a 'relativistic' melancholy (God sees things one way, human creatures another); we must assume that God knows better and thus that everything really is beautiful, good and just, and our impression is not just different, but plain wrong. It is conceivable – at any rate not logically inconsistent – that we know that this is God's view of the world and that it is correct (for instance, because God Himself has told us so), but are incapable of sharing it (except perhaps in the case of mystics who momentarily participate in the divine vision; but they have no means of conveying that vision to others).

If we fail to perceive the beauty, justice and goodness of the world, and instead see vast swathes of ugliness and injustice, does it matter that we know, or pretend to know, that the world is indeed beautiful, just and good? I believe it does. It does not change the content of our perceptions, nor does it make us more efficient in what we do; but it may affect our attitude toward the world. People who strongly believe – on the basis of divine revelation, or because of some non-transmittable experience, or (like Leibniz, for example) as a result of *a priori* reasoning – that there is a good moral order in the universe and that ultimately everything is for the best, are not protected against ugliness, injustice and suffering. But they are better able to absorb the adversities of their existence, even though their image of things cannot be formulated as an empirical hypothesis in accordance with the rules of scientific procedure.

This difference is worth pondering when the question of truth is discussed. It is hard to refute the traditional arguments against both relativist and absolutist claims about human knowledge. The gist of the antirelativist argument is as follows: the relativist denies any eternal and absolute standard of rationality. In his view, if we say that something is true to the best of our knowledge, we must assume, implicitly or explicitly, that it is true for a particular civilization, or in particular historical conditions, or by virtue of our biological structure, or within a linguistic game. But in this way, critics argue, the relativist is entangled in his own snare: he cannot escape the antinomy of the liar, for his general statement about the relativity of all knowledge falls victim to its own verdict and is as relative as any other; albeit conceivably true, it is, as it were, unutterable. The relativist could try to get around this difficulty by transforming his epistemological proposition into a normative rule; but this would be a spurious solution, even if it removed the problem of self-reference, for such a prescription would be either arbitrary and therefore unjustified, or justified by the very proposition that has just been rejected.

The same applies, for that matter, to another kind of relativism, expressed in one of the most celebrated sentences of contemporary philosophy: Paul Feyerabend's 'anything goes.' If everything is permissible, then all restrictive cognitive rules are equally permissible; in other words, the rule, 'It is not the case that anything goes,' also goes. Thus we may say that if anything goes then it is not the case that anything goes. This reckless permissiveness does not seem a very promising foundation for a theory of knowledge (to tolerate everything means to tolerate intolerance).

The Popperian variety of relativism may succeed in avoiding the self-reference paradox because it deals with empirical hypotheses and does not pretend, if I understand it properly, to be one itself; but it entails other unfortunate consequences. If we assume that, even after a perfectly thorough process of elimination, there will always be a number of mutually incompatible explanations for the same empirical phenomena, then it seems conceivable that our knowledge, accumulated in empirical hypotheses and laws, consists entirely of false statements, and moreover that this will always be so.

The distinction between truth and falsity is not abolished, but it is of little use; falsity can be established, but truth cannot. No doubt, one can formulate rules of acceptability or admissibility, but not criteria for establishing the distinction between what is merely acceptable and what is true.

In all three variants of relativism the concept of truth in the everyday sense of the word has been discarded. But to reject any of those variants on logical or other grounds is not to reassert the concept of truth. On the contrary; the ancient sceptics' traditional argument about the infinite regress that inevitably arises in the quest for criteria of truth still seems cogent.

The outcome of these well-known arguments is equally well known. There is no zero-point in the search for knowledge, no uncontaminated source from which certainty – real, unconditional, unimpeachable certainty – springs. Husserl's unflagging pleas for Truth – with a capital T – in the face of the relativist corruption of European civilization went largely unheeded. This was not because his arguments were necessarily flawed but rather because the prevailing cultural trend was in another direction, gradually eroding belief in eternally valid intellectual standards, in the regulative ideal of *episteme*, and finally in the very usefulness of the concept of Truth. This trend has reached its climax in our time, but we can trace it back, with the benefit of hindsight, to the very beginning of the Enlightenment (in the broadest sense of this loose term).

Modern scepticism, one may suppose, resulted from contact with other civilizations and concerned, as we see in Montaigne, not only moral rules and customs, but all kinds of truth. This was, to be sure, before modern science emerged in the beginning of the seventeenth century, soon to be codified in a set of distinct abstract procedures. But the great thinker, the reputed pillar of modernity, who contributed to this codification and whose work could initially be seen as a philosophical response to Galileo's physics, was to become, unwillingly, a part of the sceptical conspiracy. Descartes's attempt to restore certainty and his approach to the reality of our world of experience has of course been endlessly analysed and commented upon. But few have accepted it as a reliable method for establishing trust in our cognitive prowess; it was Descartes's sceptical questioning that most strongly influenced his readers, and was repeatedly denounced as the main source of modern idealism.

It was the Enlightenment proper which, from various directions, cast more and more doubt on our proficiency in the search for truth as it had been traditionally defined. Hume, of course, became one of the main culprits when he ultimately reduced knowledge, tautologies apart, to the content of particular perceptions, immobilized in their particularity, and everything beyond that to pragmatic values. So did Kant, at least in the popular perception of his work. Schopenhauer even argued that the Kantian distinction between phenomena and the thing-in-itself, and his insistence that objects were co-created by transcendental forms of consciousness, led to the conclusion that our world of experience is a realm of dreams (we should suppose, therefore, that once Kant had been awakened from his dogmatic slumbers by Hume, he realized that he had been, and still was, living in a dream and that the world of experience is Maya, as Vedic wisdom taught).

This might seem a somewhat exaggerated interpretation, and Kant himself did not say this in so many words, but when we look at great philosophers as cultural facts, what counts is less their genuine intentions than the way their thought influenced and was perceived by the general educated audience. When Kant said that his place was the 'fertile depth of experience,' he meant it, and his writings, sometimes opaque, were not designed to instil in his readers a feeling of tragic renunciation or a terror of the great Unknown. But his simplified message was that the world as it really is, is beyond our reach: God's existence is unprovable, and morality is severed from its religious roots. This was supposed to be 'the withdrawal from immaturity, [an immaturity] for which we ourselves are to blame,' that is to say, the Enlightenment. To be sure, one school of Kantians altogether rejected the thing-in-itself as a fictitious construct and made Kant the herald of the absolute sovereignty of Thought, but another school reduced his transcendental forms to psychological, species-related conditions of knowledge, thus reinforcing the relativistic side of his legacy.

Hegel also took part in the conspiracy; again, less perhaps through his notoriously ambiguous intentions than through the way he was read. And it was fairly easy to perceive him as a historicist for whom all products of human thought, including philosophy, metaphysics and religion, must be seen as temporary instruments of the great impersonal spirit in search of itself, and truth as time-bound and culture-related. His philosophy was frequently misread as Reason's approval for all historical contingency.

A further vigorous stimulus to relativist thinking came from the philosophical elaboration of Darwinism. From a theory implying that all development of life is guided by a single factor – the mechanical elimination of the worse adapted – it was possible to conclude that the specifically human Reason we boast of, including its power of abstraction, is merely an effective instrument in the adaptation of the species to the changing environment, and that no other meaning can be attributed to it; in other words, that the proper measure of knowledge is the ability to predict and efficiently control events in order to counteract the hostile contingency of nature. The ideas of Reason and Truth in the Platonic, Aristotelian and even Cartesian sense became empty and irrelevant to this task. This was what the empiricists of the late nineteenth century explicitly and consistently argued.

Does the reduction of knowledge to a self-defence mechanism of the species fall prey to the antinomy of the liar? Not necessarily: not if it is transformed into a prescription which can be applied to itself. It may be argued that in some interpretations the discovery of the theory of evolution is itself an instrument for improving the survival chances of the species that contrived it. For example, one could argue that it would be good for humanity as a whole to slaughter its ill-adapted members; certain English lovers of mankind like H. G. Wells and George Bernard Shaw even suggested as much at one point.

But philosophical Darwinians usually do not bother about this issue. The Darwinian theory is accepted as a scientific discovery, and the assumption that it is true (in the normal sense of the word) is stealthily smuggled into arguments which deny the meaning of truth on the basis of this same theory.

Nietzsche, of course, was the loudest voice of the cultural mutation of relativism, for all his contradictions. Quite often we glimpse
a hidden despair looming up from behind his triumphal war cry over
the dead bodies of God, Truth, Reason and a well-ordered universe.
But the crucial, poignant message was unmistakable: nothing but
pathetic wreckage remains of the lofty Platonic mirage of wisdom.
We are no longer pilgrims doggedly and tirelessly striving toward
this great treasure; the treasure does not exist – it is a figment of our
hollow craving for the impossible. We live in an aimless chaos and
try to assert our individual or collective will to expansion. Our philosophy, our religious search, often even our art, are illusions, veils
behind which we enclose ourselves in order to face the world as it
'truly' is (never mind that there is no Truth).

But civilizations cannot survive in despair, not for long at any
rate. So an effective medicine was found: an optimistic interpretation for what many people might have seen as a disaster. It goes as
follows: There is nothing disastrous in our reasonable renunciation
of the chimeras of Truth and Reason. These were merely spectres
which had been haunting our civilization for millennia, and to some
extent continue to haunt it. Why should we despair because we have
stopped trying to stalk an animal from a fairy tale? Our knowledge
has proved efficient and provides us with predictive power. What
else do we need? If parts of it prove inefficient or even counter-
effective, they are cut off like dead twigs; we accept what remains as
healthy, and science has devised good criteria of acceptability. People
have debated, for instance, about 'the existence of the world.' But
even assuming that we could define and grasp the meaning of such
a bizarre question, it is a futile and empty one. Whatever we decide
concerning the existence or non-existence of the world, nothing
changes in our life, our perceptions, our practical business or our
science. We must discard such nonsensical problems, which possibly
originated in sick minds.

Similarly with most traditional problems of metaphysics and
epistemology, except those that are of an empirical nature and
belong to psychological or linguistic analysis rather than to epistemology proper in the Husserlian sense. Neither ordinary people nor

scientists are tormented by the distinction between the coherence and correspondence theories of truth; they discriminate between the true and the false on the basis of common criteria of acceptability, which in turn depends on the answer to the question, 'What can we do with this truth?'

Even physicists, who tell us that some descriptions of the phenomena they examine depend on the observer or the measuring devices used, and cannot be made without including them, have contributed to the belief that our pursuit of Truth can never be entirely independent from the fact that we are engaged in this pursuit; and perhaps to the belief that the very idea of Truth is unintelligible. Einstein might have been dismayed by this perspective, but most scientists are not.

Replacing criteria of truth with standards of acceptability thus conceived belongs to the programme of moderate pragmatism, which invalidates metaphysics but does not affect science, which can continue to function according to rigorous standards without bothering about truth, except in the sense of acceptability. Immoderate, or extravagant, pragmatism, which instead employs criteria of usefulness or even 'happiness,' may be left aside. Not because it is false – this is an arbitrary prescription anyway – but because it is impracticable: it is impossible to specify how such criteria should be applied. No one can say how, for what or for whom they should work, or in what time scale something should be judged useful or productive of more happiness, or how 'happiness' is to be defined. (Drugs produce happiness for a while, but misery in the long run. And who is wise enough to calculate the global amount of happiness, given how unpredictable are the effects of so many human endeavours?)

Needless to say, extravagant pragmatism may not appear a compelling conclusion to be drawn from the moderate variety. But the cultural impact of ideas does not operate according to logical rules. 'Efficiency' and 'usefulness' do not mean the same thing, but in cultural and psychological terms the path from one to the other is short. The claim that there is no truth in the Husserlian or Platonic sense does not, of course, logically entail that 'anything goes,' but the road from one to the other is as easy (albeit longer) as, for example, the route from the demand for freedom to anarchy. It goes without saying that I am for freedom and against anarchy, but one can follow the changes, sometimes unnoticeable, in the prevailing use of concepts, whereby concepts eventually take on a meaning far removed from or even opposite to their original sense. And, of course, it is not just wordplay that causes such displacements but cultural processes that occur in other areas of life – in the hierarchy of values, in customs, in science, in technology, in social stratification, in religious beliefs, in information systems – all of them acting independently. For this reason isolating the precise impact of any one of those forces is usually a matter of speculation.

The path from the austere, ascetic and lucid thought of David Hume to the contemporary philosophy of hippies and flower children, often called postmodernity, is convoluted and twisting, but it can be traced. Nevertheless, it is not one step that causes the next one but external energies, often hard to identify.

Despite the massive assault on universal, intellectual and other standards, there are, fortunately, areas where standards still apply – notably in the sciences and especially in the so-called hard sciences, which do not seem to have been affected by the irresponsible philosophy of butterflies. They can do without the idea of Husserlian Truth; they have no need explicitly to assert the eternal criteria of rationality; but they have elaborated some fairly precise rules of acceptability that work, all doubts and disputes notwithstanding. Things are worse in the humanities, to be sure. But it would be an exaggeration to say that standards in historical studies have already been killed off by postmodernist propaganda, which manifests itself more in programmatic appeals than in the actual practice of science. But signs of the invasion can already be detected. The 'anything goes' creed has clearly won in the arts and made fairly strong inroads into moral beliefs.

If we are to single out a particularly powerful cultural factor that has contributed to the progressing collapse of standards, we are tempted to point to the enormous increase in mobility, both spatial and social. The virtual extinction of village life in the developed areas of the world has destroyed the spiritual organization of space as a guarantor of stability and eroded trust in tradition, which formerly provided people with a number of basic moral norms and the belief in an order of things that bestowed meaning on life. This is not a new observation. Many people have seen uprootedness as a distinctive mark of our times; this widespread feeling of insecurity, of the absence of spiritual shelter, naturally found ideological or philosophical expression. We shed our archaic 'irrational' habits of mind not in order to enter the glorious kingdom of rationality but, on the contrary, to adopt new habits which disregard the idea of rationality altogether.

There is no way back to the old unsullied order; no amount of nostalgia will reverse the course of change nor undo its alarming, perhaps calamitous, effects. But the need for certainty and Truth, to know the world as it really is, is not limited to philosophers, nor invented by them; it is simply human, and it is most unlikely that it will ever be extirpated. Various plagues of our civilization may be traced back to the loss of spiritual security. They include the widespread use of drugs, which give people an illusory and short-lived feeling of reconciliation with life; they also include the growth in violent criminality, a symptom of the refusal to find oneself a place in an order which is experienced as no longer being an order. Religious fanaticism and the search for pathetic satisfaction under the guidance of grotesque prophets also belong here. For any unprejudiced mind, as Hegel says, Truth will always remain the great word that makes the heart beat more strongly.

Quine, whose thinking may be seen as an expression of moderate pragmatism, says that both objects and God are cultural artifacts, but the former are superior in that they are more efficient for predicting events. Even if Quine is right, the fact remains that the fictitiousness of the objects which science deals with is not something many people are bothered or saddened by, whereas once God is declared an artifact and people accept this judgment, their world is really changed, both intellectually and emotionally; the absence of God is really experienced.

Science is usually trusted because it works. But it, too, has contributed, in a different way, to this same feeling of insecurity, because it is unintelligible to most nonscientists, and parts of it, especially quantum mechanics and cosmology, have become increasingly counterintuitive.

Even if we assume that truth is prepositional – and this is a discretionary decree – rationalism remains another discretionary decree. Its criteria of acceptability are based on the extent to which the truths thus discovered allow us to predict and control phenomena; this is to say, truth is conceived in terms of moderate pragmatism. This is culturally and historically explicable, but if it is understood unrestrictedly, it dismisses the idea of Logos as an unattainable mirage, a capricious fancy. Critics who attacked this scientific, or rather 'scientistic,' instrumental reason – for example, the Frankfurt School – and tried to safeguard the supremacy of Logos, were unable with precision to define its scope of domination or the criteria it was supposed to use in its discoveries. Consequently, their philosophy could be accused of being no more than a yearning after the lost Platonic or Hegelian paradise.

And then we are back at the beginning: since no compelling logical argument can be provided either for adopting so-called instrumental reason or for embracing the Logos of its critics, the ultimate justification of both lies within the realm of human needs. And no one can say, 'Your needs are not genuine; I know best what you really need.' The quest for the kind of knowledge that would satisfy our need for an all-embracing meaning of life and for valid, 'true,' moral rules, can, of course, easily be discarded as having nothing to do with truth. But so can those needs which stir or steer our curiosity when the point is to control our environment. If there is no unmediated truth, that is, no truth in which the knower and the thing known coincide, if our words are tools rather than a mirror or the carbon paper on which the universe leaves its direct mark, there seems no escape from the rules of moderate pragmatism – unless we accept that another route of knowledge lies open to us, one where words cannot be so deftly manipulated but rather suggest or draw us near a reality that is not empirical in the sense of ordinary perception. Let us repeat: to concede a monopoly to the rules of scientism would be an arbitrary verdict. Does the refusal to do so amount to groping blindly for a lost treasure in the darkness? Perhaps. As Epicharmos said, everything precious is usually found at night.

We survive uneasily in a perplexing chaos, having forfeited our belief in infallible guidelines for thought. Ours is a post-Enlightenment world in that it is Enlightenment turned against itself – the loss of Reason as a result of Reason's triumphant victory over the Unreason of the old mentality. And better not to venture into 'futurology,' since the future by definition does not exist. Strong beliefs easily breed fanaticism; scepticism, or the lack of beliefs, easily breeds mental and moral paralysis.

1996

Is There a Future for Truth?

I will argue that the question 'Does Truth Have a future?' is neither frivolous nor pointless; moreover, I believe that a reasonable answer can be found to it. I mean Truth in the very traditional sense of *adaequatio*.

Some of us, at that stage of our early youth when we made our way through a great many books, believed that one day we would hit upon the book *par excellence*: the absolute book, the book that would bring ultimate enlightenment and reveal the Whole Truth. We fairly soon came to the conclusion that, although there are many excellent books, wise books and interesting books, the absolute book does not exist. But what we had in mind, as we laboured under the illusion of its existence and waited for the Truth to be revealed, was truth in a particular sense. Most of us probably did not doubt that our chemistry or geometry or even history books contained true knowledge; but the absolute book, the book that would initiate us into the Truth, would contain knowledge of a different kind.

Believers who have never experienced doubt know that there is such a book, and even where it is to be found. It is the text given or dictated by God: the Bible or the Koran. (The sacred books of the Oriental religions, much as they are revered by believers, do not enjoy this kind of unshakeable authority; they are a source of great wisdom, but not a transcription of God's words.) Those who favour a 'fundamentalist' interpretation of religion think that they hold the Whole Truth in the palm of their hand. It may not be literally the whole truth in the sense that it does not contain all true sentences, the number of which is infinite. Still, the expression 'the whole truth' is not out of place here. But what does it mean?

The correspondence theory of truth – that is, the idea of truth as the correspondence of a thought (a sentence, a belief, an idea) with reality – gave rise to endless problems and conundrums. Philosophers from Plato to Tarski have grappled with them, and are still grappling with some of them today: does *adaequatio* apply to sentences or meanings, and what might be the consequences of this distinction? How are we to understand the Aristotelian statement that things are 'causes' of the truth of a proposition, and how can it be defended? But if what matters is correspondence with reality, can any agreement be reached about how that reality is to be conceived? Is the relation which obtains between the various components of a fact similar to that which obtains between the various parts of an utterance about that fact? If so, what does the similarity consist in? How can we escape the antinomy of the liar and other paradoxes of self-reference? (The concept of a meta-language and the theory of types in logic have helped here.) What consequences would follow if we accepted some version of the ontological concept of truth, Heidegger's, for instance, or Aquinas's? Or if we extended the predicates 'true' and 'false' to beliefs other than those that are expressible in propositions about the world, for instance to our perceptions or ideas? And if we accept the correspondence theory of truth, which says that the sentence 'Snow is white' is true if and only if snow is white, will this be enough (mathematics apart) if we do not know the criteria which allow us to distinguish between true and false sentences and to decide whether or not a sentence is true? And would this definition still work if for a sentence like 'Snow is white' we substituted a meaningless sentence with the external characteristics of a proposition, or a sentence of a kind that some philosophers, like Alfred Ayer, have pronounced meaningless – a metaphysical or theological statement, for example? What, for example, are we to do with a sentence like 'The Holy Ghost is co-eternal with the Father'?

But despite these complications, all of them endlessly discussed in an abundant literature on the subject, we can say that the idea of truth as correspondence with reality seems to fit well with our ordinary, non-philosophical intuition, which is indifferent to the squabbles of logicians, and with the ordinary, non-philosophical meaning of the words 'true' and 'truth'. We are, after all, talking about something that is perfectly intelligible to anyone who has mastered a language – any language: if Michael spoke the truth when he said that it was raining, then it was raining and he said what was the case; Joe did not speak the truth when he said he had not stolen the money, because he did steal it. We can have all sorts of doubts about whether or not something is true, but in ordinary speech we know what the word 'true' means.

Philosophers, however, are not content with this. They insist that when we use the words 'true' and 'false' as they are used in everyday speech, in a natural and unthinking way, we actually mean something different from what we think we mean. They maintain that when we say that something is true we do not mean to say that a thing is 'really' the case, independently of anyone's knowledge of it, but something quite different.

So what is it that they think we mean? One explanation that has been put forward of what we mean when we say 'It is raining' or 'The earth is round' is the so-called coherence theory of truth. It has caused even more trouble than the correspondence theory. According to the coherence theory, the sum of our knowledge is a coherent, internally connected system, and particular bits of this knowledge – that is, particular propositions – are acceptable insofar as they fit into the whole. We have no unmediated perception of facts, independently of any presuppositions; the words in which we express our knowledge are comprehensible by virtue of being parts of a whole, a system where every component is referred to the whole and also presupposes the whole. Nothing is true or false without reference to the whole, and Truth in the full sense, without restrictions, is only the system as a whole. For this system is not simply a collection of true sentences, which together make the whole true. Rather, it is the other way round: sentences are true (but only partially true) by virtue of being elements of the system. There is, however, no way of evaluating and deciding between different systems without additional assumptions. Some propositions – for example, those which express religious and metaphysical beliefs – can be true in a system that allows them but untrue in one which does not. Let us suppose that I say to someone: 'Yesterday my guardian angel saved my life'. If the other person inhabits a mental world in which no such entities as guardian angels exist, he will reject my statement, even though it is perfectly valid in my system. On the other hand, we can both accept the statement 'It is raining'. So the same sentence can be a valid sentence, true or false, in different, mutually incompatible systems. But can we say that such a sentence has the same meaning in both systems and that it is true only by reference to the whole? This is one of many problems that beset the coherence theory of truth. The idea that particular sentences are only partially true, and that only the system as a whole contains Truth without restrictions, has also been criticized. (If particular sentences are only partially true, are they therefore also partially false?) The suggestion has been made that the coherence theory works well in axiomatic deductive systems (although such systems can be mutually incompatible), but this does not seem tremendously interesting; mathematicians know the rules of their discipline and the coherence theory does not seem greatly to enrich their skills.

Coherence can be conceived as a criterion of truth or a definition of truth. If it is only a criterion, we need not refer to any reality independent of our methods of verification. But then we no longer need (and can probably never attain) truth in the traditional sense; all we have, and all we need, are the criteria which allow us to establish which sentences are acceptable.

The idea of reference to a whole can, however, be construed in a way that leaves intact the idea of correspondence. It can be argued that the truth of any particular sentence, factual or theoretical (and possibly mathematical or logical as well), can never be perfectly certain unless and until it is confronted with the Absolute Truth, since we do not know how the Absolute Truth might change it or limit the scope of its validity; but we can never attain the Absolute Truth, for it resides in, or rather is identical to, the Absolute Divinity. In other words, it is identical with God. Consequently we can never apply this definition. It does not function as a tool to discover the truth or to tell truth from falsity; it only states the conditions on which something can be said to be true. On this version, the correspondence theory remains valid (although inapplicable) as the definition of truth, while the criteria of truth must be established separately, independently from the definition; they are thus – again – no longer criteria of truth, but of acceptability.

Truth in the traditional, Aristotelian sense also disappears in the pragmatist theory of truth, in both its moderate and its radical versions. In both, truth is not only unnecessary but probably indefinable as well.

In the moderate version, propositions and questions are accepted as meaningful if there is some practical operation that can (at least in principle) be performed which would establish their truth or provide the answer. The answer thus obtained can be called true, but this does not imply that there is such a thing as 'being true' in itself, independent of our processes of verification. There is no truth whose acceptance or rejection has no empirical effects. To ask about the speed of sound or the distance from the Earth to the Moon is to ask a meaningful question because we have tools that allow us to answer it and to determine the practical effects of the answer, but to ask whether or not there is a supreme idea of the good which is prior to all particular instances of good things, or what exactly it means to say that justification is by faith or by works, or what is the relation between the Holy Ghost and the Son of God in the Trinity, is not to ask a meaningful question. Pragmatism in this sense boils down to the traditional anti-metaphysical doctrine of empiricism. It does not need a concept of reality that is independent of experience – or rather it firmly sets such considerations aside as a waste of time. Whether we call the anticipated and empirically confirmed results of our verification process 'truth' is a matter of linguistic convention.

The radical version of pragmatism is not satisfied with the efficiency of our actions as a criterion of truth; it goes on to suggest the utility of our beliefs as such a criterion. In this perverse sense what is true is what is useful. The fact that something can be useful at one moment and of no use at another, or useful to me and of no use to someone else, is considered acceptable, however absurd it might be on the traditional interpretation of what it means for something to be true. One of the bizarre consequences of this version of pragmatism is the rejection of the moderate version: there is no doubt that religious and metaphysical beliefs of various kinds can be useful, in the sense that they can be helpful in our lives, and so, in this strange sense, they are true. I can believe that I am protected by my guardian angel even though I have no empirical evidence for it of the kind that a physicist would endorse, and my belief can be true. Both variants of pragmatism require that we give up the idea of any reality independent of our verification procedures. This is something that cannot be salvaged, for it does not help us in getting to grips with the world; it does not make our lives better or more comfortable or more just, and nothing changes when we give it up.

Pragmatism is a very old philosophy. It can be found in Christian Platonists of a mystical persuasion, who argued that while we cannot say anything true about God in the normal sense – for the truth about God is inexpressible – there is a practical sense to what we say about Him, for it impels us to worship and love Him. Intimations of a pragmatist interpretation of science can be found in late medieval physics, for instance in Burdanus; Osiander wrote a preface to Copernicus's main work in which he argued that the true meaning of the heliocentric theory is practical: it makes it easier to calculate the movements of the heavenly bodies. David Hume defended a pragmatist concept of knowledge insofar as he claimed that while for practical reasons we cannot avoid going beyond individual impressions, what we have when we do so is not knowledge properly speaking. His followers, in particular Avenarius and Mach, argued similarly: truth in the traditional sense was, for them, both unnecessary and unattainable.

None of this is particularly revelatory; it can be found in any dictionary of philosophy. But we can persist in thinking that the question, 'What is the concept of truth as correspondence with reality *for?*' is neither trivial nor futile. To be sure, we can say that truth in this sense is of no use or significance either in empirical science or in everyday life and that all we need are pragmatic rules which tell us what is or is not acceptable. We can say that the idea of 'reality' is unclear and that we do not know what criteria to use in order to distinguish what is real from what is not. And we can say that our empirical knowledge, whether scientific or everyday, can be applied in technical operations and used to predict the effects of our actions without the need for debating metaphysical puzzles about reality-in-itself, independent of our observations. What we need is knowledge that we can apply; metaphysics is useless. This sort of defence of pragmatist philosophy is still popular today, possibly even more than in the past; Richard Rorty is perhaps its best-known proponent. But the question I put above – 'What is the concept of truth as correspondence *for*?' – persists.

However, it requires an important distinction. It is indeed true that a rational person who does not make a living by teaching philosophy knows perfectly well what people mean when they say 'It is dark outside,' or 'Polyphemus was a Cyclops,' or 'Hemlock is a poison,' or 'Water is a compound of oxygen and hydrogen.' These sentences express certain truths about the world (though we must remember that Polyphemus has a different kind of existence from hemlock). This rational person might not even understand a thinker who told him that there was no reality-in-itself and that the above sentences could be considered true (with the exception of the one about Polyphemus) only in a certain sense: not in the sense of reproducing in words any facts about a world that exist independently of us, but only in the sense that we can carry out practical operations in which these facts are assumed and those operations will stand a good chance of being successful: for instance, we can give hemlock to someone we want to kill or take a torch when going outside at night. These facts are embedded in a variety of linguistic conventions and human biological reactions to the world – reactions which, a pragmatist can admit, display certain regularities on which we may rely without implying that they refer to being-in-itself, of which we know nothing. And if the rational person listening to all this (who, let us repeat, does not make a living by teaching philosophy) does understand the thinker's explanations, they need not drive him to despair or hysterical protest or mental breakdown. He may even say: perhaps it is as you claim, and perhaps not, but if I understand you properly, none of this changes anything in my attitude to the world, my practical endeavours or my thinking. Perhaps sentences like 'It is dark outside' or 'Water is a compound of oxygen and hydrogen' presuppose certain specifically human ways of perceiving and certain linguistic conventions; perhaps 'hydrogen' and 'hemlock' are artefacts we have constructed for practical purposes; but since everything remains as it was, why should I worry about it?

There is, however, a class of propositions with regard to which we cannot expect such indifference. They are propositions which express a view of the world as a whole in a religious or metaphysical sense. Asking questions in this sphere is not some sort of extravagant whim or idle amusement for fanciful dreamers. Such questions are part of the legitimate interests of human beings as rational animals – creatures endowed with reason. And the answers to them provide mental and moral nourishment for ordinary people who have never so much as encountered the word 'metaphysics'. As rational animals, we want to know how we came into the world: was it simply as a result of parental reproductive activities? Is that all there is to it? Or was it, perhaps, by decree, in accordance with the mysterious plans of some higher power? As rational animals we also feel a need to know about the world, its purpose and meaning and goal: is it guided by some wise hand, directed towards some end, tending towards good? Or is it no more than the random movement of material particles, devoid of meaning, purpose or direction? And does all our striving and suffering have any meaning, or is it merely the accidental result of that aimless movement of particles? Will it all perish in the abyss of time? Or will something of that striving and suffering remain for eternity? And if so, what will it be, and how will it be preserved? We want to know these things. And we also want to know about good and evil: do they really exist? Are they part of the universe, or merely something we have invented for our convenience?

These are the questions which the rational animal asks about meaning. It asks them because it wants to know the Truth – truth in the traditional sense. It wants to know how things really are, not just whether such-and-such an answer accords with the rules of coherence, or is good or bad in the pragmatist sense – i.e., useful or useless – or whether it can help us in making predictions, or come in handy in practical matters. The rational animal wants Truth in the proper sense: the real McCoy, Truth *simpliciter*, Truth without restrictions. It wants to know how things truly are: whether they are indeed as those sentences say they are – *ita ut significant* – and whether the questions we ask are the right questions, properly put. The rational animal has little use for the various definitions of Truth suggested by philosophers; it wants to know how things are.

Is there any reason to believe that one day the rational animal will stop asking such questions, having realized that they serve no purpose, that there are no answers which would satisfy the requirements of chemistry and physics, and that the questions are therefore meaningless and futile?

No. There is no reason to think that such questions will ever stop haunting the mind of the rational animal. The rational animal will persist in asking them. It will not ask all those other questions which philosophers have tried to foist on it, questions like: does the answer (whatever it might be) meet the requirements of coherence? Is it useful? Is it pragmatically justified? But it will go on wanting to know the Truth: how things really are. And since it is highly unlikely that the rational animal will ever desist from asking questions of this sort, it is equally unlikely that the question of Truth in the traditional sense, the sense in which the philosophically untrained, commonsensical mind understands it – truth as *adaequatio*, or correspondence to reality – will vanish in the foreseeable future. Its roots are cultural, not epistemological. If we were to find ourselves in a civilization where such questions are forbidden and those who ask them jailed or hanged or locked up in an asylum, we would know that the human race had undergone a cultural mutation. We have no way of predicting what the effects of such a mutation might be, except for the large degree of probability that the rational animal would revert to a non-rational state: it would lose the reason with which it had been endowed. But since we have no grounds for making such a prophecy, it will be better and more sensible to assume that there is still a future for Truth.

Theologians used to speak of *'gaudium de veritate'* – joy from truth. They meant by this mainly the joy that we – or some of us – will feel once we have crossed over from our perishable world to a new life where illumination will descend upon us and the truth of the divine will be revealed. I believe there is *gaudium de veritate* in this perishable, profane world as well. We simply like knowing things, quite apart from any practical benefits to be derived from knowledge; we like truth for no better reason than that it is truth. Without the joy of truth we would no longer be rational creatures.

2001

On Reason (and Other Things)

There is, as we know, an abundance of proofs of the existence of God. This fact alone is enough to arouse suspicion. If, for any statement on any subject, we have one proof – genuine, valid, certain proof – then that is enough; there is no need for more. If there are more proofs, most likely none of them is a valid proof. God's existence, however, is not something we can prove in the way we can prove that the series of prime numbers is infinite. But this does not mean that the proofs we do have are worthless or absurd.

For they are not intended as proofs, but rather as reminders which point the way. This is why St Thomas Aquinas called his proofs of God 'ways'. 'Way' is probably a better word than 'proof', but it, too, is not entirely satisfactory if it involves the assumption that these ways will unfailingly lead us to our goal. They do not lead us to it unfailingly. But they do point us in the right direction. Aquinas has five ways to God; one of the greatest Thomists of the twentieth century, Manser, even tried to prove that five is the most there can be and that there can be no sixth.

But people get their proofs in all sorts of ways and from all kinds of things; almost anything will do. This is because the world is strange. And for some people the strangeness of the world is in itself proof of God's existence. Czesław Miłosz recently recalled a remark by the Polish writer Józef Wittlin that another Polish writer, Julian Tuwim, was proof of God's existence because there was no other way to explain how someone so stupid could be so brilliant. I read somewhere that Salvador Dalí, upon learning of the discovery of DNA, decided that here was proof of the existence of God. Salvador

Dalí was not an authority in the field of genetics, but one can see what he meant.

There is, then, no certain proof of the existence of God. But this should not worry us; it might be owing to the nature of our cognition and language. Many Christian thinkers, like Pseudo-Dionysius or Nicholas of Cusa, argued that we can literally say nothing about God because whatever we say, we can only say in language, and language is shaped by our experience of material things and the ordinary phenomena of our world. Language cannot reach God, and we must accept the fact. Even the resort to analogy fails, for what kind of analogies can there be between the finite and the Infinite? The Christian thinkers who argued that our language is unsuited to capturing divine reality were deeply convinced of God's existence, but they thought that even the verb 'to exist' was inappropriate when applied to God, for it, too, was shaped by our experience of material objects and could not therefore describe the divine being. We can say that a tree exists, and we know more or less what we mean. But what does it mean to say that God exists? They did not, however, find this a cause for despair, nor were they expressing despair when they argued as they did; they were merely pointing out how very limited were the capacities of our reason, and thus also of our language. And (they further pointed out) since our reason is limited, it should not overreach in its aspirations, for this only makes us succumb to excessive pride.

There has always been a current in Christian thought according to which we should be concerned with God only to the extent of praying to Him, worshipping Him and thanking Him for the gift of existence. There were even those who considered that only God is the proper object of our interest; all that went by the name of philosophy, i.e., all secular learning, was dismissed by them as worthless, and they thought it a sin to devote any attention to it. This was the line taken by Lactantius and Tertullian, and later by the medieval anti-dialecticians, among others. Petrus Damiani was famous for his pronouncement that we learnt grammar from the devil, for he (the devil, not Petrus) said to our ancestors: 'You shall be as gods'; in other words, he taught them how to decline the word 'God' and use it in the plural. He (Petrus, not the devil) is also famous for saying that monks who study secular matters are like men who abandon their chaste wives to seek pleasure in the arms of whores. This current was of course strengthened by the Reformation. Luther and Calvin made 'philosophy' into a term of abuse. Luther used to say that once you begin delving into the mysteries of the Holy Trinity with the aid of human logic, you will cease to believe in it (in the Trinity, that is, not in logic). He knew how perverse we could be.

There was some justice in what they said. If we try to grapple with theological problems with the aid of ordinary logic, the result will be only uncertainty and chaos. Moreover, if in spite of this we come to believe that we have achieved results, it will turn out that we have merely been feeding our *libido scienti* – our lust for knowledge; and lust for knowledge is considered one of the very worst sins. Despite these warnings, no one has succeeded in destroying secular reason, though not for want of trying.

We are born into a world of incomprehensible chaos. With time we succeed in acquiring tools which enable us to control that chaos: they are reason and what is known as religion or – as it has become fashionable to call it in recent decades – the sacred. The role of reason is to provide explanations of physical phenomena and enable us to predict and control them, that of religion to reveal the meaning of the world. Religion's ambitions are greater than reason's, for religion encompasses the meaning of the whole, and the whole is something reason will never be able to grasp.

There are three kinds of reason, and two of them have their source in the animal world. The first is empirical reason: the ability to register experiences and through them to acquire knowledge about the world, to transmit that knowledge to others and to devise practical ways of applying it. But the use of tools is not in itself a uniquely human characteristic. Birds can manoeuvre twigs in their beaks to extract worms from their hiding-places; monkeys use sticks to shake fruit down from trees. The use of tools had its inchoate forms in the animal world. But humans use tools in a different way: we can make them, and we can transmit our knowledge about them to others.

Nor is the ability to remember connections between phenomena limited to humans. Conditioned reflexes are common to all creatures endowed with a nervous system. Apparently even snails are (albeit with difficulty) capable of them. What *is* unique to human reason is the ability to register the knowledge gained through experience and pass it on. In this way we accumulate truth, or what we take to be knowledge – though there are those who say that what we call knowledge is purely pragmatic or utilitarian and not really truth.

The second kind of reason is the ability to organize collective life. We can observe various forms of this among animals, starting with ants and bees: the division of labour, hierarchies, the defence of territory and so on. But it is only humans who have devised specific tools for the organization of society. The most important of these are laws, money and writing. These powerful tools organize society and make life predictable, at least to a degree that allows us to survive at all; they limit chaos and impose order.

We have the first and second kind of reason as social animals; both involve contact with other people. But this is also what makes us aware of the gulf between our experience and our expression of it. Uncertainty creeps into what we think we know; we realize that the order we find in the world is not guaranteed, not absolutely reliable, and that our world is constructed of probabilities. So our reactions to events cannot be the purely instinctive responses of animals. This is the price we pay for the use of reason: uncertainty and the realization that our efforts are never absolutely successful, that nothing is guaranteed for ever.

But there is also a third kind of reason – reason *par excellence*, we might call it. This is the reason involved in mathematics and logic. Its results are not subject to falsification; it gives us certainty. It is also furthest removed from all that lower forms of life are capable of. We can, if we like, feel smug about this, although there are those who say that here, too, we have nothing to be particularly proud of, for both mathematics and logic consist simply of analytic statements, which are true by virtue of the meaning of their words alone, and this, they say, cannot in any sense be called knowledge, for it tells us nothing about the world.

From its earliest stages modern philosophy undermined our certainty from two sides. On the one hand it undermined our trust in the value of knowledge obtained through reason; on the other, it questioned the religious or theological knowledge – knowledge about God – which we had also acquired, or imagined ourselves to have acquired. All Descartes's works seem to be about God: how He can be reached and what traces of Him we can find in the world. But Voltaire claimed that many of his acquaintances became atheists after reading Descartes. How could this be? Descartes was not a deist in the sense of subscribing to a theory according to which God, although He created the world, does not interfere in its affairs, so that His presence in it is indiscernible and we derive no benefit from it, at least not of an intellectual kind. In his view, maintaining the world in existence requires no less power than creating it; the presence of God is thus an essential condition for the continued existence of the world. Nevertheless, the charge of deism (which, according to Pascal, is almost as distant from Christianity as atheism) was not entirely unjustified. Descartes argued that although God exists and the soul is immortal, the physical world is governed by a few simple mechanical laws which admit of no exceptions; consequently we do not need God's presence to acquire knowledge about the world, and there is no way from nature to God. Descartes did not explicitly deny that miracles could occur, but in fact his philosophy entailed such a denial. God, for Descartes, is absent as far as knowledge and science are concerned, and can safely be forgotten about. The human body is a machine like any other, and the medical sciences can tell us nothing about the human soul; so in the study of anatomy and physiology the immortal soul, too, can safely be forgotten about.

In this sense Descartes was indeed a proponent of the world of the early Enlightenment, a world which had lost the ability to discern traces of God in objects, people and physical phenomena. The cosmos was now merely a machine and no longer, as it had still been in Renaissance theories, an organism whose life we could observe just as we observe other living organisms. This was pure mechanicism, and from here the path to atheism was a straight and easy one.

But worse than this was still to come, for the late Enlightenment gave birth to the doctrine of David Hume: a severe doctrine, hemmed round with iron rules. This was another thing altogether, quite different from Cartesian philosophy. Here knowledge was divided into two kinds of data. One consisted of our individual sense perceptions: what we see, hear and touch. These perceptions are immobilized in their individuality; if we make generalizations based on them, it is only for practical reasons. Of course we must remember that if we pick up a stone and let it go, it is much more likely to fall to earth than to rise up into the air, that if we go for a swim in a lake we could drown, and so on. But this is just practical information; it contains no real knowledge, for there is no valid way of getting from individual perceptions to the general statements of which science is made up. The other kind of data consists of what later came to be called analytic statements: logic and mathematics. This is a sphere of knowledge in which we cannot be said really to know anything. Mathematical statements add nothing to our knowledge; they merely simplify its codification and help in remembering it. Hume was rigorous in setting out the limits of our knowledge because, he said, he wanted to follow the search for truth through to the end. But his analysis led him to the conclusion that there is no such thing as truth. So he was left empty-handed – although nowhere did he admit this.

This was the turning point. Truth, once lost, was hard to recover. Human reason, having excommunicated God, seemed to go on to excommunicate itself; nothing was left of truth in the sense in which we had understood it since the time of Plato. Reason has not recovered since it fell on hard times, and distrust of reason has continued into our own age. It took Nietzsche's evil genius to bring home to us the full extent of the disaster and its consequences: the world is nothing but eternal chaos; nothing exists but individual centres of power, each struggling to wrest more power for itself at the expense of the others; there is no meaning in the world, and God is a figment of our imagination, perhaps the result of the human need for protection. A large number of the modern theories which excommunicate truth in the traditional sense have their roots in either Hume or Nietzsche.

Thus reason manoeuvred itself into an impossible situation from which there is no way to God. Yet it is in the sphere of the divine that people are most in need of truth. If we are told that the ordinary objects of our everyday life are nothing but artefacts, and that it is these artefacts that make up the world which our sciences describe, this is something we can accept without horror. We can live with it; it is not cause for despair. But if we are told that God and the divine reality which encompasses our world and gives it meaning are also artefacts, then the situation is quite different, for people want to believe that these things really exist, that they are true, not merely figments of our imagination.

So there is a conflict between our need to seek hidden meaning in the world and the absence of truth in the traditional sense. We seek safety in both religion and reason – safety in the sense of being able to control the physical reality around us and in the sense of being able to believe that the world does have meaning, an invisible mean-ing that cannot be derived from empirical facts or from our own experiences. The need for safety can sometimes have paradoxical consequences: in its extreme form it can lead to the voluntary aban-donment of one's personality and the loss of one's sense of self.

Mysticism in its radical form is such an abandonment of the self: a dissolving in the divine. On the other hand, we have the (some-times grotesque) efforts of reason to rid the world of all contingency and bring it under total control. An extreme form of this aspiration is the utopia where people are reduced to their function in the whole and perfectly interchangeable; here, too, personality disappears. The most perfect utopia of this sort is perhaps the one thought up by the eighteenth-century French Benedictine Deschamps, who said quite clearly that in his ideal society people would be like bricks in a wall: entirely interchangeable and identical in all respects, even in their external appearance. These are two extreme expressions of the nos-talgia Freud wrote about: our longing to be rid of all responsibility and return to the womb.

We know that the need for safety conflicts with the need for freedom. We want safety and we want freedom, but we cannot have both to any large extent; one limits the other. And here is what happened. A small revolutionary Jewish sect, which later took the name of Christianity, managed to dominate the world – but at a price. At the beginning Christianity was an alien enclave in a hostile world, a haven for truth in pagan surroundings. But in order to gain a spiritual hold over the Roman Empire, Christianity had to turn for support to Greek philosophy. Without this it could not have irrupted into the world of the empire's educated classes, and so could not have fulfilled its missionary role. It had to absorb the Greek philosophical and scientific tradition – in the form of works as splendid and incomparably beautiful as Euclid's *Elements*. The Neo-Platonist tradition also gave us the concept of the Absolute – an Absolute not entirely separate from us, allowing some kind of contact with it, albeit of a nature very hard to encompass with our linguistic tools.

But how could the God of the Old Testament and Plotinus's One be one and the same? How can we reconcile Plotinus's One – a timeless being we cannot fathom (for we do not understand what it means to be beyond time, or to be omnipotent, or to be omniscient without ever going outside oneself) – with the God of the Old Testament, God as a Person? How could the ineffable One of the Neo-Platonists have made a covenant with Abraham, instructed Noah in ark-building and talked with Moses? This is something we cannot fathom. And this is what Christianity had grappled with. Whether it did so successfully I cannot say, but reconciling these two images of God borders on the impossible.

Another difficulty, a tremendously important one that emerged with the fall of both reason and truth, concerns our ability to distinguish between good and evil. This, too, we inherited from the religious tradition. Whether it will be able to survive independently of that tradition is something we do not yet know. Of course we could all make up our own criteria of good and evil and they could be whatever we like, but why would anyone else accept them? This is another disaster brought about by the changes which robbed our world of meaning and in the twentieth century led to the spread of the sense of the absurd which now permeates all areas of culture: philosophy, theatre, the arts.

I remember once reading an interview with Ionesco in the Italian Catholic journal *Avvenire*. Ionesco said that it is absurd to call his work the theatre of the absurd because it is always about the search for God. I found this astonishing; I wish someone would show me how to go about finding traces of the search for God in Ionesco's work, for it seems to me to be an impossible task. But I suppose we must believe the author rather than our own impressions of his work.

So we have a sense of the absurd and a sense of uncertainty in distinguishing between good and evil. But we must surely know something about good and evil; we must have some tool that allows us to assert with conviction that freedom is better than slavery or equality better than servitude. But where is this tool? Can it be that we have lost it? I do not know.

2003

Lot's Wife or The Charms of the Past

The so-called sin of Sodom, recent studies have shown, is a myth – a fairy tale, fabricated by enemies of that city to evoke disgust and turn people against it. Even in Scripture the story is far from clear. The truth is that the inhabitants of Sodom ended up in conflict with the higher powers for entirely different reasons. They decided that everyone was equal, free and endowed with the right to life, and they issued an edict declaring equality, universal freedom and the abolition of the death penalty. In order to give this edict the necessary force, they also issued the following supplementary decrees:

1. Whoever denies that people are free and calls for the imprisonment of anyone whosoever shall be imprisoned for an indefinite term.
2. Whoever denies that everyone is equal and calls for the introduction of inequality shall be sentenced to slavery and deprived of all rights.
3. Whoever calls for the introduction of the death penalty shall be sentenced to death, the sentence to be carried out immediately.

In order to enforce these decrees the Sodomites organized a vast network of secret police whose task it was to eavesdrop on people, in their houses and in the street, and to proceed to the immediate arrest of anyone heard to express opinions not in conformity with them. And since many people expressed doubts as to the advisability of abolishing the death penalty, there were a great many executions, following swiftly one upon the other: thousands of people were brought before the courts, summarily sentenced and shot. Similar numbers of prison sentences were pronounced for expressing doubts about the principle of universal freedom, and thousands were enslaved for questioning universal equality.

For greater efficiency, the police organized themselves into three sections, one for each of the three offences. But sometimes agents from the Section for Safeguarding Universal Equality expressed doubts about the principle of universal freedom and were then arrested by agents from the Section for Safeguarding Universal Freedom. These latter in turn were sometimes heard to express not entirely sound views about the abolition of the death penalty, whereupon they were seized by the Section for Safeguarding Life, brought before the courts, sentenced and summarily executed. And so on. The situation that ensued became intolerable. The three sections began to harbour an intense loathing for one another, and each was more vigilant in sniffing out offences committed by agents of the other two than in spying on the rest of the population. Executions, prison sentences and slavery attained mass proportions; as people began to inform against one another, with the overwhelming majority of the accusations coming from police agents informing against their fellows, the decimated ranks of each section had constantly to be supplemented by fresh recruits. These were easily found among the general population, for naturally no decent, self-respecting person could refuse to cooperate with an organization devoted to upholding Freedom, Equality and Life. Within a year a quarter of the population had been shot for opposing the abolition of the death penalty, another quarter was in prison for opposing the principle of freedom, a quarter had been enslaved for questioning the principle of universal equality, and of the remaining twenty-five per cent almost all worked for the secret police.

Jehovah observed all this with concern and dismay. He took a very dim view of the theoretical principles of the Sodomites, for he considered freedom and equality to be absurd inventions, while the idea of abolishing the death penalty was clearly to be interpreted as an act of subversion against his rule. He also found the Sodomites' obstinacy in defending these principles irritating in the extreme. He therefore sent down some emissaries, charged with the task of propagating his own ideas in the infected city. To wit: that people were neither free nor equal and that the death penalty must be maintained. These emissaries made contact with a man by the name of Lot, who had long been considered suspect by the secret police. Not without reason, for very soon, after only a brief acquaintance with his guests, Lot admitted to them that in his view a large portion of the population was of inferior race and should be locked up in concentration camps and put to death in case of disobedience – views which were an affront to the laws of the city of Sodom. The agents then initiated him into their superior's plans: Jehovah, his patience stretched beyond bearing by the Sodomites' philosophy, had decided to burn down the whole city. But since he, Lot, did not share that philosophy, he was to be led out of the city and saved from death in the conflagration.

And this is indeed what happened. Just before dawn the emissaries led Lot and his family out of the city. As soon as they had left, a rain of fire poured down from the heavens and within a moment the whole city had been swallowed up in flames.

It is at this point that the famous story of Lot's wife begins. Jehovah's emissaries had strictly forbidden them to look back during their flight. 'If you look back,' they said, 'it will mean that you long for the past, and for the principles of Freedom, Equality and Security which God has condemned. Remember that such whims carry the death penalty, which Jehovah will be all the happier to carry out in order to strengthen your family in the conviction that the death penalty is just.'

Now as soon as they were beyond the city gates, Lot's wife, unlike her husband, began to long for Freedom, Equality and Security. She began, in other words, to long for the past which had been so brutally torn from her. She left her city with a heavy heart, and as the screams of Sodomites being burnt alive receded in the distance the temptation to look back tormented her more and more, until it became overwhelming. It seized her with such force that she could not resist. She looked back; she saw the city in flames. And at that moment, as we know, Jehovah turned her into a white lump of sodium chloride, bearing, in its shape, only a very vague resemblance to the human form.

Consternation seized the group of refugees. Lot ran up to the emissaries and cried:

'My wife! A mineral for a wife! Do something, for God's sake! Bring her back!'

'Too late. It's her own fault,' replied one of them. 'We warned her. What possessed her to want to go back to the past?'

'But she *didn't* want to go back to the past! She only wanted to look at it in the moment of its destruction.'

'To want to look at the past is to desire its return,' replied the emissary sternly. 'Otherwise why look at it?'

'Precisely to rejoice in its destruction! To gladden her eyes with the sight!'

'Oh no, my friend. One thing you should learn: delving into the past is among the most grievous sins under Jehovah's sun.'

'But why?'

'So that people do not acquire knowledge which it is undesirable for humans to possess.'

'But we already know our own past! What new secrets could we learn from it?'

'Jehovah does not wish what is past to be compared to what is and will be. The past must be forgotten because –'

' – because otherwise people will not appreciate the future enough,' Lot supplied.

The emissary smiled kindly.

'You are clever, my friend. But you do not know everything. People long for the past not because it was better but because it is past. For – heed my words well – a person *is* his past, and the past is all that he is. You are made up of the whole of your life until this moment. In other words, you consist of the past. Apart from that you are nothing. To take away your past is to kill you. The past can be taken away gradually and imperceptibly, by degrees; that is possible. But if it is taken away suddenly and all at once, you cease to exist. Your wife saw her past go up in flames all at once, in one moment; that is why she had to die.'

'You contradict yourself, my good Angel. First you said that Jehovah killed my wife because she did not want to forget the past. Now you are saying that she brought her own death upon herself because her past was destroyed.'

'Self-contradiction is part of Jehovah's mystery,' said the emissary, somewhat less politely now. 'By longing for the past your wife incurred Jehovah's wrath. She wanted to be saved, but by looking at the past in the moment of its destruction she destroyed herself. So in a sense her death resulted from a combination of her own actions and Jehovah's.'

'But if that is the case, then Jehovah, since he wants to take away my past as well, wants to destroy me, too.'

'Not in the physical sense,' said the emissary, now with a distinct note of impatience in his voice. 'He only wants you to become a different person and to forget all those absurd notions of Freedom, Equality and Security. You will enter a land of despotism and inequality, a land with no security from death, and once you identify with it you will be a different Lot. You will lose the identity that was shaped in this world.'

'But then why was my wife destroyed physically?'

'That's enough!' roared the emissary, by now thoroughly enraged. 'No more explaining of divine mysteries. You seem to think you are my equal and can argue with me as much as you please. Enough of this! You yourself agreed that the idea of equality was a subversive absurdity. Please have the goodness now to act accordingly and accept the explanations of your superiors with the respect due to them. No more trying to be clever, no more argument. I consider this conversation closed. My patience has been strained enough as it is.'

So Lot crept sadly into his new land, pondering in secret the mystery of the Past, Equality, Freedom and Jehovah's Self-Contradictions.

And these are the morals that can be drawn from Lot's predicament:

First moral: regarding the past. We think the past belongs to us. But in fact it is the reverse: it is we who belong to the past, for we are unable to change it, while it fills the whole of our existence.

Second moral: regarding the past. The authorities which forbid us to look back on the past are only thinking of our own good. Indeed, my friend: look back and you will turn to stone.

Third moral: ditto. Since to lose one's past is to die, and since to delve into the past is also to die, only one option remains: to carry the past with us while at the same time pretending it is not there. You say this cannot be done? And yet not a few have managed it. Long live not a few!

1957

This essay was written as part of a collection of Biblical tales, but was removed by the censor. It remained unpublished in Poland until after the fall of communism.

Our Merry Apocalypse

The first vehicle with a combustion engine attained a top speed similar to that of a good horse. The steam locomotive was somewhat faster. Today we can read about the breaking of the sound barrier. (Why break it? Who knows. It is worth noting, in passing, that the average speed of traffic in London at rush hour today is the same as in Queen Victoria's time, when horse-drawn carts and carriages filled the streets.) From the birth of man until the middle of the nineteenth century, our speed of locomotion remained unchanged; it began to increase at the end of the century, until it reached what it is today. Things have speeded up in similar ways in various areas of our lives. We can follow (more often with anxious dismay than with pleasure or excitement) the various growth functions, some of them exponential: the increase in world population, pollution, violent and non-violent crime; the speed of travel and the production of books, journals and films; the number of television channels, huge cities, enormous airports and vast universities that are impossible to manage. And, looking at them, we tremble at the thought of what the future will bring. But extrapolation, while easy, is of little predictive use: we know that the lines on such graphs cannot keep going up for ever; they can become S-curves or suddenly plummet. Generally we don't know which is the more likely, but the predictions of demographers and chemists are not encouraging.

To take a simple example: imagine that one day the population of China and India attains the same standard of living as Western Europe, and acquires the same democratic rights and privileges. Each inhabitant of these two countries – altogether two billion people today – will want to visit England at least once in his life, which does not seem an extravagant desire to harbour. Let us now try to calculate how many airports the size of Heathrow will need to be built in order to make this possible. But those airports will not be built; they cannot be built. So the dreams of the Chinese and the Indians will never be realized.

Bertrand Russell once remarked that his children, since they were born in the twentieth century, will never know what it is to be happy. One is tempted to reply that while 'happy' may be a suitable adjective to qualify the lives of the aristocracy in Victorian England, it is doubtful whether the poor look back on those times with the same nostalgia. The observation seems obvious, even trivial, but on closer inspection it may prove not entirely convincing. Certainly neither happiness nor suffering can be quantitatively measured – whether we define happiness positively, as a good feeling or, like Schopenhauer, negatively, as the absence of suffering. But a brief look back at the century now ending does not suggest to our common sense that the amount of suffering in the world is smaller than in the previous century, even if we take into account the progress medicine has made in the alleviation of pain. We can say with almost no hesitation that no previous century witnessed the killing of so many people, both in absolute numbers and in relative terms: in massacres, by armies in the two great wars and in countless small ones, in death camps or in great famines. Although genocide is not an invention of our age, the word itself is, because techniques of killing have made such strides. But such tools as gas chambers or artificially induced famines are not essential for large-scale massacres; primitive instruments like machetes in Africa have proved quite efficient. The art of torture continues to flourish, as reports from Chinese prisons and concentration camps testify.

I began with those remarks about the progress in our speed of travel because that particular area of progress seems to be a decisive factor in the changes that have come about in the modern mentality, and because it has contributed enormously to that loss of 'community' which everyone today deplores – a loss to which we ascribe, not without reason, many of the catastrophes of our century, as well as some of its triumphs. But it is worth noting that people have been bemoaning this loss for at least two centuries; they were at it even when the inhabitants of the most developed parts of the world were still travelling at the same speed as their Neolithic ancestors. Recent decades have enriched the vocabulary of their lamentations with the new word 'communitarianism', which is nothing more than a general name for their complaint. The '-ism' suffix contains the vague (and false) suggestion that those who use the word know what should be done to turn back time and recover the beauty of the past. The complaint is understandable and perfectly well founded, but the loss seems irreversible. We have all read works of anti-science-fiction whose authors dream of a return to the simple life before the invention of electricity; the Amish in Pennsylvania, a radical branch of the Dutch Mennonites, live without tractors and automobiles, cultivate their land with hand tools and seem fairly content with their lives, though it seems reasonable to suppose that their mentality, too, has remained unchanged since the seventeenth century. We all remember the films of Jacques Tati which make fun of progress; one of them is about the adventures of a postman who, told that we should emulate the achievements of the Americans, pedals about on his bicycle enthusiastically repeating: *'rapidité! rapidité!'*

But it was precisely speed that swept away the mythological dimension of our world, the sacred dimension without which, as Mircea Eliade argued, the universe cannot reveal its hidden meaning. It is this mythological dimension that allowed us to perceive laws, the fundamental norms of our lives, as inherent in the very constitution of being rather than freely created by man. But today we inhabit Cartesian space, and my village is no longer the centre of the world.

Together with the mythological dimension we have also lost (or destroyed) our belief in natural law. In fact, we lost it in large measure even before technological progress gave us the vertiginous speeds of which we are so proud. It was destroyed by the Enlightenment, and its destruction removed the foundations of our moral, and soon thereafter also our cognitive, certainty; both were undermined by sceptical rationalism.

Should we, then, condemn the Enlightenment? Many today do,

mostly, but not only, from a Christian perspective (Eric Vogelin is perhaps the best known and most radical, or most relentless, of such critics). From that perspective the Enlightenment is defined essentially by its hostility to the Christian tradition. It was, its critics say, an idolatrous and semi-gnostic plan for man's self-redemption in the world, and reconciliation between the Enlightenment and Christianity is unthinkable. The Enlightenment (they further say), by exalting man and endowing him with the dignity of a potentially omnipotent creator, in fact degraded him to the status of an animal; the distinction between good and evil was supplanted by utilitarian criteria. The fundamental ties which bound the human community – religion and the family – were ridiculed or violently sundered. In short, the Enlightenment was a huge cultural catastrophe. It reduced human existence to its purely biological determinants; in consequence human persons became entirely interchangeable, like bricks in a wall. And this is how the foundations of twentieth-century totalitarianism were laid.

But however widespread the custom of seeing the Enlightenment as the source of all the evils, horrors and sufferings of our age, it does not have a monopoly as such a source – not even in Christian literature. It is sometimes pointed out that the main ideas of the Enlightenment, although expressed and propagated in a non-Christian or anti-Christian context, have their historical origins in Christianity. Among them is the idea of human rights and of the equality of the sexes (although finding Christian roots in the idea of religious freedom or free speech is somewhat harder). Assuming this to be indeed the case, a confrontation of these two traditions – not exactly a friendly one, perhaps, but without hatred – could be imagined, especially since the Church of Rome has in large measure abandoned the tradition of seeing liberalism as the main enemy.

But is it really the case? It is still hard to be sure – even with a lot of good faith, which is often lacking. Even if we reduce the definition of the Enlightenment to the Kantian minimum, to the ostensibly innocent slogan '*sapere aude*', we are already confronted by the hard kernel of a permanent and incurable conflict. For this slogan, if taken to its logical conclusion, presupposes not only that reason has the right to penetrate wherever it will, but also that it has a monopoly on pronouncing on the legitimacy of every question and the validity of every answer which might present themselves to our minds, and that the criteria of validity are established in accordance with the corpus of knowledge that exists at a given moment. This scientistic (for one cannot call it scientific) doctrine was admittedly essential to the development of modern scientific knowledge, but at the same time it was clearly anti-Christian. Indeed it was hostile to all religion, since religion in all its varieties draws its strength and legitimacy from inherited tradition and divine revelation. There is no such thing as rational religion; and if a rationalist religion exists, it is nothing other than the Enlightenment.

I do not think that what we call secularization, or the widespread indifference to the question of religious belief, can be explained by the conflict between the content of science and the content of religious belief. It is of course true that there have been such conflicts in the past, violent ones and much regretted by the Church today. However, we are not, at least most of us, prone to a rigorous scientism; most of us are to some extent superstitious. All sorts of absurd and even appallingly dangerous beliefs circulate happily and gain currency in the world, not least among the educated classes. At the same time, large numbers of books written by scientists – physicists, for instance – take great pains to explain that modern physics and cosmology do not by any means abolish God; on the contrary, they tend (some of these authors claim) to provide arguments for His existence. So the causes of this indifference are probably simpler. What has changed is the hierarchy of needs and their fulfilments. The sciences provide goods that are palpable and quantifiable; faith provides spiritual and invisible ones – trust in life and the certainty that Providence is watching over us – but it does not increase our supply of worldly goods. Such a spiritual mutation no doubt has a certain price, but it is one we are prepared to pay.

The Enlightenment, however, has turned against itself. In retrospect we can clearly trace its suicidal steps, starting with Hume in the eighteenth century. Hume's rules of empiricism eventually became the basis for epistemological nihilism, which recognizes no reason to cling on to the concept of truth in the traditional sense. If practical considerations are the only authority we have for judgements about the world that go beyond individual perceptions, then the concept of truth is useless; utilitarian criteria are perfectly adequate, both in science and in everyday life. But the Enlightenment saw itself as the bold and relentless pursuit of truth – the whole truth, as Hume required. Truth was supposed to defeat and supplant religious superstition, Christian myths, tradition and history as sources of certainty. And we can see how this struggle for truth in secular culture reached a cultural impasse, leaving us to confront, unarmed, a new situation where truth is absent, degraded, in pragmatist thinking, to the status of an old superstition. But the philosophy that killed off truth proclaims unlimited tolerance for the 'language games' (i.e., opinions, beliefs and doctrines) that people find useful. The outcome is expressed in the words of Karl Kraus: *'Alles ist wahr und auch das Gegenteil.'* 'Everything is true, and also its opposite.'

Is truth dead? That would be too hasty a verdict. We have seen so many elements of our civilization not only condemned to death but effectively guillotined, only to find them again alive and well. It would be hard to count the number of times the death of the novel has been announced, in tragic tones. But despite its execution new novels continue to appear, some of them quite good ones. Figurative painting was supposed to have died a violent death a considerable time ago, stabbed by the dagger of photography. But it continues to flourish, and photography itself evolved into a new art form. Philosophy, and in particular metaphysics, has been killed off again and again, day after day, the deed done by a variety of assassins: eighteenth-century empiricists, Hegel, Marx, positivists of every hue, Wittgenstein, and so on. But behold, after all these massacres the poor thing rises from its grave, oblivious to the fact that it is supposed to be dead, and starts walking. Where it is going it admittedly does not know, and nor does anyone else, but that is a different question.

But this is not all. It has also been announced, this time in scholarly, erudite, scientific (of course) tones, that man no longer exists;

there are only structures. And that the word 'I' has no referent. The end of history, the end of love, the end of ideology . . . Nothing but corpses and cemeteries – and then a resurrection. But even God, dispatched by Zarathustra over a century ago, although in fact killed hundreds of times over before Nietzsche and after him, does not resemble a corpse that has been buried for very long; on the contrary, from time to time He still makes use of people to destroy His enemies.

People sometimes point out that the death of the novel or of figurative painting need not mean that no one will ever again write novels or paint pictures, only that there will be no more Flauberts or Prousts or Velázquezes or Rembrandts. Well, it is certainly true that Flaubert, Proust, Velázquez and Rembrandt are dead; that much we can agree on. But the claim that there will never again be works of art comparable to theirs in their imaginative power has not been demonstrated, and never can be. We cannot imitate Flaubert or Rembrandt; the result would be poor by definition, for every great artist is unique. But the artistic imagination is alive and well, even if great talents have to overcome greater obstacles in clearing a path through the surrounding mass of mediocrity.

In short, the life of our culture is intense, interesting and vigorous. What, then, are the reasons for our pessimism and gloom, our feeling of chaos and sense of unease? The Churches say: 'It's because you have forgotten God.' But it is far from clear which is the cause here and which the effect. 'You have forgotten God,' they say, 'because God is constraining and inconvenient, because He imposes duties you consider too heavy, although in reality they are not hard to bear.' 'Not at all,' we might reply; 'God is not in the least inconvenient. On the contrary, He endows us with serenity and certainty; thanks to Him we can believe that the world has meaning and is essentially good, even though experience might suggest otherwise. As for duties, it is true that we are all sinners, like our ancestors; but they seemed to manage quite well, and succeeded in coming to various arrangements with heaven. We, too, could manage in a similar sort of way: by believing in God but not to the extent of believing that all His demands are seriously binding.'

In any case, this business of forgetting God is far less advanced than people claim. Sociologists have often criticized the idea of an unstoppable and ineluctably triumphant trend towards what is called secularization; they have demonstrated that the process can be observed on a large scale only in Western Europe, that counter-trends, some of them hostile to modernity, can be observed every-where, and that the traditional forms of religiosity still tend to attract more adherents than those which attempt to incorporate or adapt themselves to Enlightenment ideas.

Nevertheless, our fears and our sense of chaos are real. Perhaps we ourselves do not know what it is we are afraid of. Even if we set aside all the well-known curses of modernity – pollution, crime, noise, loss of authority by political parties and elites, government corruption, drugs – nothing in our intellectual life seems firmly rooted; everything is continually being put to the test. Religion is no longer an unfailing solace and prop, even for the faithful; science has become incomprehensible and counter-intuitive to the overwhelm-ing majority of us; in history everything seems uncertain and liable to revision. At the same time, the vertiginous speeds at which things take place in most areas of our lives provide some escape routes. Who – we might ask – needs seventy television channels? The spon-taneous answer that no one needs them will at once be questioned: on the contrary, almost everyone needs them, for they provide a way of escape from we-know-not-what to we-know-not-where, or per-haps from absurdity to absurdity.

Uncertainty is the stigma of our times – a stigma both in the sense of a mark branded on the forehead of a criminal and in the sense of a mystical wound.

We have lived through the experience of totalitarian regimes. What was new in them was not genocide, or even ideological geno-cide, so much as the successful technique of total intellectual expro-priation. This was of course possible only on condition that the tyranny could achieve a perfect monopoly of political, economic and cultural power, including systems of communication and edu-cation, art, literature and so forth. Despotism on that scale had prob-ably not been possible earlier; medieval Europe, in defiance of the semi-theocratic aspirations of the Church, maintained the separation of spiritual and secular powers and mercifully failed to invent economic central planning. If it had invented that institution, the modern era, including the Enlightenment, would most probably never have been born.

It is hard to find a convincing answer to the question of why totalitarian regimes should have appeared in our century. But we can probably say that among the necessary conditions of their appearance were those changes which allowed the masses to participate in the political process. In other words, the development of democratic institutions in the preceding period made possible the birth of the anti-democratic monster.

We sometimes ask ourselves whether the totalitarian experiment can ever be repeated, or whether it was something unique to our brutal century. On the face of it, a repetition seems unlikely because total control of information and communication – the absolute condition of totalitarianism – is no longer possible; the instruments of the so-called IT revolution are dispersed and in the hands of individuals. Moreover, we have grown accustomed to the belief that the free market and democratic institutions, including political and religious pluralism, go hand in hand and that neither is imaginable without the other. Admittedly, China, where a barbaric form of despotism coexists with the market, provides a counter-example, but we may comfort ourselves with the thought that this coexistence is barely a few years old and hope that the market will in the end force through democratic change. Perhaps it will. For the moment the world market seems to be operating to China's benefit: enormous numbers of slaves in the Chinese Gulag manufacture a huge variety of merchandise at practically no cost, which makes that merchandise unbeatable in competition. Thus does the free market support despotism and slavery.

Nevertheless, the conviction that the totalitarian threat is definitively behind us may be somewhat premature. It is true that the triumph of democracy in Eastern and Central Europe and in Latin America in recent years is encouraging: this, we think, this is the road our species will take! Well, perhaps; but it is far from certain.

We all know that we live in a ruthless age, but we also know that it is a hedonistic age. We forget too easily that freedom cannot be guaranteed for ever, that it requires constant watchfulness, and courage, and readiness to come to its defence. In our societies there will always be forces prepared to destroy it; they may seem insignificant, but in a large-scale social or economic catastrophe they can spread with lightning speed. We have seen it happen. And all sorts of things can bring about a cataclysm. We have grown accustomed to the liberality of the welfare state, and demand more and more of the goods and services it provides. But we are told that the burden will be increasingly hard to bear, if only for demographic reasons, and that this liberality will have to be sharply curtailed in the very near future. Sensible ideas for stemming the growth of huge cities, explosive concentrations of extreme poverty in the Third World, do not seem thick on the ground. The combination of growing populations and limited water and space can always lead to war, while the expansion of the market can create extreme inequalities, and thus a dangerous mass of resentment. And resentment is a feeling which gives rise to particularly large amounts of destructive energy.

The ideology itself is not important: it depends on chance and circumstance. We have, after all, had more than a few lessons in how a killing tool can be made out of any ideological material. It could be the God of the Old Testament; it could (not as easy, but not impossible) be Jesus. Or, of course, the Koran. Or it could be the idea of equality; the radiant socialist future; race, tribe or nation (nation above all: that is confirmed every day). Reason, too, can serve quite well as a justification for revolutionary terror, of both the Jacobin and the Bolshevik variety. The Enlightenment, Romanticism, religion – anything will do. The symbols themselves can be quite innocent: there is nothing bad in the symbol of the hammer and sickle, simple tools used for centuries by peasants and labourers; but circumstances were such that they became the symbols of Soviet tyranny. Nothing bad, either, in the swastika – a symbol found in many ancient civilizations, both pre-Hellenic and pre-Columbian; but for us the swastika is irresistibly associated with the horrors of Nazism.

Once again: ideologies and symbols are not important. Ideologies tend on the whole to be weaker than their advocates and those advocates' interests and aspirations. Our sky is never entirely unclouded; it was ever thus, and people have always known it. I do not say that we are rushing towards catastrophe; only that, like Alice, we must make a huge effort and run very fast to stay in the same place.

1997

First-time Publication Details

I.

The Death of Gods
1956

Translated by Agnieszka Kołakowska, published here in English for the first time.

What Is Socialism?
1956

First published in English in *The New Leader*, February 1957.

Communism as a Cultural Force
1985

Originally a lecture, published in *Survey*, summer 1985. This version, revised by Agnieszka Kołakowska, was published in *My Correct Views on Everything* (South Bend, St Augustine's Press, 2005).

The Heritage of the Left
1994

First published in *Balkan Forum*, 1994.

Totalitarianism and the Virtue of the Lie
1983

First published in *1984 Revisited*, ed. Irving Howe (New York, Harper and Row, 1983).

What Is Left of Socialism?
1995

First published in English in *First Things*, no. 126, 2002.

Genocide and Ideology

1977

First published in English in *Western Society After the Holocaust* (Boulder, Westview Press, 1983).

The Marxist Roots of Stalinism

1975

First published in English in *Stalinism: Essays in Historical Interpretation* (New York, Norton, 1977).

My Correct Views on Everything

1974

Published in *The Socialist Register 1974*, vol. 11. E. P. Thompson's Open Letter, to which this is a reply, appeared in *The Socialist Register 1973*, vol. 10.

II.

Jesus Christ – Prophet and Reformer

1956

Translated by Agnieszka Kołakowska. First published in English in *My Correct Views on Everything*, (South Bend, St Augustine's Press, 2005).

Leibniz and Job

2002

First published in English in *The New Criterion*, December 2003. Originally a lecture delivered at the Nexus Institute in 2003.

Erasmus and his God

1965

Translated by Agnieszka Kołakowska. Published here in English for the first time.

Anxiety About God in an Ostensibly Godless Age

1981

New translation by Agnieszka Kołakowska. First published in English in *First Things*, June/July 2003.

An Invitation from God to a Feast

2002

Translated by Agnieszka Kołakowska. Published here in English for the first time.

Why a Calf? Idolatry and the Death of God

1998

Originally a lecture delivered at the Nexus Institute, published here in English for the first time, revised by Agnieszka Kołakowska.

Is God Happy?

2006

Originally a lecture delivered at the Nexus Institute, published here in English for the first time, revised by Agnieszka Kołakowska.

III.

In Praise of Unpunctuality

1961

Translated by Agnieszka Kołakowska. Published here in English for the first time.

In Praise of Snobbery

1960

Translated by Agnieszka Kołakowska. Published here in English for the first time.

Crime and Punishment

1991

First published in English in *The New Criterion*, November 1991.

On Natural Law

2001

Originally a lecture, first published in English in a shortened version in *Critical Review*, 2003. This version was published in *My Correct Views on Everything*, *op. cit.*

On Collective Identity

1994

First published in *Partisan Review*, 2003.

The Demise of Historical Man
1989

First published in *Partisan Review*, 1991.

On Our Relative Relativism
1996

First published by the Institute of Philosophy and Sociology of the Polish Academy of Sciences in *Debating the State of Philosophy: Habermas, Rorty and Kołakowski* (Santa Barbara, Praeger Publishers, 1996). This is a revised version, published in *My Correct Views on Everything, op. cit.*

Is there a Future for Truth?
2001

Translated by Agnieszka Kołakowska. Published here in English for the first time.

On Reason (and Other Things)
2003

Translated by Agnieszka Kołakowska. Published here in English for the first time.

Lot's Wife
1957

New translation by Agnieszka Kołakowska. Published in English in *Tales from the Kingdom of Lailonia and The Key to Heaven* (Chicago, University of Chicago Press, 1972, 1989).

Our Merry Apocalypse
1997

Translated by Agnieszka Kołakowska. Published here in English for the first time.

Leszek Kołakowski was born in 1927 in Radom, Poland. He studied philosophy at Łódź University and Warsaw University, where he took his DPhil in 1953, taught as an assistant professor, and in 1959 was appointed to the Chair of the History of Modern Philosophy. For a number of years he also worked in the Institute of Philosophy of the Polish Academy of Sciences. In 1968, because of his political activity, he was expelled from the University by the government and banned from teaching and publishing. Later that year he accepted an invitation from McGill University in Montreal to a Visiting Professorship. In 1969–70 he was Visiting Professor at the University of California at Berkeley and in 1970 went to Oxford, where he was Senior Fellow of All Souls College until his retirement in 1995. In 1975 he was visiting professor at Yale University. From 1981 to 1994 he was also Professor in the Committee on Social Thought at the University of Chicago.

He was a Fellow of the British Academy, Foreign Fellow of the American Academy of Arts and Sciences, member of the Polish Academy of Sciences, the Academia Europea, the Bayerische Akademie der Künste and the Académie Universelle des Cultures.

He was widely honoured, and received, among others, the Jurzykowski Prize (1969), the Friedenspreis des Deutschen Buchhandels (1977), the Prix Européen de l'Essai (1981), the Praemium Erasmianum (1982), the MacArthur Fellowship (1983), the Jefferson Award (1986), the Prix Tocqueville (1993), the Premio Nonino (1997), the Jerusalem Prize (2007), and numerous doctorates *honoris causa*. In 2003 he was the first recipient of the John W. Kluge Prize of the Library of Congress for Lifetime Achievement in the Humanities.

Leszek Kołakowski is the author of over thirty books. Those written in or translated into English include: *Toward a Marxist Humanism* (1968), *The Devil and Scripture* (1973), *Husserl and the Search for Certitude* (1975), *Main Currents of Marxism* (1978), *Religion: If There Is No God . . .* (1982), *Bergson* (1985), *Modernity on Endless Trial* (1985), *Metaphysical Horror* (1988), *The Presence of Myth* (1989), *The Key to Heaven* and *Tales from the Kingdom of Lailonia* (1989), *God Owes Us Nothing: A Brief Remark on Pascal's Religion and the Spirit of Jansenism* (1995), *Freedom, Fame, Lying and Betrayal* (1999), *The Two Eyes of Spinoza* (2005), and *Why Is There Something Rather than Nothing? 23 Questions from Great Philosophers* (2008).